MIDLAND STEAM

By the same author
BRITISH STEAM SINCE 1900

MIDLAND STEAM

W. A. TUPLIN DSc FIMechE

DAVID & CHARLES : NEWTON ABBOT

0 7153 6193 7

Set in 11/13pt Plantin
and printed in Great Britain
by W J Holman Ltd Dawlish
for David & Charles (Holdings) Limited
South Devon House Newton Abbot Devon

Contents

Illustrations

Note: Each m-number is a means of identifying a class of locomotive with the list of its dimensions in Table 3, and has no other significance

Line illustrations

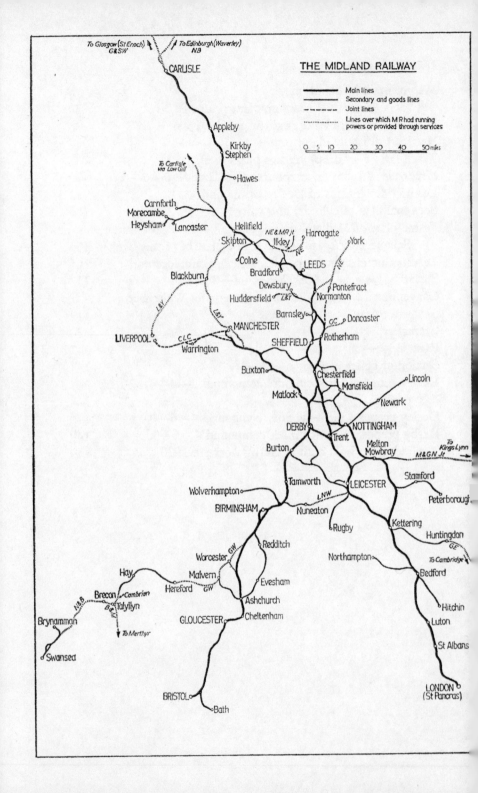

THE MIDLAND RAILWAY

——————	Main lines
————	Secondary and goods lines
– – – –	Joint lines
· · · · · ·	Lines over which M R had running powers or provided through services

0 5 10   20   30   40   50 miles

To Glasgow (St Enoch)
G & SW
To Edinburgh (Waverley)
NB

CARLISLE

Appleby

Kirkby
Stephen

To Carlisle
via Low Gill

Hawes

Carnforth
Morecambe
Heysham   Lancaster

Hellifield

Skipton   NE & MR Jt
Ilkley   Harrogate   York

Colne
Bradford   LEEDS
Dewsbury
Huddersfield   Pontefract
Normanton

Blackburn

Barnsley
Doncaster
GC
MANCHESTER
Rotherham
LIVERPOOL   CLC   SHEFFIELD
Warrington

Buxton   Chesterfield   Lincoln
Mansfield
Matlock   Newark

DERBY   NOTTINGHAM
Trent
Burton   Melton
Mowbray   To Kings Lynn
M & GN Jt

Tamworth   Stamford
Wolverhampton   LEICESTER
Peterborough
BIRMINGHAM   LNW
Nuneaton   Kettering   Huntingdon
Rugby   GE
Redditch   To Cambridge
Worcester   GW   Northampton   Bedford
Malvern   Evesham
Hay   Hereford   GW
Brecon   Cambrian   Ashchurch   Hitchin
Brynamman   Talyllyn   GLOUCESTER   Cheltenham   Luton
To Merthyr   St Albans
Swansea
BRISTOL   LONDON
(St Pancras)
Bath

Preface

The Midland was a great railway, one of Britain's Big Three, but one would hesitate before saying that Midland steam was great steam. The cause of the hesitation is simple but not entirely logical. It was that Midland main-line locomotives were limited to eight wheels whereas most British railways were using ten-wheelers before 1923 and some had even gone to twelve. In the twentieth century the Midland was a 'small engine' line and, while size is not in itself a virtue, lack of it hints of inferiority.

In the nineteenth century, however, Midland locomotives were not noticeably small. The Midland was indeed ahead of the North Western and the standard gauge Great Western in building eight-wheelers. The competition that faced the Midland demanded high quality in its locomotive department; Kirtley and Johnson in succession provided that quality in Victorian style; Deeley and Fowler were Edwardian.

The Midland, not notable for high speeds, did not compete in the 'Races to Scotland' in 1888 and 1895 and claimed no 100mph spurt, although one or two of its engines ran nicely over ninety before many British ones did. Foxwell and Farrer wrote in 1889:

> Here is a line with magnificent pluck and enterprise—too much sometimes for the peace of mind of its neighbours. English people, at least those who live north of the Thames, must for ever thank this company for the fact that third class travellers may go by any express, and that third class accommodation has been raised to its present standard of excellence. Perhaps in the long run the abolition of second class, initiated by the Midland and since adopted in part by the Great Northern and Scotch

lines, will prove to be another benefit both to the public and the shareholders. The Midland again must be credited with most of the quicker running introduced on the North-Western during the last ten years, for with the entry of the former company into Liverpool and Manchester, and later when it pushed boldly over the hills to Carlisle, it became necessary that the North-Western should smarten up its time-tables unless it wished to suffer from a serious defection of passengers.

Comparing the Midland total of 11,000 daily train-miles at over 40mph with those of the Great Northern (8,900) and North Western (14,000) and bearing in mind that the Midland engines have to face much the hardest gradients, there can be no doubt that this is, as it stands, the finest record in England. But, as we remarked before, since in so many cases the Midland does not observe punctuality, we hardly know what to say. Certainly the *journey speeds*, ie the speeds including stops, are not as good as they look on paper, for the journey so often takes longer than it is advertised to take. But the actual running-speeds, ie the speeds *excluding* stops, are probably *greater* (because the trains are delayed at stations) than on paper. At any rate, the Midland engines perform wonderful feats of hauling heavy loads at high speeds up severe gradients; and a Midland express is rarely late from any fault of engine or driver. But yet one other thing must be considered; these plucky high speeds on the Midland are very often performed with *two* engines, whereas the Great Northern scarcely ever (if ever), and the North-Western very rarely, deign to employ double engine power.

So double-heading, a Midland characteristic in the twentieth century, was not a new development. It was not economic and most railways strove to minimise it, but the Midland thrived in spite of it. Derby believed that, with the help of a little old engine, an ordinary middle-aged one was as good as a big new one. Only Deeley's 'flat iron' tank engines and Fowler's Lickey banker had over eight wheels. This was a notable achievement; not a 'big engine' line, it was able to manage its affairs so that it kept its passengers, traders and shareholders happy with medium-sized engines and a few fairly big ones.

CHAPTER ONE

Introduction

Running a railway is properly a dull business. Efficiency requires a fixed routine that everybody understands so that no time or effort is wasted in wondering what to do. Only when things are going wrong need railway staff be stirred out of their normal serenity, and even then although perhaps slowed, they are not stopped as the Rule Book covers every contingency.

At least when judged on this basis, the Midland was a good railway. It ran trains regularly and well but it provided no superfluous excitement. Its locomotives were not notably large, powerful, beautiful or fast. There was nothing distinctive in their design, or in their performance. No Midland locomotive designer saw any advantage in leaving the slow stream of conventional development from the six-wheel inside-cylinder locomotives that came soon after the Stephenson *Planet* of 1830. The one notable exception to this safe policy was the 'Midland compound' introduced by Johnson. When superfluous complication had been removed from this engine by Deeley, it worked well and it was one of the few designs that saved compounding from perpetual ignominy in the eyes of British locomotive engineers. It was realised at Derby that a compound must, above all, have simplicity if it were to compete successfully with a simple. With everything in its favour on the Midland, the compound principle just got by. In locomotive Britain the word 'compound' had to be preceded by 'Midland' if it were to be tolerated with comfort. In Britain the Midland was distinguished in that it found compounding good enough to be tolerated. It was tried and it was not discontinued. Indeed its use was expanded when for non-technical reasons the Midland gained technical control of motive power on the LMS. The expansion there was permitted, not because compounding had proved itself in any specific way to be specially worth expanding, but because inertia seemed to prevent ex-Midland officials from thinking that anything else might be better.

This, however, is part of the LMS story. More important is it to remember that on absorption into that large group at the beginning of 1923, the Midland had only 45 compound locomotives in a total stock of over 3,000. Only one of them was notably large, and none was technically outstanding, but they were all good enough for what they had to do. The veriest Victorian schoolgirl could discern their one distinction: they were red.

Yes, their colour was magnificent and their golden numbers stood out large and magnificent upon it. This became so in Deeley's time and the new style was a fitting accompaniment to a complete locomotive renumbering that might have been devised to provide something to occupy the mind of any locomotive enthusiast who should direct his attention to the Midland. It might have had a more profitable motive but it did at least show to all the world that someone on the Midland was stirring things up a bit. Nearly forty years later someone else was to do just the same thing on an impressively greater scale on the London & North Eastern Railway. If you should rebuild a locomotive you might spoil it, but re-numbering could not harm it. It introduced novelty without risk.

But although any student of the steam locomotive might regret that the history of Midland lacked dramatic incident, he would have to concede that the engines were at least reasonably good. It must have been so, because otherwise the Midland could not have recompensed its shareholders so well as it did. Some other British railway companies did even better at times, but still others did not.

The name 'Midland' was appropriate in that the railway grew from a group of small railways in the middle of England. Even when fully developed, its centre of gravity and its technical centre were both still in the middle of England, but its extremes were well spread. From Southend-on-Sea to London, Derby and Carlisle is a far and varied cry. From York through Derby to Bristol is not so far and not so varied. From Lincoln through Birmingham and Hereford to Brynamman near Swansea is a very odd cry, but Midland engines worked at both ends of it, although not at every place in between. And let it be added that no hair will be split here about exact ownership of every yard of track regularly traversed by Midland engines. It is all regarded for the present purpose as Midland territory.

The Midland was much involved in joint railways and this has attracted a good deal of attention from students of railway activity. Recent memory of search through the literature of the subject suggests that as much has been written about the Midland & Great Northern Jt Railway the Midland & Great Western Jt Railway and the Somerset & Dorset Railway as about the Midland itself. The influence of Midland steam was clearly apparent in the first-named and last-named of these railways, but less so in the other.

The geographically outstanding part of the Midland Railway was, of course, the seventy-odd mile line from Settle Junction to Carlisle. This railway, laid at enormous expense to break the North Western monopoly of railway access to Carlisle from the south, was unique in being a British mountain-road with no speed-restriction. In South Wales, Midland engines regularly worked over an unfenced mountain road of quite different character to reach a detached part of the Midland Railway with a terminus in Swansea. They did so by using another detached portion extending from Hereford westwards to Three Cocks Junction. Ten years before the end of its separate existence, the Midland 'took over' the London, Tilbury & Southend Railway, an outer-suburban commuter line with intense rush-hour traffic.

13

Introduction

Between Manchester and Liverpool, the Midland helped in another kind of commuter service in competition with two other rail-connections between those cities. Midland engines also entered Liverpool from a different direction and into a different station in connecting the city with Midland trains running between Leeds and Carlisle and calling at Hellifield. Most of these trains ran into the Wellington terminus at Leeds and this afforded opportunity for quicker 'engine change' for the next part of the journey than is possible without reversal of direction of running.

Between Swinton and Clay Cross (at the least) the Scottish trains shared the route with Midland trains running between Bristol and York (for Newcastle) and with a dense traffic of Midland goods and mineral trains. In South Yorkshire, Derbyshire and Nottinghamshire the Midland system was complex and congested. This was the origin of its most lucrative business, that of conveying coal to London and the south. It was the congestion and associated inefficiency that stirred the Midland into developing a traffic control system that the other large British railways found it worthwhile to copy. In the same area lay the remarkable junction of Trent, from which extended eastwards over the 40 miles to Lincoln the only part of the Midland railway that could be said to be level, although some fifteen miles of it are at positively-posted inclinations. A good deal of the Midland was markedly switchback, although not on so large a scale as the 40-mile hump between Settle Junction and Appleby.

By joint lines or running powers the Midland reached the North Sea at Yarmouth, the English Channel at Bournemouth and the Bristol Channel at Swansea. Not even the North Western had quite so wide a coverage. The main long-distance passenger trains handled by the company were those running between

1   St Pancras and Carlisle for Glasgow
    St Pancras and Carlisle for Edinburgh
2   York (from Newcastle) and Bristol and/or points south
More numerous were the Midland express trains between
3   St Pancras and Manchester

14

4 St Pancras and Leeds
5 St Pancras and Sheffield

All of these trains, except (2), travelled via Leicester or Nottingham and might call at either of those towns. The Manchester trains might call at Derby. The north-east to south-west trains (2) did call there and (usually) at Birmingham (New Street).

The Midland routes to Scotland were about ten miles longer than that of the North Western and its trains were normally booked to take about half an hour more on the way. Their main advantage over the rival trains was that they could pick up passengers from the Midlands, whereas the North Western did not attempt this except in so far as travellers from the Black Country and the Potteries could join the Scottish trains at Crewe. The function of the St Pancras–Scotland trains in providing for travellers to Scotland from the Midlands persisted even after nationalisation in 1948. It was the origin of an at-first-sight contradictory note in a time-table column referring to the sleeping-car train from St Pancras to Edinburgh which read:

> Sleeping cars London to Edinburgh.
> Does not convey sleeping car passengers from
> London to Edinburgh.

Trains from St Pancras to Manchester were in competition with the North Western, those to Leeds with the Great Northern and those to Sheffield with the Great Northern and (later) the Great Central. To Manchester the Midland was handicapped by a slightly greater distance and by the climb over Peak Forest. To Leeds, the handicap was ten miles plus intermittent speed restrictions in coal-mining areas. The Great Northern had an even greater advantage in respect of Bradford and the 'Heavy Woollen' district of the West Riding, so much so that the Midland planned a new route from Royston to Bradford and indeed opened it as far as Thornhill. More remarkable still was a detached Midland line, very expensive to lay, from Mirfield to Huddersfield.

In 1910 there were about twenty-eight daily express passenger

15

trains from St Pancras for destinations at least as far as Trent. Of these, twelve ran to Manchester; the first left at 2.45am and the second, at 5am, included a restaurant car!

Between York and Bristol the Midland had no strong competition until in 1908 the opening of a new line north of Cheltenham enabled the Great Western Railway to fight keenly for some of the traffic between Birmingham and Bristol, while using about twenty miles of the Midland line between Gloucester and Bristol in doing so.

It is clear from this that Midland steam had to match that of other British railways in running fast passenger trains. Less clearly it had to do so in respect of local services and of most goods and mineral trains. Right back in the 1880s some through-the-night goods trains were booked to run quite fast over long distances (eg Bradford via Leeds to London at 35mph) to ensure 'next-day' deliveries of specially despatched freight, but for the general run of the lucrative goods traffic speed was not essential and indeed for long loose-coupled goods trains it was not practicable. The Midland was no different from other British railways in this respect and they all shared the same story of almost imperceptible development of goods engines in half a century or more.

On the passenger side things were not quite so placid. Very early in railway history Brunel had remarked that travellers would always prefer the fastest conveyance that they (or their employers) could afford. This still seems to be the case and it was the need for power and speed in the engines for main line passenger train service that led to the more noticeable experiments and advances in locomotive design. This was certainly so on the Midland Railway right from Kirtley to Deeley.

Midland passenger train speeds were well in line with the best of those on other British main lines. A list prepared by Mr C. J. Allen and published in the *Railway Magazine* for July 1910 shows that in the summer of that year, 115 daily runs totalling over 5,800 miles were booked by the Midland at over 50mph

Page 17 (above) No 35 (m4) as rebuilt in 1879. Horns connected by tie-bars. Withdrawn in 1894; *(centre)* No 639 (m5) was Johnson No 39. Note ejector near smokebox. Furness lubricator on steam-chest; *(below)* No 2601 (m8) was the first of the largest Midland singles. Not conspicuously more successful than the earlier ones. Note the impressive 8-wheel tender which, when fully loaded, was heavier than the locomotive in working order

Page 18 (*above*) No 1 (m12) was Johnson No 156. Note boiler feed clack-box and springs for two safety-valves. Someone had to decide whether to place the numeral ahead of the vertical joint in the tender side-sheet or behind it; (*centre*) No 166A (m14) Johnson chimney, numbering and lettering. Became No 24 in 1907; (*below*) No 1075 (m16) as originally built for running on the Derby-Manchester line. Became No 132 in 1907

start-to-stop. The fastest were between St Pancras and Kettering, 72 miles in 76 minutes at 56.8mph. The slowest was at 50.2mph between Hellifield and Leeds.

The longest non-stop runs regularly made by Midland engines were those over the 196 miles between St Pancras and Leeds. In some pre-1915 summer time tables a train was shown to leave St Pancras at 11.50am and to reach Carlisle at 5.58pm without any intermediate call. On the face of it this meant a non-stop run of 309 miles and, according to one story, a representative of another railway company rode as a passenger on one early occasion in order to find out what actually happened. There was a non-stop run over about 206 miles to Shipley Curve (beyond Leeds) where one Deeley compound was replaced by another, which then ran non-stop over the 103 miles to Carlisle. Unfortunately the engine-changing point was reported as Shipley Gate (in the Erewash Valley, 128 miles from St Pancras) and though this seemed strange it was not so much so as to be quite incredible. It does suggest however that it might have been sensible to adopt some different name for the station misleadingly called Shipley Gate. 'Cotmanhay' would have been equally accurate and much more distinctive.

The 11.50am averaged 50.7mph to Shipley Curve and 51.5mph from there to Carlisle. If it were allowed 4 minutes for engine changing, its total running time of 364 minutes was exactly the same as that of the preceding 11.30am train which was booked with a total of 16 minutes standing time at Leicester, Leeds and Hellifield. By 'Shipley Curve' was meant that short length of line at Shipley between the 'Leeds Junction' facing down trains and the trailing 'Bingley Junction'. Time for engine-changing could have been shortened by stopping at Leeds Junction instead of running on to the curve, because it could have held the relieving engine ready to back on to the train as soon as the London engine had moved off in the Bradford direction.

While trying to discover whether such a change in plan would

19

B

have delayed other trains, the writer found some interesting features of train-running in this vicinity. According to Bradshaw for April 1910, one might leave Leeds (Wellington) at 1.52pm and be conveyed so rapidly over the $10\frac{3}{4}$ slightly uphill miles to Shipley as to enable one to cross on foot from the most easterly platform to the most westerly one, and leave by another train for Keighley all in eleven minutes. This is not, however, any proof of exceptional vivacity in Midland engines, but merely a suggestion that even printed figures may be incorrect in spite of all the efforts of proof-readers. In other words, it was almost certainly an example of what Rous-Marten called 'Bradshavian eccentricities'.

But some equally strange Bradshaw figures about doings in Yorkshire were true. The Midland worked a 'shuttle service' of ten passenger trains per day between the Great Northern's Westgate station at Wakefield and the Midland's Sandal & Walton station on its London–Leeds main line. These trains were 'express' in covering the distance of $2\frac{3}{4}$ miles in seven minutes as they did not stop at the Great Northern station at Sandal. The Midland station was in fact in the old-world village of Walton, a full mile by country lanes from the village of Sandal Magna. Rejection of the name 'Walton' for the station may have been associated with the fact that there were nine other 'Waltons' with various qualifications in the Bradshaw index or with Midland desire to be associated with the greater community of Sandal. The Midland's Wakefield–Sandal service is just one example of the host of details by which old Bradshaw may entertain anyone interested in the running of railway trains. It is mentioned here as a reminder that long fast runs were not characteristic of engine-operation in general. There were a great many short slow ones and a great deal of standing still. This is why such small mileages had to be placed on the next to the last line of the table on p237.

The steam locomotive was not able to work for 24 hours a day because it had to stop to take on supplies of coal and water, to be oiled and, every week or so, to be withdrawn from service for cooling, emptying and washing-out the boiler. These unavoidable delays did not account for any large fraction of the standing time in average locomotive duties. The main factors were the nature of the passenger train service (determined by users' needs) and the traffic delays to goods trains whose stops and starts had to fit in with movements of passenger trains. When a locomotive was at rest it was not usually because it was unable to run but because there was either no need or no opportunity for it to do so. When it was running, it could be useful to its owner and specially interesting to an admirer. Foxwell, for one, admired the running of Midland engines but commented markedly on the use of two of them per train. Something has to be said about this in any dissertation on Midland steam.

It was an old practice to attach a second engine in front of one that was judged to be unable to keep time with its train over the next stage of the journey. If that stage were short and steeply adverse, 'double-heading' was a reasonable artifice, and the same remark applies to the alternative course of applying a helper-engine to the rear of the train. Nevertheless one cannot escape the feeling that there was something fundamentally uneconomic in double-heading a train to run over an ordinary route, just because the load was 5 per cent greater than some officially specified maximum. It was clearly uneconomic to use two engines where 1.05 would suffice, and yet a great deal of this kind of thing was done on the Midland in the last fifteen years of its independent existence. The obvious and usual alternative was to work the regular engine 1.05 times as hard as usual so as to keep time with the 1.05 size train. It might multiply the coal consumption and the wear and tear by something rather more than 1.05 but that was much less expensive than an extra engine on the journey. Two men were required to run the extra engine but, as they were paid whether they made the trip or not, there might be no additional expense on that account.

On the other hand, there was no need for the men or the extra engine if it were established that any train might be overloaded by 5 per cent now and again and that the regular engine could still be required to run it on time. Pursuance of this policy might well admit 1.05-size trains so frequently that it would come to be accepted as normal, and even 1.1-size trains occasionally taken. This is what tended to happen on railways in general and it is in fact the way in which the real capabilities of different classes of locomotives were gradually established. It explains why many 25-year-old locomotives regularly did far harder work than was expected of them when they were first built.

On the Midland this kind of development stopped abruptly on the establishment of 'traffic control' by Paget in 1909. Goods train traffic was overloading running lines and sidings; goods trains were suffering long delays as a matter of course and passenger train punctuality was rarer than it ought to have been. Complaints on this score were taken more seriously by the management than were the inconveniences and expense of the bad running of goods trains, and so conditions in that field got worse and worse. The Paget traffic control made a very great improvement and, in order that its effect on passenger train punctuality should not be spoiled by loss of time by locomotives, loads were so limited as to make the engines' jobs very easy. If the weight of a passenger train came out at only a couple of tons above the specified limit, an extra engine had to be put on, whether anybody liked it or not.

In consequence a great deal of Midland double-heading of passenger trains was just mechanical inefficiency but on the other hand regular double-heading of certain goods trains might be justified. It became common Midland practice to double-head coal trains from Toton sidings (near Long Eaton) over the 129 miles via Melton Mowbray to Brent sidings (near Cricklewood). It was justifiable because each load could be made up to the allowed limit for the pair of locomotives concerned and so there was no waste of engine-power. So far as the mechanics of the matter were concerned, the load might have been moved as two separate trains, each with one engine, but in respect of line-occupation, one train—even a long one—was better than two.

It may be asked, 'Why not triple-head a combination of three standard trains and gain even more?' An answer lies in the limited strength of the wagon-couplings. Even with all appropriate skill and care, the running of a long loose-coupled goods train over an undulating road was a difficult job, and shock-loads in couplings could be very high. The standard Midland double-headed coal-train was probably as heavy as it was sensible to try to run from Toton to Cricklewood.

It may also be asked whether it would not have been rational for the Midland to develop, for these trains at least, a single locomotive to replace the two 0—6—0s normally used and thus save the wages of one crew if nothing else. This question is bound

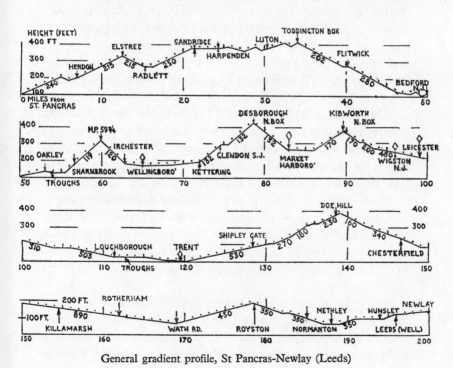

General gradient profile, St Pancras-Newlay (Leeds)

to have been raised with Fowler and it does seem that his designers were unable to find an answer acceptable to the Midland management. An answer materialised on the LMS in 1927 in the form of the Garratt-type 2—6—6—2s of which 33 were eventually built. These engines did the work they were intended for and kept at it for many years, but they were unsatisfactory in ways that have to be attributed to Midland features in their design. They were features that 'got by' in the easy working conditions of the Paget system but showed up as unnecessary weaknesses when railways were coming up against the harder facts of life. It may be that one of these weaknesses—axleboxes of poor design—had been recognised as trouble-spots if Midland engines were to be worked really hard, and had therefore been a factor in determining the lenient load-limitations laid down for the various classes of Midland locomotives. But even if Derby in Midland days saw no way of building a single locomotive tractively equivalent to two 0—6—0s, it might have produced (and did produce for the Somerset & Dorset line) a 2—8—0 equivalent to one-and-a-half 0—6—0s. This was in fact the eventual solution reached in 1935 when the Stanier 2—8—0s began to appear.

A bad fault of Midland double-heading was that it was with 'pint size' locomotives, each with two men whereas one man and a boy might well have sufficed. On every railway there were plenty of jobs for small 0—6—0s, but when there was real haulage to be done then each locomotive should be at least big enough to use all the coal that an adult fireman could be expected to handle. The big goods engines should have boilers as big as those of the big passenger engines. But the Midland preferred to use and to repair its small goods engines in large numbers rather than to build, for the heavy jobs, larger ones that would have made better use of man-power.

The application of a second locomotive to a Midland passenger train, while conveniently called 'double-heading', was not usually so in every literal sense as the helper was normally smaller than the train engine. For example, a 'single' or a 2—4—0 would normally be coupled in front of a 4—4—0. It was desirable that any leading engine, even though less powerful than the train engine, should not be pushed. It was felt that any locomotive needed a steadying backward pull to restrain it from running off the road when riding roughly and therefore that, however fast a double-headed train might run, the helper-in-front should be able to go faster so that it could keep its coupling tight.

An official instruction was that the driver of the leading engine of a multiple-headed train was responsible for observing signals and for stopping at the right places at the right times. The driver of the second engine was also required to observe signals but of course steam from the leading engine could make this difficult or impossible. It sometimes happened, however, that the driver of the leading engine was much less experienced in the working of heavy fast passenger trains than was the driver of the train engine. Because of this it was common for the drivers to confer, while the helper engine was being coupled, and to decide who was going to apply the brakes. Misunderstanding on this point was a partial explanation of collisions of double-headed trains with buffer-stops at terminal stations.

It had also to be decided, before starting away with a double-headed train, what was to be done at water-troughs. Was each engine to pick up at alternate troughs, or was each to have a go each time? If the latter, the right way was for the leading engine to dip on the second half of the trough and the second engine to lift from the first half. A disadvantage of the alternative procedure was that if the fireman of the leading engine was unable to lift his scoop (because, for example, the water pressure on the scoop was too strong for him), then the scoop would take the top water from the second half of the trough and the second scoop could get nothing useful from it. The second engine might indeed get plenty of water by overflow from the tender in front of it, but that was no good to the engine or to its crew. Specially vulnerable by water were the leading axleboxes of the second engine, and so in Deeley's time protective plates were attached

25

to the buffer beams of Midland engines with leading bogies.

Railway enthusiasts who enjoyed watching engines probably approved of double-heading as it made visible engines more numerous than trains, and of course two engines working together might give a more vivid impression of power than either could produce alone. Double-heading was an easy way of coping with emergencies of certain types and with short steep gradients, but wholesale and persistent double-heading was inevitably more costly than the use of locomotives big enough to do all ordinary jobs single-handed. On the other hand it cannot be said that the usually published annual figures for cost of haulage on British railways showed Midland practice to be noticeably extravagant in this respect and so the shareholders had little cause to grumble about details in procedure. Whether the published statistics really meant what they seemed to mean is another matter.

While the cost of extensive double-heading of trains over their full journeys may be questioned, the practice of providing a train with a helper-engine over a short length of steeply graded track is more readily justifiable. It is therefore natural to examine the gradient-profiles of Midland main-lines, and to consider to what extent the use of extra engines on the steeper inclines may have been an influence in tempting the locomotive department into its rather liberal double-heading policy.

CHAPTER TWO

Midland Roads

The earliest steam locomotives were very heavy in relation to their propulsive effort. It was apparent that, if the steam locomotive was to become a commercial proposition, railways would have to be laid either with no steep gradients at all or, if that were impracticable, with the steep gradients limited to a few short lengths over which special assistance could be provided. George Stephenson originally aimed to avoid any gradient steeper than about 1 in 300, but soon found that in many localities such a restriction would be quite unrealistic.

On the Liverpool–Manchester railway, in what is certainly not hilly country, there are near Rainhill two inclined planes each about $1\frac{1}{2}$ miles long at about 1 in 90. The start from Liverpool (Lime Street) is up $1\frac{1}{4}$ miles at 1 in 93 to Edge Hill. In the early days of the railway assisting engines were used on the inclined planes, and rope-haulage in the Lime Street–Edge Hill cutting. The prospect of locomotive haulage on railways in really hilly country cannot have looked bright. Development of the steam locomotive raised power-weight ratios so that steep gradients looked less disconcerting, but improvement on the 1830 position was never enormous. A goods train normally composed for an average road could threaten to overtax the locomotive on any gradient much steeper than 1 in 100. Passenger trains were not so readily affected because they normally ran at double the goods train's speed on the level, and so stalling was hardly a threat on anything flatter than 1 in 50.

When the Birmingham–Gloucester line was first contemplated it was accepted as reasonable that the climb over the escarpment of the Lickey Hills should be concentrated into one short but very steep incline up which every train would be assisted in the rear besides being pulled at the front. Rises of three or more miles at 1 in 90 up to Peak Forest on the Derby–Manchester line were accepted as possibly demanding help for goods trains but not usually for passenger trains. On the formidable Settle–Carlisle line the heights attained are greater and the rises are nearly as long but they contain only a few short lengths steeper than 1 in 100. Help was in the form of double-heading from Hellifield or from Carlisle. Rear end assistance was not normal practice on this route.

Apart from the three obvious 'big hills' just mentioned, the gradients on the Midland main lines were fairly severe; south of Leicester the average bank is at about 1 in 180. An exception on the main line is found in the 3-mile rises at 1 in 120 to the summit at mile post $59\frac{3}{4}$ from St Pancras in a cutting between Sharnbrook and Irchester. This post was a useful timing point (in daylight).

Even after concluding that, by and large, the gradients of the Midland main lines were about average and therefore that the general job of Midland steam was not an unusually severe one, it may be useful to ask to what extent an undulating road is harder for the engines than is one of uniform gradient. Is there any sense in the suggestion (sometimes heard) that the latter is harder because unlike the former it includes no easy section on which the effort may be relaxed? How much easier is it to cover 10 level miles in 10 minutes than to go down for 5 miles at 1 in 200 and then up a similar gradient? It was claimed by some people in the early days of railway projection that the high speed gained on the descent gave such assistance in the subsequent ascent that it could be completed 'on time' without demanding from the engine any greater overall effort than it had to make on the level. Is this true?

The answer depends on the fact that in order to go from A to B in a specified time with minimum expenditure of energy the speed must be constant. Consequently the dip demands neither extra time nor extra energy, provided that the engine takes the train up the gradient at a speed equal to the average for the journey. If it cannot do this, then it must exceed that speed on the down gradient to gain enough time to offset the loss on the climb. Near the bottom of the dip its speed must exceed the average for the journey and it is the extra resistance at speeds above the average that makes the dip more toilsome than the level for any specified average speed. So a saw-tooth gradient profile is slower than a uniform slope from start to finish, but at least for climbs flatter than 1 in 200 the difference is not great. All this assumes of course that there is no speed restriction in the dip and that it is V-shaped with no appreciable level length on which speed is reduced by windage rather than by gravity.

The foregoing remarks apply to trains of vehicles safe up to 90mph but not necessarily to slower trains. It certainly cannot be assumed that loose-coupled goods trains could use switchback routes as easily as flat ones, unless the conditions were such that the engine could be allowed to continue to pull on the downgrades without attaining speeds too high for safe running of the goods vehicles. But even apart from easily expressed limitations of this kind, the handling of loose-coupled trains on up-and-down lines demanded skill and experience that cannot be defined by figures.

It is fair to say that, even apart from speed restrictions where speed would otherwise be high (Wellingborough and Market Harborough were the marked examples), the Midland main line south of Leicester was distinctly more difficult than a level one in running passenger trains even with unrestricted downhill speeds. For goods trains, unable to have anything in the nature of a flying start on the main climbs, it was laborious.

The immediate start out of St Pancras is not much harder than level and, as it was Midland practice for each departing train to be helped out of the platform and for some distance further by the engine that had brought the empty coaches into the terminus, fast starts were usual. The average gradient to the summit beyond St Albans is only 1 in 400, but the distance of 21 miles includes a good many steeper than 1 in 200. The 3-mile descent from Elstree to Radlett often produced a maximum of over 70mph but the effect of this would be dissipated within the three miles on to Napsbury and the engine then had to cope with 1 in 177 from there to the top. Thence to the summit beyond Leagrave the serrated gradient averages level, and as the dips are short it is little harder than level, but the local top speeds between St Albans and Luton could be noticed by a passenger without timing anything.

Then comes the big dip, over 25 miles from crest to crest with no speed restriction, and Midland maxima were commonly up to 75mph near Bedford. The effect of this had disappeared before the 55-mile point, the beginning of the climb, mostly 1 in 119, to the summit at mile post $59\frac{3}{4}$. This summit is the highest point between Bedford and Wellingborough and it almost equally divided the six miles between the stations of Sharnbrook and Irchester. It was usually called Sharnbrook Summit although it is nearer to Souldrop and there was a signalbox of that name. The summit is in a cutting, featureless except for ventilating shafts for the adjacent goods-line tunnel, but the Sharnbrook - Souldrop

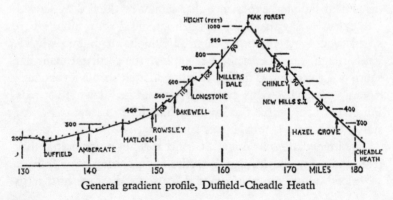

General gradient profile, Duffield-Cheadle Heath

area is one of the most delightful bits of wooded country between London and Carlisle, or indeed anywhere else. Drivers of north-bound goods trains had time (if not always freedom) to appreciate it as even the eased goods-line gradient enforced low speed. Passenger trains could run over the summit at 50mph, but lower speeds were common and were sensible if the train was on time. An undulating road such as this gives to every intelligent driver the problem of deciding how to handle the engine on each climb so that it works no harder than is necessary. He can allow the boiler pressure to drop below the rated maximum when the train goes over the crest, so that there is a margin for it to rise when the engine is eased without wasting steam by blowing off at the safety-valves.

With the regulator kept open, speed would pick up fast on the slope from mile post $59\frac{3}{4}$ towards Irchester, and it could be closed before that station was reached, and left closed so that the train drifted on to Wellingborough and ran through at the restricted speed prescribed for that vicinity. The actual figure varied from time to time. Fifty miles per hour was not unreasonable in the Midland period but British Railways allowed as much as 65mph. Unrestricted speed would have been useful as 75mph would have been easily practicable and would have helped in the approach to the 9-mile rise from Burton Latimer to Desborough.

As things actually were, the driver's problem was to decide where to shut off steam on the way down from mile post $59\frac{3}{4}$. If he were running late and anxious to get back onto schedule he might keep steam working to within a mile of Wellingborough and then brake hard. If he were in good time his aim would be to shut off as soon as possible consistent with running through Wellingborough at something like the specified maximum allow-able speed without deliberately applying the brakes at all. Or, if he judged that the train would run too fast through Welling-borough if it were not braked, he might shut off the small ejector and allow leakage to put the brakes on hard enough to do the trick. There were many possibilities that might interest a driver

31

who had nothing else on his mind, and most of them included some 'drifting'—running with the regulator closed. Very similar circumstances applied to the descent from Desborough to speed-restricted Market Harborough, where again drifting was common. Drivers' experiments in drifting might cause trains to run past restrictions even more slowly than the official limit and this could puzzle a train-timer who did not suspect what was happening.

After Market Harborough, three easy miles enabled speed to be picked up to help on the climb to Kibworth. From there it was a fast easy run to Leicester, spoiled only by the speed restriction round the curve at Wigston North Junction. From Leicester to Trent Junction is a 20-mile speedway followed by about eight gently rising miles to Derby on the one hand or by about the same length of slightly adverse gradient past Trent station and up the Erewash Valley as far as Ilkeston Junction. Beyond that point, the steeper rises and speed restrictions for coal-mining subsidences hampered Midland trains on the climb to Doe Hill. In the succeeding 50-odd miles only the speed restriction at Rotherham (Masborough) and the more severe one at Normanton suggested any slight difficulty in achieving a mile-a-minute average to a stop in the Wellington station at Leeds.

In the opposite direction, the most irritating feature was the speed restriction at Market Harborough, right at the foot of the $4\frac{1}{2}$-mile climb at 1 in 133 to Desborough. From Desborough was a lovely 13-mile swoop down to Wellingborough, but even after ignoring the speed restriction there, the rise to Irchester prevented the engine from getting anything like a run at the $2\frac{1}{2}$ miles at 1 in 120 to Sharnbrook top. After half a mile on the fall, the regulator could be closed for five miles or so to Oakley troughs and there is some easy going beyond Oakley station.

At Bedford, however, hard facts had to be faced and the 16-mile climb from Bedford to Leagrave could worry the fireman of an engine that was not steaming as she should. Even after passing Leagrave, the men could not relax until nearing St Albans, 13 miles further on. From there the engine could be allowed to drift for two or three miles and so get a bit of breath back in preparation for the 3-mile climb from Radlett to Elstree. Here again the driver might set himself a little problem. Was it better to shut off altogether or to keep a little steam working on the way down to Radlett so as to start the climb faster? Once into the tunnel at Elstree the train was home, provided only that the engine had enough steam to make the one-mile climb at 1 in 196 to Cricklewood.

THE LICKEY BANK

It must have been a comfort to the engineer of the Birmingham & Gloucester Railway that the principle of using helper-engines on steep gradients had been accepted in working the Liverpool & Manchester Railway in 1830 and afterwards. Having aimed his line from Birmingham directly at Gloucester and brought it to the edge of the Lickey escarpment, he could send it down for two miles at 1 in 37.7 and announce without arousing too much comment that banking engines would be needed to get trains back. With this makeshift already used on what was perhaps the most famous British railway, he had no need to bother about devising a route over which passenger trains might be worked without banking. As Stephenson had set the Liverpool–Manchester inclined planes at 1 in 90, it was surely permissible to adopt 1 in 37.7 ten years later. Could not improvements in locomotive engines in ten years be expected to offset steepening the gradient in the ratio of $2\frac{1}{2}$ to 1?

So this monstrosity was incorporated in what would otherwise have been a fast main line, opened in 1840, and no compromise softened its severity. At the bottom of the incline, at the northern platform ends of Bromsgrove station, the change from 1 in 37.7 to flat was made in a few rail-lengths, producing a vertical curve of such severity that even descending passenger trains were enjoined not to exceed 30mph on a line that is dead-straight in plan and to slow to 10mph at the bottom. The Lickey was bound to

33

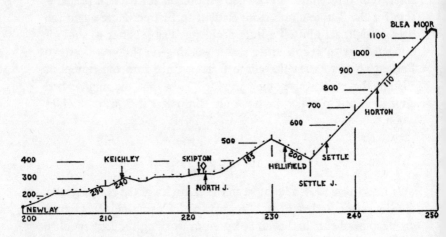

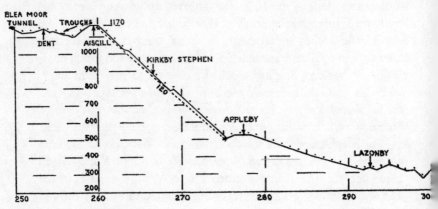

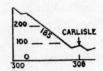

General gradient profile, Newlay-Carlisle

Page 35 (above) No 113 (m17) as built by Johnson. Became No 219 in 1907; *(centre)* No 278 (m18) was Johnson No 1498. Shown with Fowler chimney; *(below)* No 270 (m19) was Johnson No 1530. Shown with Fowler chimney

Page 36 (above) No 306 (m20) was Johnson No 1318. Shown with Fowler chimney; *(centre)* No 323 (m21) was Johnson No 1341. Rebuilt with extended smokebox and Fowler chimney; *(below)* No 1563 (m22) substantially as built. Became No 329 in 1907

delay northbound trains by its adverse gradient; it also delayed descending trains by its bad design at the bottom and by an injunction to stop at the top. This latter mandate was a necessity for goods trains and in the early days for passenger trains but when, after 1880, such trains had continuous brakes, the top stop became merely a pompous ritual. The Lickey was excusable in a pioneer railway, but the continued acceptance of its inefficiency for over a century was no credit to the Midland Railway.

It must be admitted that any alternative route would be costly and that any decision as to whether it could justify itself would necessarily depend on an estimate of traffic for perhaps fifty years ahead. Sufficient pessimism on that score could defeat any proposal for amelioration and no doubt that happened several times in Midland history. It may be that the Lickey was laid with the idea that, although its use demanded banking engines at the time, improvements in motive power would eventually obviate such a necessity. This certainly did turn out to be the case but not until well after a century of banking. Early in that period the original hope perhaps subconsciously persisted in the minds of those in authority and suppressed all suggestions for alleviating the situation by modifying the route, by improving the operating details or by employing steam locomotives specially designed for the banking job. For by far the greater part of a century, banking on the Lickey was by ordinary steam locomotives that worked in 'full gear' and were therefore very extravagant in coal.

Perhaps the most extraordinary feature of early train working on the Lickey is that the very first locomotives provided for banking trains on it were 4—2—0 single-drivers, and yet they proved to be more successful than a four-coupled Bury engine tried in competition with them a year after they started work. The singles were built by Norris of Philadelphia (USA). It is hard to believe that no British manufacturer was able to supply locomotives for the job, but price may well have been the controlling factor. The American engines were not accepted without a lot of technical objections and price-cutting, and it could well be that British

37

c

manufacturers had enough work to keep them busy at good prices and so were not at all interested in any bargaining.

In the 1840s, spots of bother with locomotive boilers were not uncommon on British railways but a famous boiler explosion at Bromsgrove in 1840 was not on a Norris engine. The American engines did well with the train loads that were common on the Lickey in the early 1840s, but traffic was outstripping them and in 1845 a much heavier (30 tons against 12) engine entered service. This was an 0—6—0 saddle tank engine (*Great Britain* designed by J. E. McConnell) with the obviously desirable feature that all its weight rested on the driving wheels, and for a century that remained a characteristic of Lickey bankers.

For eighty years at least the track layouts at the top and bottom of the Lickey remained in the original primitive form which was excusable when traffic was sparse. Banking engines were not attached to the trains they assisted. When the bulk of a pulled-and-pushed train had passed the top of the 1 in 37.7 and the train could be accelerated by its own engine, the banking engine was eased, to let the train leave it, but continued to run through Blackwell station and beyond a cross-over line that it would use on reversal to reach the down line and so return to Bromsgrove. This it might do provided that the down line was not required at the time for a train coming along from Birmingham. If, for this or any other reason, the banking engine could not go down immediately, it backed into a siding on the up side of the running lines. There it had to remain until both up and down lines were clear for it to come out and get across to the down line. The Midland never got round to providing a siding for banking engines between the running lines; it was left for the LMS to do this.

Not even the LMS did anything about the layout at Bromsgrove, where there had to be a storage siding with supplies of coal and water for banking engines. It was naturally placed on the up side of the running lines and it could be reached by a returned banker on the down line only when the up line was clear. The Bromsgrove layout could have been improved in various ways.

An obvious one was to splay the up and down running lines and to place the banking-engine siding and a coal-wagon siding between them.

The specified maximum permissible loads for unassisted engines up the Lickey were so low that very few trains qualified for permission to climb without a push at the back. When this circumstance had become well recognised, it was tacitly accepted that *every* train, however light, should stop to be banked and this was nice and simple for everyone. But when the train had stopped it still remained to be decided how many banking engines should be called out of the siding to cover the job. The answer depended on the number of vehicles in the train and on the class of train engine, and rules were laid down in print on this point. But it was hardly possible to ignore a complaint from the driver of a train-engine that it wasn't steaming properly, that the coal was bad, that the fire was dirty and so on. Consequently main-line enginemen, who believed that banking-engines were there to be used, could make enough fuss to get banking assistance strong enough to enable the train-engine to take the bank very easily indeed. So jiggery-pokery was sometimes an invisible addition to defilement of the serene beauty of the Lickey Hill countryside by smoke and uproar from locomotives worked far outside their economic ranges of development of push and pull.

The Lickey Hills were (and are) beautiful and there must have been lamentations and expostulations from those who found a long embankment being built close to their homes and later discovered what noisy and noisome use was made of it. The particularly affronted ones were not numerous as Bromsgrove station was $1\frac{1}{2}$ miles from Bromsgrove town and many human beings find that they can co-operate with the inevitable. Moreover, as the years went by, houses began to be built close to the Bromsgrove station despite its smoke and noise. Even after 130 years of use of the Lickey incline, the traveller on it may discern beauty in its rural surroundings and especially at certain seasons of the year.

The locomotive enthusiast was always fascinated by the sight, sound and scent of hard-worked steam locomotives and for him there was nothing quite like the Lickey. Its greatest thrill was obtained by leaning out of the rear window of the last vehicle of a banked train where one might be within ten feet of the blasting chimney of a hard-thrashed tank engine. The uproar was so impressive as to be termed music by some. A following wind could persuade hot cinders to fall on to the observer's head and this would leave him in no doubt as to whether he was enjoying himself. It is sad to reflect that it was the inefficiency of the steam locomotive that produced its greatest glamour. Apart from its very much higher initial cost, a diesel locomotive is more efficient than a steam locomotive and is far less impressive as a spectacle. It can pull a train up the Lickey without a banker, and so it ought in view of the amount of money taken from the taxpayer to buy it.

THE PEAK FOREST LINE

The Midland Railway as formed in 1844 by combination of the Birmingham & Derby Junction Railway, the Midland Counties Railway, and the North Midland Railway embraced Leicester, Nottingham, Birmingham, Derby, Chesterfield and Leeds, and had nothing to do with steep gradients. Its routes encountered no mountains and included nothing to disconcert the gradient-sensitive steam locomotive. It joined industrial towns at reasonably short distances and was able to run trains with good pay-loads without requiring anything exceptional in locomotive power.

The boring of Clay Cross tunnel, between Ambergate and Chesterfield, revealed a gold-mine in the form of coal-measures and a consortium including old George Stephenson did well out of minerals in this area. So plenty of haulage business originated in this fairly rural stretch of the Midland railway and there was no immediately powerful incentive to push north-westwards from Ambergate up the Derwent valley, although the existence of the Cromford Canal suggested that there could be something worth fighting for. Matlock was a small town, although hardly an industrial centre. But eventually a move was made in that direction and by 1849 there was a Midland branch to Matlock and indeed even beyond it to a terminus at Rowsley near, but not too near, to Chatsworth House, and therefore forming a convenient railhead for the current duke.

For more than ten years Rowsley was the end of the Midland branch from Ambergate. Inducement to extend it was limited to Buxton, thirteen miles away over a considerable hill, and Manchester, forty miles away over a more considerable one. But eventually the urge to expansion prevailed and by 1863 the Rowsley branch had been extended by ten sharply climbing miles (most of them between 1 in 120 and 1 in 100) to Millers Dale, within five miles of Buxton, and a more formidable five miles to the top of the hill at Peak Forest. Up to Millers Dale from Rowsley the only considerable tunnel was the one prescribed by the owner of Haddon Hall so that no sight or scent of the railway should reach him. For the last four miles the route was on a ledge on the steep side of Millers Dale.

Not until early in 1871 (eight years after attaining Millers Dale) was the Midland route into Manchester (London Road) completed by an extension from Millers Dale over Peak Forest, down to New Mills and thence by Marple and Reddish. By 1880 a diversion from Romilly led Midland trains into Stockport (Tiviot Dale) and on through Heaton Mersey and Throstle Nest Junction into Manchester Central which then became the Midland home in Manchester. Not until 1903 were Midland trains running by a gloriously swooping line right down from a junction south-east of New Mills to Throstle Nest Junction, a rising mile-and-a-half short of Manchester Central. The philosophy that inspired a route with no speed restriction over the mountain between Settle and Appleby was at work when this Midland entry into Manchester was projected. If you want a competitive railway, don't make one with sharp curves however undulating may be the countryside. Gravity is bound to hold you back when climbing; don't cramp its style by being compelled to apply brakes when you're coming down. To comply with this philosophy between Peak Forest and Manchester, the Midland had to bore the 2.2-mile Disley tunnel, ten miles from the top. In going from Derby to Manchester, the last three miles to the top were up at 1 in 90, but the regulator might be closed as the engine began the descent and left closed till after Cheadle Heath, 17 miles

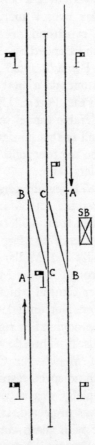

Track layout for dropping two pilots at once

further on. The Derby–Manchester line conformed to the general British gradient-pattern for east-west routes in occupying 35 miles to get to the summit, but only 25 to come down.

The extension of the line from Rowsley towards Peak Forest could not be beyond Rowsley station because that lay in the Derwent Valley above its junction with the Wye Valley which was to be followed up to Bakewell. The turn onto the new route had to be made at a point south of Rowsley, and a new Rowsley station was therefore erected on the new main line where it curved westwards from the old one. The curve here imposed a speed restriction on main-line trains when passing through Rowsley in either direction. The rise beyond Rowsley was broken by three half-mile bits of downhill, one between Haddon and Bakewell, one between Longstone and Monsal Dale, and the third just short of Millers Dale. Psychologically these were welcome breathers, but in plain physical fact a uniform gradient would have been more economical of effort.

Between Rowsley and the next station to the south (Darley Dale), a shed was opened to accommodate engines used in banking goods trains from there to Peak Forest. Eventually an array of goods train reception sidings and sorting sidings extended along the west side of the main line on this stretch, the Midland thus producing more cause for Ruskin's anti-railway fulminations than it did between Bakewell and Buxton, the two towns specifically mentioned by him in inveighing against mechanical transport in the Peak District. The comparison between the triviality of what offended him and the poisonous horror that fouls every British road a century later merely underlines the thought that the human race may survive if it can adapt itself to continuously coarsening conditions.

It has to be admitted, however, that pollution and bloodshed came to the roads only when the roads themselves had been made good. The nineteenth-century rail-traveller from Derby up to Peak Forest might revel in the splendid scenery in a way impracticable for the road traveller. Derbyshire roads were in general bad; in wet weather their limestone character made them into mud of the most slippery description. The observer might or might not think that light-coloured limestone walls defining fields were an embellishment to the landscape; no road traveller could doubt that limestone as a road material was the absolute end.

In the writer's mind, limestone country and the Midland are very closely associated; certainly the two most mountainous Midland lines are in such country, and the Derby–New Mills section is one of them. It goes over a big hill with miles at 1 in 90 and it may be called a hard or a difficult main line. When an engine that has pulled a train over 130 miles at about a mile a minute with occasional dashes at 75mph is observed to be slogging at about 30, it is natural to think that it is now on a road that is hard because the gradient is steeply adverse. But is the engine really working harder? Does the low speed really imply hard work? The answer is not necessarily, but a steep gradient does demand a hard pull and the Midland recipe for hard pull was an additional engine either behind the train or in front of its engine.

Passenger trains were not normally double-headed on the Peak Forest line, but many goods trains were assisted in the rear from Rowsley to the top. In the opposite direction such assistance was obtainable at Gowhole sidings, south of New Mills. If the assisting engine were attached to the front of the train engine and was free to make the full journey between Rowsley and Gowhole, then the extra braking thus made available for the downhill run might avoid any need to stop just over the brow for the purpose of pinning-down wagon brakes. A hard road was always harder for goods trains than for passenger trains and provision for adequate braking of the former could be more troublesome than for pulling them. Downhill speeds attained by passenger trains on hard roads were usually determined as much by the temperament and current mood of the driver as by the essential mechanics of the matter. As was common everywhere on British railways, normal running was characterised by caution rather than by haste and even the occasional occurrence of what might seem by comparison to be reckless running rarely involved any approach to serious risk.

In running down to Rowsley, passenger trains were usually, but not always, kept below 70mph. Speed was similarly restrained on the western slope, and although a little steam would have produced 80 or more without risk below New Mills, drivers were normally content to let the trains drift in accordance with normal practice on that part of the route. For enginemen the outstandingly bad feature of the Peak Forest line was Dove Holes tunnel, two miles slogging in sulphurous smoke up 1 in 90 immediately after a 15-mile rise not quite so steep. There was nothing worse anywhere else on the Midland.

THE LONG DRAG

A glance at the gradient profile of the Midland main line suggests at once that if it contains a really hard road, it is the one from Settle Junction over Blea Moor and Aisgill down to Appleby. It is interesting, however, that railwaymen refer to the Settle Junction–Blea Moor climb as the 'Long Drag' and not the 'Hard Drag'. It includes nothing so steep as the 1 in 90 of the Peak Forest line and it is less than half a mile longer than that from Rowsley to Peak Forest. Moreover, passenger trains commonly started the Long Drag at Settle Junction at a far higher speed than was permissible at Rowsley. While the adjective 'long' is (just) justified in comparing these climbs, the Derbyshire one is the more difficult in that it ends with three miles at 1 in 90, which is 10 per cent steeper than the southern slope of the Long Drag. On the northern side the climb from Ormside viaduct to Aisgill is $15\frac{1}{2}$ miles long, whereas it is 17.4 miles from Cheadle Heath to the top of Peak Forest, including about 7 miles at 1 in 90. There is thus some justification for calling Cheadle Heath to Peak Forest the Longer Drag and even more for calling it the Steep Drag (see gradient profile, p34).

The Yorkshire line is obviously a mountain road in that it runs

45

through what is—apart from the town of Settle—very sparsely inhabited country for some forty miles straight off, whereas considerable stretches of the other route are in what might be called outer suburbia. Although the nature of the visible countryside is of interest to some train-travellers (but a very large proportion of them do anything but look out of the window), it is hardly a factor to be taken into account in considering technical details in the running of railway trains. The occasional traveller may well find joy in pleasant scenery, but those who use the same route professionally day after day can hardly be expected to find similar joy every time. So long as everything was working properly the Long Drag was a very easy job for drivers of express passenger trains and a not very difficult one for firemen; once embarked on the descent the enginemen had nothing much to do but look for signals and as they were neither numerous nor hard to find in normal weather, there was no strain on anyone. There was plenty of time to look around and plenty to see if you liked grim hills and moors; between Appleby and Carlisle it is pleasantly pastoral except where it is dramatically craggy and wooded. The Vale of Eden may not be exactly like the Garden of Eden but it is not in every way inferior. Did environment have any effect on enginemen as they rode without effort on the long downhills of the Long Drag? If so, were they themselves aware of it, or would they have been just as happy running condensing tank engines underground on the Metropolitan Railway? The answers would vary widely between different individuals.

The Long Drag suffers a haulage handicap not shown by the gradient-profile, and that is wind. Wind can hardly be dismissed as a negligible nuisance on any open stretch of railway and it can be very strongly felt even down at sea level, as for example on viaducts across arms of the sea on the way from Carnforth to Furness. But when a train is over a thousand feet above sea level on a viaduct a hundred and fifty feet above the ground, where the fells funnel a gale across the track, a rip-roaring south-wester can transcend the most imaginative interpretation of the word 'wind'.

Not only might a gale stop a train that was by its weight alone a sufficient drag on the engine, but it could trim down the coal-heap on the tender and could blow out of the lee gangway any coal that the fireman might try to feed to the fire with the shovel. (You would think that Midland locomotive engineers would hear of this and counter it providing side doors between engine and tender, but you would be wrong. Nothing was ever done officially about it.) In those circumstances Blea Moor tunnel, though much disliked for its damp, was a peaceful haven and the only place for miles where you could be sure of getting some more coal into the firebox. Ribblehead viaduct was the worst place for wind when a westerly gale was raging, but a great deal of the tableland from Blea Moor to Aisgill was nearly as bad.

But while west winds were a worry to enginemen, the weather that was reported to the Midland's Holbeck shed at Leeds was that observed at Crosby Garrett, not near the summit but some ten miles from Aisgill, some 400 feet lower and nestling in the north-easterly lee of the 1,200ft Crosby Garrett Fell. The menace here was not the south-west wind, but the almost exactly opposite Helm wind that is apt to come down from Cross Fell with a resistful force not easy to explain. It may be associated with a peculiar stickiness that cyclists and golfers have noticed in certain east winds; they seem to oppose as much by viscosity as by velocity. It must be added that notwithstanding the peculiar malice of the Helm wind, Crosby Garrett ceased to be a railway weather-reporting point when in 1938 Ribblehead station was given an official status as a meteorological observation point and the station-staff were specifically trained in its practices. Ribblehead is certainly in the path of the commoner wild winds but what happens there is not an infallible indication of what is going on down near Appleby.

The Settle–Carlisle line is about 72 miles long between Settle Junction (nearly two miles south of Settle station) and Petteril Junction trailing into the North Eastern line from Newcastle to Carlisle a mile short of the Citadel station. On the way there was

47

a facing junction with the Hawes line at a station called Hawes Junction (much later, Garsdale) and another at Appleby leading onto the North Eastern line and thence to Penrith. In the opposite direction there is no facing junction on the Petteril Junction–Settle line nor indeed beyond it until Hellifield is reached after a run of some 75 miles. In Midland days there was no speed restriction until Skipton North Junction, 85 miles. This last was far from being a British record (the Great Western held it with 106 miles from Paddington to Bath) but was notable in a line that included ten miles above the 1,100-foot contour.

Absence of speed restriction might merely mean that the motive power was not able to make trains run fast and so it may be useful to remark that speeds up to rather more than 90 miles an hour have been noted near Settle, near the bottom of the 15-mile drop from Blea Moor. This was in the first few years of the twentieth century and was exceptional. In later years it became rare to note speeds much higher than 80mph anywhere on the Midland. This was partly because there were on the Midland a number of stretches where good passenger train speed could be maintained with steam shut off and so Midland men developed the habit of drifting whenever it could be done without losing too much time.

The speed that can be maintained by gravity on any particular descent depends on the relation between the total moving mass and the running resistance. Coaches behind a locomotive have much less resistance in relation to weight than have locomotives, and so when a train is drifting the locomotive is holding back the tender and the coaches. A Midland compound with a train of 200 tons drifting down a long-enough gradient of 1 in 100 would eventually attain a speed of about 85mph. For the engine and tender alone the figure was roughly 60mph. These figures suggest that no big flow of steam was required to get a 250-ton train up to 90mph or so in coming down past Settle or Crosby Garrett. They also suggest that the rarity of such speeds in those vicinities was due to drivers' disinclination to use any steam at all on the steeper slopes of the Settle–Appleby line. Any ordinary passenger train would run so fast without steam that very little time could be gained by using steam.

Some of the foregoing remarks apply to passenger trains but not to loose-coupled goods trains. The former were much the easier to handle over any hilly road; on the Long Drag this was particularly the case, because with continuous vacuum brake available for instant application, a passenger train might be allowed to drift as fast as it could unless and until it came to an adverse distant signal. No loose-coupled goods train could be safely handled in any such free manner. On the long drops, brakes had to be continuously applied on engine, tender and brake-van to keep speed down and the driver made every effort to see each distant signal at the earliest possible moment. Goods engines usually had to slog pretty hard on the rises and firemen were kept busy, but equally important were the brakes in keeping trains on schedule and on the rails when going downhill. Great experience and judgement were required in drivers and guards in deciding how fast a loose-coupled goods train could safely be allowed to go down a given stretch of road in particular weather conditions. 'Letting down' a goods train from the top could be as tricky as letting down an aircraft on to a runway, and the results of an error of judgement could be almost as striking in the one case as in the other.

Vital and exciting though the braking of goods trains could be (and many of the most dangerous episodes never came to official notice), they find a place under the literal heading of 'Midland Steam' only to the extent that steam-brakes were applied on the engines when things were getting out of hand; normally hand-brakes on tenders and in brake-vans did all that was wanted. It was the up-grades that really demanded steam and made firemen at least believe that some roads were hard.

For a particular power output and a particular train, the steeper the gradient the harder the engine must pull and the lower the speed. To withstand the draught produced by the stronger blast associated with the harder pull, the fire-bed must be deeper than it need be for the gentler and more nearly uniform draught at high speed. To deepen the fire on the immediate approach to a steep gradient, the fireman has to work harder for a few minutes than was necessary in running steadily on the flatter road. But once on the gradient, no Midland combination of engine, passenger train and booked speed called for any higher combustion rate than sufficed on the level. On narrowly academic grounds, it can be claimed that ideally an engine for steep climbing should have a higher nominal tractive effort than that of an engine for running the same train on the level. In actual practice the adaptability of the steam locomotive in suffering little loss of cylinder-efficiency anywhere over a 2 to 1 range of speed and pull made it able to cope with ordinarily steep gradients without any need for any specially high combustion rate anywhere. But where load and gradient demanded continuous working of an engine in full gear, coal could be consumed very fast and it became a hard road for the fireman at least.

The real difficulty about a steep gradient is that it may stop the train altogether if for any reason the boiler pressure falls far below the normal running figure which is usually close to the blowing-off point; on level track a passenger train could be kept moving by its usual engine with very low boiler pressure. So by a hard road is meant one with steep gradients; it does not mean or imply that either engine or fireman need work unusually hard to keep time with the normal load in normal conditions. A hard road creates difficulty only if the engine becomes unable to work as hard as usual because a steep gradient then increases the risk of an enforced stop out of sight of signalmen. This could cause much loss of time not only to the train particularly concerned but, by reason of signalmen's anxiety, to many others.

When subnormal conditions on any engine threatened beforehand the possibility of stalling on a steep gradient, the driver would stop before reaching it at any station where an assisting engine could be conveniently provided. Failing that, he would stop at a signalbox and use the blower to urge the fire to regain full boiler-pressure as quickly as possible. Before resuming his journey he would tell the signalman that he might have to stop again 'in the section' before reaching the next signalbox. The signalman there would also be informed and this would minimise the chance that the train stalled in the section would be over-looked.

When the Paget traffic control and its corollaries had become established on the Midland there was a lot of double-heading of trains and it was common for the extra engine to be added and removed at places where the train was booked to stop in any case. But where the pilot (the helper-engine) was removed at a wayside station or signal box after helping up a steep gradient it was immediately backed into a siding alongside the running line, and remained there until a gap in the traffic enabled it to come out again. It did not seem to occur to the Midland that where such operations were common, or likely to become so, a special track layout could be a help.

On the Settle–Carlisle line, pilot engines on south-bound trains were always attached at the front and this was normally done at Carlisle. At Aisgill, just over the brow of the last climb, the pilot could be taken off as little adverse gradient faced the train-engine for the rest of the way to Leeds. A pilot engine detached at Aisgill had to return to Carlisle, but to run tender-first for 48 miles would have been far too cold for the enginemen at most times of the year. Because of this, and instead of provid-ing pilot engines with tender-cabs so that tender-first return to Carlisle could be tolerable, the practice was for detached pilot engines to go south to Hawes Junction and to use the turntable there before returning to Carlisle. This meant about ten extra miles, perhaps an hour extra time, and more occupation of the main lines. Northbound trains also stopped at Aisgill to drop their pilot engines which had been superfluous over the last ten miles from Blea Moor; these too stopped at Hawes Junction on their return journeys in order to use the turntable. In consequence Hawes Junction and the adjoining lines could become congested with pilot engines that had called there for no other purpose than to be turned before going home. Congestion of this sort was a circumstance preceding the disastrous collision between Hawes Junction and Aisgill on 24 December 1910. A pair of returning pilot engines were allowed to stand on the down mail line for some time and, owing to flagrant rule-breaking negligence of the enginemen, remained unnoticed by the signalman. An obvious comment is that where sidings exist they should be sufficiently commodious to avoid any need for engines to stand on the main line. It is interesting to consider what track layout would minimise the fuss and bother of dropping pilots and setting them off on their way home. (The simpler alternative of making engines big enough for their work needs no discussion.)

The first point is that the pilot should be dropped as soon as the train engine no longer needs it. This means at Aisgill going south (as was common practice) and at Blea Moor going north, but no provision for pilot-dropping was made there. The second point is that no time should be spent in putting engines on and off turntables. Engines likely to be required as pilots on the Hellifield–Carlisle line should be provided with tender-cabs or other comparable protection for backward running, and come down tender-first. At each pilot-dropping point there should be a siding between the up and down running lines so that no disengaged pilot should ever need to cross either of them to reach the other.

On p42 is shown a track layout that permits pilot engines to be dropped from up and down trains at the same time. The leading engine of a double-headed train stops at A, and the fireman of the train engine uncouples the pilot engine which then runs ahead past the points B which are spring-loaded to divert it into the siding when it comes back to them. After it has come abreast of the train engine at A, the train can resume its journey as soon as the brakes have been released. None of this requires any action by the signalman, but no engine can run from the siding onto either running line until he has 'made the road' by moving and locking points C and cleared the correct signals.

Page 53 (above) No 360 (m24) was Johnson No 1740. Rebuilt with larger boiler and cab and re-numbered in 1907. Shown running over Dillicar troughs on the L & NW main line south of Tebay; *(centre)* No 399 (m25) was Johnson No 1886: rebuilt with larger boiler and cab; *(below)* No 386 (m25) was Johnson No 1816: rebuilt with Belpaire boiler and extended smokebox

Page 54 (above) No 760 (m31). Note bogie-brakes and water-splash guard-plates for leading bogie axle-boxes; *(centre)* No 999 (m33) as built in 1907. Smokebox on saddle. Note operating arm for MacAllan blast-pipe cap. A snifting valve on steam-chest; *(below)* No 483 (m34). Smokebox carries mechanism for working the superheater damper. Mechanical lubricator on frame-plate. Fowler-Anderson by-pass valve beneath running board. Bogie brakes

Reflections on matters of this sort are interesting but they are concerned not so much with steam as with movements of engines under the direction of the operating department. To an onlooker the distinction may appear trivial but to railwaymen it was paramount. Departmental limits were rigorously maintained and disputes over borderline circumstances were part of the way of life. The working of the Aisgill pilots affords a typical example. The operating department could have been saved a great deal of time and mileage if the pilot engines had gone downhill tender-first, but to make this reasonable for the enginemen, tender-cabs would have had to be provided and the locomotive department could refuse to accept the expense involved. To the outsider, circumstances of this kind are regrettable. The insiders may see things quite differently; an anomaly is usually evidence of a declaration that this or that department is not going to be told by any other department what it shall or shall not do.

Even in what might be expected to be the logical field of engineering development there are oddities ascribable to what are gently called 'personalities' exerting non-technical influence on technical matters. Great economies could have been effected by providing the Leeds–Carlisle line with locomotives able to run the passenger trains without piloting at all. Six-coupled engines might well have been deemed necessary for this purpose, but after the chairman's son had made an unsuccessful experiment (p166) of this kind, it might have been impolitic for Deeley or his successor to do any better. So there was never any Midland 4—6—0 and the management seemed content to see traffic on the Hellifield–Carlisle line cluttered with engines running hundreds of useless miles per day.

The Settle-Carlisle line was twice brought prominently into public notice by disastrous collision followed by fire. Both accidents occurred in the dark small hours above the 1,000ft contour and have been many times reported with the sort of detailed relish to be expected by those who regard this kind of thing as drama in the high fells. Inevitably the essential facts have been

55

D

buried under masses of irrelevant details such as the numbers of the engines, the origin of the coal used and the inclemency of the weather.

The Hawes Junction accident on 24 December 1910, already mentioned, was followed on 2 September 1913 by a collision on the up line not far north of Aisgill. In this case a train which had stalled had been standing for some minutes, but the guard had broken a rule by neglecting to protect it by placing detonators on the rails at an appropriate distance behind it. So the preoccupied driver of a following train (which had run for miles since he had last looked where he was going) did not receive the officially prescribed last warning of approach to a train stopped in a section and a collision ensued.

It is obviously possible to use each happening as the foundation for a whole book of stories about relevant and irrelevant details without dropping any hint about the fact that in each case the accident would have been avoided had the responsible railwayman worked to the relevant rule. It required no skill, judgement or even high intelligence in taking a simple defined action at a time when he had absolutely nothing else to do. If it were rational to spread blame on to antecedents of these lapses (if you do, you don't know where to stop and end with such dilution of responsibility as to suggest that it was nobody's fault), the next thing to be mentioned is that the Midland prohibited signalmen from using any artifice that could remind them that trains were standing in dangerous places. But it did not prohibit engine drivers from walking round their engines when running on lines used by passenger trains.

One other Midland accident is mentioned here only because nearly all the published accounts of it present an entirely misleading picture. It happened on 2 September 1898 at Wellingborough, where a train running at about 50mph was destructively derailed by a platform-truck that had fallen from the down platform on to the down main line track, unnoticed by the signalman. Two men were trying to move this truck and one may be tempted to think of them as heroes risking their lives in attempting to snatch disaster from under the racing wheels of an engine at speed. In actual fact their efforts had been going on for some *ten minutes*, but they had made no attempt to inform the signalman who had no reason to suspect that when he cleared his down main line signals he was admitting a train to disaster. The clearing of the signals gave some two minutes warning of the arrival of the train, but neither man made any use of this.

CHAPTER THREE

Eighty Years' Expansion of Steam

Development of the steam locomotive was in general a slow process. After Trevithick had been instrumental in winning a bet by almost casually throwing together a steam locomotive in 1804, some twenty-one years elapsed before a railway was formally opened for the transport of goods and passengers in steam-hauled trains. Four more years went by before the performance of the *Rocket* at Rainhill convinced everyone that the steam locomotive could revolutionise land-transport with power and speed. It was in the next fifteen years that it developed most quickly, and so much experience had been gained by 1844, when Matthew Kirtley took charge of Midland steam, that he could use certain styles of construction with confidence that they would meet immediate needs. He adopted double-frames and inside cylinders in locomotives of the 2—2—2, 2—4—0, 0—6—0 and 0—4—4WT (well-tank) wheel arrangements. During his twenty-nine years at the head of Midland locomotive affairs, successive designs of 0—6—0 showed in cylinder-volume, boiler-pressure and heating surface an average increase of $1\frac{1}{2}$ to 2 per cent per year.

During S. W. Johnson's thirty-year tenure of the top job at Derby, the corresponding average annual increases were about 0.2 per cent in cylinder-volume, 0.8 per cent in boiler-pressure and 0.6 per cent in heating surface. During the twenty years over which R. M. Deeley and H. Fowler were successively in charge, the figures were about 1.2 per cent, zero and 0.4 per cent. It must be added that both Johnson and Deeley had made some use in 4—4—0s of boiler pressures higher than the final 175psi for 0—6—0s. From 1862 to 1923 grate areas in 0—6—0s had advanced from 15.5 to 21.1sq ft, an average of less than 0.5 per cent per year. The change in size of Midland goods engines over the years may therefore be described as representing steady progress. Averages may, however, be a little misleading in some ways and the progress in grate area (for example) might have been made in (say) two big steps rather than in about ten small ones, but the fact is that if it had been made in just a single step, that would have been only about 36 per cent.

The low rate of increase in size of 0—6—0s after about 1850 was not peculiar to the Midland; something similar could be seen on most railways. The reason is that after the phenomenal development of railways and locomotives from 1830 to 1850 the average 0—6—0 had attained a size that enabled it to cover a wide range of duties during the whole subsequent history of the steam locomotive. In the twentieth century eight-coupled goods engines became numerous but there still remained a vast amount of railway haulage that ordinary 0—6—0s could handle.

The greater majority of Midland tender engines in fact had only six wheels. No main line passenger train locomotive had more than eight, as Paget policy on the Midland found no need for anything bigger than 0—6—0s for goods or 4—4—0s for passengers. Moreover it forbade any hard working of Midland engines with the result that the full abilities of the Midland compounds—which were big 4—4—0s—were never demonstrated in normal service until after the Midland had been merged into the LMS. In technical development, as distinct from mere increase in size, the readily identifiable achievements of the four Midland engineers may be summarised thus:

Kirtley—Introduction of the eventually universal device to enable locomotives to burn coal instead of coke (1859)

Johnson—Introduction of a sound design of compound engine (1901)

Deeley—Simplification of the Johnson compound (1905)

Fowler—Introduction of superheating on the Midland (1911)

Of these, the Kirtley development was incomparably the most important as it affected not merely the Midland, but the steam locomotive all over the world. It is usually associated with the name of Kirtley, although production of the first successful device and the experimental work that led to it are ascribed to Charles Markham, one of his assistants. The earliest steam locomotives were built to haul coal from collieries and they naturally burned coal as there was plenty of it lying about to be picked up 'for nothing'. It had its disadvantages as a fuel, but they were as nought in face of the fact that the coal did not need to be 'bought out'. For locomotives on railways in general, coal did not have quite the same overmastering advantage, as railway companies did not (usually) own coal-mines and so they had to buy their fuel.

But coal did make black smoke and, while that might be tolerated in the neighbourhood of a colliery, it could arouse fierce objection if it came from a locomotive running in any ordinary residential area. Coke was quite different in this respect, and as smoke was specifically a possible cause for rejection of any candidate in the Rainhill contest in 1829, coke was used by all of them and continued to be the normal fuel for steam locomotives for many years afterwards. Coke is much more expensive than coal and this seems unfair when it is remembered that coke is simply coal with a lot of the goodness roasted out of it. A lot of money could therefore be saved by any device that permitted a locomotive to be fired with coal rather than coke, without producing too much smoke. So a lot of ingenuity was displayed, and tedious and experimental work done, in trying to find a sound practical way of designing and making locomotive fireboxes that could get smokeless heat from coal, and in thirty years a solution was found.

The essential facts about production of black smoke from coal are simple enough now and have been known for many years back, as far indeed (one may think) as 1829. This may well have been the case in respect of physicists and chemists, but not necessarily for engineers. Coal placed on a fire immediately emits hydrocarbon gases which, if the fire is hot enough, are ignited by it and burn as they are swept up by the draught. If there is enough air in the stream of gas above the fire, both hydrogen and carbon find all the oxygen they need for combustion and no smoke is produced. If not, flame that is white where it starts with hydrogen combining with oxygen is dull red and smoky where it ends on its way to the chimney. If you can provide heat and air above the firebed, you give the carbon a much better chance of combining with oxygen to produce a smokeless outcome.

Markham's solution was the combination of a brick arch and a deflector. He placed over the front part of the fire a roof that compelled hot gases to pass backwards and then upwards before going forward into the tubes. He made the roof (or arch) of refractory brick that became yellow-hot when the fire had been going for some time and was thus a stimulus to combustion even when other conditions were unfavourable. To lead oxygen into the critical region, he fixed a downward-pointing inverted trough (a deflector-plate) in the fire-box over the fire-hole and this directed the inward-rushing stream of air to the underside of the arch. Collision of gas streams running in markedly different directions caused thorough mixing and this provided plenty of oxygen to burn off the smoke. The instruction to firemen was to close the door after each round of firing and then immediately to open to the smallest extent that would clear the smoke.

It may have seemed odd to build a brick structure inside a boiler that would be jolted and jarred whenever the engine was running, and optimistic to expect that the bricks would hold together while very hot and shaking, and indeed brick arches were always expendable items liable to partial failure without much warning. The deflector plate, unless carefully made to fit precisely and securely, could make accurate shovel-shots difficult and so give trouble to the fireman, but nevertheless the basic principle was simple and sound. As nothing superior was ever devised, few locomotives were designed after 1860 to use any alternative. This Midland contribution to the fundamental design of the steam locomotive was the greatest since Henry Booth proposed the multi-tubular boiler that gave the *Rocket* victory at Rainhill. Provided that the fireman took a bit of trouble, it enabled a locomotive to burn coal without turning out too much smoke, but there were many occasions when taking that bit of trouble was too much effort and black smoke came out of the chimney.

The Midland was also a pioneer in the development of air-sanding and of steam-sanding of driving wheels. Steam-sanding persuaded Johnson, Pollitt (Great Central) and Ivatt (Great Northern) into building singles after locomotives of that type had begun to be regarded as outmoded.

Deeley's simplification of the Johnson design of three-cylinder compound made compounding viable in Britain and led, very slowly, to the realisation that if you must have compounds, let them be three-cylinder ones. After sixty years' domination of the French railway-scene by four-cylinder compounds, M Chapelon adopted the three-cylinder principle in a large 4—8—4 built for the French national railways in 1946. It is perhaps to be regretted that a Derby design prepared in 1924 for a three-cylinder compound 4—6—0 never materialised, although it may be doubted whether it would have had any advantage over the corresponding three-cylinder simple sensibly designed to make full use of knowledge at that time.

Midland practice was distinguished by early use (1893) of piston-valves in certain classes of locomotive. These were 4—2—2s and 4—4—0s, from which speed was required, and it was no doubt believed that piston-valves were less advantageous at low speeds. This is true to the extent that it was less difficult to design and make piston valves to give plenty of port opening than was the case with flat valves, but on the other hand it must be remembered that flat valves did not in themselves prohibit high speed. Some Great Western performances made that quite clear. Piston-valves were not necessarily superior to flat valves in steam tightness but they were less troubled by superheated steam. Some British railways adopted piston valves only when they took up superheating, but that was not the case on the Midland. On the contrary, Derby found it possible, by dint of special attention to lubrication, to apply superheaters to existing wet steam engines while retaining their flat valves.

The simplest possible steam locomotive had only four wheels and only two of them were driven by the pistons and connecting rods. Stephenson's *Rocket* is the most famous example of a locomotive of that description. If the conventional type of locomotive boiler is used, a four-wheeler cannot be either big or fast as the fire-box must overhang the wheelbase. A four-wheel engine is good for getting round very sharp curves very slowly but not for speed on curves or straight. A 'flyer' must have at least six wheels and it is sufficient if one pair are driving wheels. The simplest arrangement is for the fire-box to lie between the middle pair and the trailing pair and for the cylinders to lie ahead of the leading pair. The Stephensons soon developed from the double-frame 2—2—0 *Planet* of 1830 the double-frame 2—2—2 and many railways afterwards used this type of locomotive.

The Midland obtained two 2—2—2s (ml) from Kitson in 1845 and probably also some similar ones in the next few succeeding years. By 1852 Kirtley, then with some eight years of Midland working, placed orders with Stephenson for six larger 2—2—2s and with Sharp, Stewart & Co for ten generally similar ones (m2). These two classes had detail variations in accordance with the standard practices of their builders, but they were identical in having double frames with axleboxes working in hornblocks in the outside frame-plates.

Kirtley's general practice was to use chimneys with well-flared rims, tall domes with Salter-type safety-valves and a raised flat seating on top of the outer fire-box. This seating looked as if it had been provided to accommodate a safety-valve, and in some cases it did; in other cases it carried only a whistle, in others nothing at all, and consequently looked like a mistake. Kirtley favoured 'sandwich frames', which was not just another name for double frames but meant that each plate was actually a large flat piece of wood clamped by bolts between two thin plates of iron or steel to form a sandwich. Frames for successive designs of locomotive tended to become deeper but were cut away in places where this would save weight without materially reducing strength.

Rectangular side-plates on foot-plates gave the enginemen's legs some protection against side winds but no other part of their bodies was so fortunate. As the years went by, however, a spark of humanity occasionally inspired someone to specify weatherboards to protect the men against wind caused by the speed of the locomotive through the local air. Later on, manufacturing drawings began to show weatherboards bent backwards at the top so as to shield the men better from falling rain. Under pressure from a series of remorseless trends of this character Midland enginemen found themselves on footplates with superimposed structures that might almost be called cabs. After sixty years, things had gone so far that when an engine was standing in still air and falling rain, anyone on the footplate had to lean out if he wanted to get wet, unless indeed there was a leak in the roof.

But Kirtley never enclosed his enginemen to this extent, nor did Johnson. It was only after the twentieth century was a few years old that the Midland had got round to usefully roofed cabs and it was Deeley who had them made. Early weatherboard roofs were very low and so were the slightly more elaborate coverings provided by Johnson. For fifty years or more the typical Midland locomotive had a tall chimney followed by a less tall dome, then by a less tall safety valve and then by a low cab-roof. After the engine came the tender, lower still. Engine and tender had a 'head-first' appearance, the highest component being at the front and the remaining ones in quickly descending order of magnitude. Even the largest nineteenth-century Midland engines were dwarfed by the highest clerestoried coaches that were often attached to them in the twentieth century.

The Kirtley 'singles' were very light but they could take the light passenger trains nicely along the easy early Midland lines and Kirtley 2—2—2s were being built as late as 1865. Engines of the '30' class (m4) had deep frame-plates cut from the solid and not 'built-up' in any way. They were strong and lasted for many years. Until St Pancras station was opened in 1868, Midland trains for London ran to King's Cross over the Great Northern line from Hitchin and engines of the '30' class got them along at the same kind of speed as the Great Northern trains were achieving on that route. The best booked times between King's Cross and Hitchin represented some of the fastest running in Great Britain at the time.

Many Midland passenger trains were, however, tending to become too heavy to be reliably hauled by singles, and Kirtley went over to 2—4—0s for passenger trains and of course continued with 0—6—0s for goods trains. So also did Johnson for a long time, but nearly twenty years after Kirtley had ceased to build singles Johnson started to produce some. What had happened to make singles viable once more? One change was that over the intervening period heavier and stronger track had become standard on the Midland, and so greater axle-loads could be taken. Kirtley had been limited to about 12 tons, but in 1887 Johnson was allowed $17\frac{1}{2}$ and ten years later still was building singles with $18\frac{1}{2}$ tons on the driving wheels (these are 'official' figures; spring-adjustment decided the load and it could be measured only by use of special equipment).

Another change was that steam-sanding of the rails had been tried and the indications were that it was more effective than dry sanding. If rails could be reliably sanded to neutralise the lubricating effect of anything else that might drop on them, a 17-ton adhesion weight could cover the needs of Midland main-line passenger trains for a long time ahead. The design and construction of sanding gear on locomotives had rarely been given the attention that it warranted. Many designers appeared never to have learned that greasy rails on an up-gradient could render any steam locomotive helpless unless it could get sand between the rails and the treads of its driving wheels. In those conditions, sand was as vital as steam.

The essential need seems simple. If dry sand is admitted to a nearly vertical pipe with its lower open end over the rail, and within a foot of the region of contact between wheel and rail, then the sand will be dropped on the rail and, a fraction of a second later, will be doing its stuff between wheel and rail. Now when practical sizes of pipe and supporting brackets are considered, it may be found that 'within a foot' is not easily attainable and that some greater separation of pipe from contact-region may have to be tolerated. As a consequence, a strong cross-wind may blow the dropped sand off the rail before the wheel can reach it.

Ruminating on this, the Derby works manager, Holt, conceived the idea that a very strong artificial wind in the right direction might blow sand between the wheel and the rail despite the deviatory effect of any natural cross-wind. It may well be that what inspired the idea was the Midland trial of the Westinghouse compressed-air brake. A locomotive equipped to work this brake carried a reservoir containing air at a pressure of 90lb per square inch and air led from it could produce a gale-force wind in any limited locality. Any Westinghouse-fitted Midland locomotive needed only the addition of ten or twenty feet of small piping to try out this idea. So it was tried, and it worked very well indeed. A couple of 2—4—0 locomotives were converted to 2—2—2s by removal of their coupling-rods, fitted with 'air-sanding' and sent with trains over Aisgill to find whether they worked as well as singles with air-sanding as they had as 'doubles' without it. This did in fact turn out to be the case and so it was concluded that Johnson might usefully resume building of singles.

The Westinghouse Company heard of this new development and raised objection to it. The only way in which they could have enforced any such objection would have been to refuse to supply any more air-compressors to the Midland if the objection were ignored. So it was not really sensible for the Westinghouse Company to make such a complaint at a time when it was trying to persuade the Midland to adopt the Westinghouse brake as standard. The outcome was obvious and inevitable. The Midland, with steam at 160psi in its locomotive boilers, told Westinghouse that it could get by without compressed air for sanding and indeed for braking, and rejected Westinghouse brakes in favour of vacuum brakes. In this way arose steam sanding, and gave a new lease of life to singles.

It has been claimed in favour of steam sanding that water formed by condensation of steam as it strikes a cold rail has some useful effect in removing the microscopic layer of lubricant that is making the sanding operation necessary. But if sand gets to the right place, it makes no difference whether there is also a lubricant there or not. Under pressure, sand grains dig into the steel and no lubricant can stop them. On the other hand, if no sand reaches the rails, then the condensate of a steam jet may diminish the effect of a lubricating layer even if it does not remove it.

Long before steam sanding was developed, Johnson had progressed from 2—4—0s to 4—4—0s and a good many of them were running on the Midland. So when singles came to be reconsidered, it was natural for Johnson to build 4—2—2s rather than 2—2—2s and in doing so he produced some very handsome-looking locomotives. A 2—2—2 rather overhangs its front wheels whereas the front of a 4—2—2 rests on a spreading bogie that looks very important and safe. Only the Dean singles on the Great Western may have surpassed the Johnson engines in captivating students and admirers of the steam locomotive. Many of them positively drooled over the beauty of the Johnson singles in their successively enlarged forms. The writer understands this perfectly, even though he rates the Dean engines more highly in this purely personal matter in spite of their raised fireboxes.

The earliest Johnson singles (like contemporary Johnson

engines of other classes) had a chimney that looked as if it might have been built up of top, bottom and middle, although it probably was not. Had the top part been copper-sheathed, it would have been more readily noticeable that the profile was almost identical with that of the chimney used by Beyer, Peacock & Co as standard for many years. Outside frames gave to the lower parts of Johnson singles a strong, massive appearance enhanced by the prominent axleboxes and springs for the driving and trailing axles. If outside frames had been used for the bogies, the engines might have equalled the Great Western ones in purposeful beauty. Inside bogie frames can obviously be made lighter and this is a functional advantage, but did it outweigh the very much easier accessibility of axle-boxes working in outside frames? These first '25 class' Johnson singles (m5) were evidently able to handle a great deal of Midland passenger traffic as 60 of them were built in the period 1887-93. One of them (No 1853) built in 1889 was sent over to the Paris Exhibition of that year in order to fly the Midland flag in France, and returned with a Grand Prix for excellence in the *concours d'elegance*.

A prominent variation in this class of engine was that after the first twenty-five, the driving axle was loaded through long helical springs instead of the original laminated springs. Friction between the plates of laminated springs is useful in killing the vertical vibration that follows impact with a high spot in the track, but it makes the springs not quite fast enough to keep the wheels fully pressed on the rails in getting over a low spot. Even momentary easing of the grip of driving wheels on rails could allow a slip to start. It became common practice to use helical springs for driving axles and laminated springs for the others.

Johnson's multiplication of these engines shows that, at least with the aid of steam sanding, their low adhesion weight was no serious disadvantage but—it used to be repeatedly hinted—the driving wheels might be slipping imperceptibly all the time the engine was pulling and this would mean a continuous waste of power. It is interesting to read (*The Engineer*, p113, 1884, vol 2) that the Midland had investigated this point by counting the number of driving-wheel revolutions made by a four-coupled engine in hauling a ten-coach train over a particular stretch of line at 50mph and by repeating the observation during a second run by the same locomotive without coupling-rods. The difference was found to be about ten per cent of the distance travelled by the train. This meant that, relative to the coupled engine, the single wasted power equal to ten per cent of that used in pulling the train, by virtue of extra slipping of the driving wheels.

On the other hand, it is recorded on p397 of the *Railway Magazine* for November 1913 that in another test the number of driving-wheel revolutions made by a Midland single was noted while she was hauled 'dead' over a particular length of line. The same observation was made while the engine hauled a regular express train over the same length. There was no significant difference between the counted revolutions and so it was concluded that if there was any slip of the driving wheels, while they pulled the train, it was too small to bother about. Two tests thus gave markedly different results. The writer finds the second one to be the more readily credible because once a slip starts, the coefficient of friction drops, the resistance to slipping is thus diminished and there is strong encouragement for the small slip to develop into one big enough for the driver to notice.

Soon after completion of the first sixty Johnson singles, the design was modified to include piston-valves instead of flat valves and ten engines of this description became the '179 class' (m6). They were the first Midland engines to have piston-valves and they had them in that odd position underneath the cylinders. Steam approaches cylinders from above and leaves them by going up to the blast-pipe; why place the valves in a position that compels steam to squeeze past the cylinders before it enters them and then to squeeze past them again (stealing heat this time) to get away?

When a designer was compelled to use cylinders too fat to leave room for flat valves in the usual space between them, he had to find some other place for the valves. The obvious other place was above the cylinders, but if it were adopted the boiler would have to be set a few inches higher than was otherwise necessary, and in the nineteenth century some designers were terrified of high boilers. But, at least where the cylinders were ahead of the leading axle (as in conventional 2—2—2s, 2—4—0s and 0—6—0s), valves might be placed below the cylinders. So far as steam-flow was concerned this was bad, but on the other hand it had the practical advantage that after a flat valve had been withdrawn through the opening in the front of the steam-chest, and the cover underneath it removed, the port-face was open to direct inspection by anyone who didn't mind lying on his back under the front of the engine. Such a position was not comfortable, but from it one could see the port-face in a way that was quite impossible where valves were between the cylinders. There was, however, no such advantage (or any other) in placing piston valves below cylinders rather than above them. But fashion requires no reason and, round about the change of century, quite a number of British locomotive engineers had a go with piston valves below cylinders. (There were similar crazes with compound engines, bogie-brakes and piston rail-rods.)

It was deemed essential that piston valves should collapse under pressure induced by water trapped in the cylinders and Johnson used a design developed by W. M. Smith on the North Eastern. Johnson reported that certain piston valves showed a much lower rate of wear than that of corresponding flat valves, but not all experience with piston valves in those early days was so encouraging. Piston valves were claimed to be drivable with less power than that required for flat valves, but as Aspinall (Lancashire & Yorkshire Railway) had shown particular flat valves to be workable by about 2 per cent of the power developed in the cylinders there was no scope for sensational economy in that direction.

There were four distinguishable classes of Johnson singles (m5 to m8) but the differences between them were quite small.

Page 71 (above) No 2632 (m32). One of the first two Johnson compounds as built. Reducing valve on smokebox. Rear splasher combined with cab in L & NW style. Ahead of it a sheet conceals some of the length of the reversing rods. Clasp brakes on coupled wheels; *(centre)* No 1025 (m32) Deeley compound as built in 1906; *(below)* No 1000 (m32). Original Johnson compound No 2631 as renumbered, rebuilt and superheated in 1914.

Page 72 (above) No 1528 (m36). Stove-pipe chimney. Coal carried on side-tank. Reflections suggest that it is not easy to make large plates quite flat; (*centre*) No 235 (m37). Side-tank engine with condenser built by Beyer, Peacock & Co in 1868 for Midland trains on the Metropolitan Railway. Rivet heads show where the bottom of the tank is curved to clear the cotters in the coupling-rod; (*below*) No 695 (m38). Well-tank engine with condenser, built by Beyer, Peacock & Co in 1869. Re-numbered 1205 in 1907

General trends in dimensions included small increases in grate area, firebox heating surface, adhesion weight, engine weight, boiler pressure, cylinder diameter, driving wheel diameter and nominal tractive effort. Heating surface of tubes, however, went gradually downwards and some commentators viewed this with the greatest misgiving intensified by the fact that cylinder-diameter had gone up. Indifferent steaming of the 'Princess' class (m8) was ascribed to the combination of $19\frac{1}{2}$in cylinders and 1,070sq ft of heating surface. A remark of this nature was made in writing by a well-experienced locomotive engineer who knew perfectly well that any engine could be made to steam by appropriately contracting the blast orifice. But the remark, and dozens of similar ones, were taken up and enlarged by people who never stopped to think about what is involved in steaming. It helped to establish a wide and firm belief that if the cylinder-diameter of a locomotive were even a quarter of an inch greater than some figure that only a genius among designers could determine by outstanding instinct, the engine might as well be relegated to station-shunting duty.

The 'Princesses', with some 24sq ft of grate area (more than that of most of the contemporary 4—4—0s), were potentially powerful engines although the starting pull was limited to about a quarter of the adhesion weight and therefore to about 10,000lb. With a nominal tractive effort of 17,000lb they needed a severely restricted regulator-opening to start in full gear without slipping, but once well under way they could develop their full power at any speed higher than about 35mph. On most of the Midland main lines this was no hardship, but on the steeper ones where the engine might be forced down to slogging at much below 35mph, sanding might be necessary to prohibit slipping, even on dry rails. But sanding gear did not always work as it should because some sorts of sand are far more reluctant than others to flow through pipes, and a combination of greasy rails, adverse gradient and inadequate sanding could stop a single more effectively than a coupled engine. Sand that flows intermittently and unequally on

73

E

the two rails can impose a sudden obstruction to rapidly spinning wheels and this was commonly held to be a possible cause of breakage of crank-axles.

In contributing to a discussion on a technical paper read before the Institution of Mechanical Engineers in 1933, Sir Henry Fowler mentioned that the crank-axles of the Johnson singles had been a continuous source of trouble. Cracks developed and extended so commonly that no axle lasted longer than eight years. It is not to be assumed that this short life was in any way associated with stresses set up when slipping wheels ran onto sanded rails as there were other origins of undue stress. It has been suggested that bending moment due to flange-pressure on the large driving wheels could induce stresses high enough to start cracks in the crank-axle and to propagate them.

As all singles used to do most of their work in an effortlessly-seeming manner (because they were not in fact making much effort), it is natural to believe that they did not burn much coal and figures in the region of 20lb per mile have been quoted for the Midland engines. No such figure can show whether the engine was notably economical or not; to obtain any information on that point it would be necessary also to know about routes, speeds and weights of trains. In the *Railway Magazine* for February 1910 are recorded figures derived from tests on Midland singles of the 115 and 2601 classes, and they quote 2.9lb of coal per indicated horsepower hour for both classes. (This is closely comparable with contemporary results from North Eastern Class R 4—4—0s.) The figures correspond to about 450ihp for the smaller engine and 550ihp for the larger one and to 21.3 and 23.0ihp per square foot of grate area, the train weights being 123 and 160 tons respectively and the average speeds about 54 and 52mph.

This implies very gentle rates of working the engines but a rather high train-resistance per ton of train weight. An odd feature of some of the data is that 'Train and Passenger' weights are quoted to the last hundredth of a ton and alongside each is given the same number divided by 12 in a column headed 'No of vehicles at 12 tons each including Passengers and Luggage'. A photograph was reproduced of single No 26 fitted on her left side with a small but highly protective indicator-shelter containing some apparatus driven by a pulley on the driving axle and a *crossed* belt.

The classic high-power run of a Midland single was that of No 125 (m7) in taking 325 tons from Kettering to Nottingham, $51\frac{1}{2}$ miles, at a start-to-stop average of 51.3mph. This corresponds to a mean drawbar horsepower of about 25 per square foot of grate area and this is not remarkably high even for a wet steam engine. The greatest difficulty on the run was that of getting a total mass of over 400 tons really going up the initial gradient of 1 in 132. The resistance due to weight alone is over 3 tons and, with adhesion weight of $18\frac{1}{2}$ tons limiting the frictional force at the treads of the driving wheels to a maximum of about $4\frac{1}{2}$ tons, there was not much margin left to cover the frictional resistances in the wheels and axles of engine, tender and train. Although acceleration must have been low on the subsequent rise of 2 miles at 1 in 160 the first 5 miles from Kettering were covered in 11 minutes, and from there to the stop at Nottingham, with more downhill than up, the average was $56\frac{1}{2}$mph.

This run of No 125 shows a Midland single at its best and it also shows why it was not possible to rely on such engines for loads over about 300 tons. Acceleration up such a gradient as 1 in 132 was bound to be slow even with a driver working the engine to the verge of slipping on dry rails; if the rails were greasy and the sanding gear imperfect, there might be no acceleration at all. Nevertheless singles were to be seen on the Midland main line south of Derby right until the grouping of 1923 and even afterwards. They could take the lighter trains and they were also useful in double-heading trains that exceeded the modest tonnages specified after 1909. In later years Midland mineral trains were sometimes assisted by singles and in this duty they were at their least effective. It was said that they were used because their coal consumption was low. Of course it was! They could not develop much power at the low speeds of mineral trains and so there was no reason why they should burn much coal. The only justification for double-heading a mineral train with a single was that it was better than nothing.

Between the 0—6—0 as a 'puller' and the 2—2—2 as a 'flyer', the 2—4—0 was an obvious compromise and most British railways made wide use of that wheel arrangement in the nineteenth century. Compromise or not, the 2—4—0 could also be a flyer and the exploit of North Western 2—4—0 *Hardwicke* in making a start-to-stop average of 67mph from Crewe to Carlisle in 1895 is a well-known demonstration of the fact. No Midland engine was ever quite so scintillating as was *Hardwicke* on that special occasion but Midland 2—4—0s worked all the best Midland passenger trains for many years. They were in charge of expresses on the Settle–Carlisle line at its opening and for some years afterwards, even though 4—4—0s were then being multiplied on the Midland. Some of the 2—4—0s competed severely witn Great Western 2—4—0s in races on the parallel lines between Gloucester and Standish Junction and others similarly challenged North Eastern engines between York and Church Fenton after the quadrupling of that line.

The foregoing remarks apply to Midland 2—4—0s of the conventional type. Some of the earliest ones, however, were long-boiler engines with outside cylinders which means that the cylinders were ahead of the leading wheels and the firebox was behind the trailing wheels. All the wheels were closely packed together so that the long-boiler should not be too long. Four such engines were supplied to the Midland in 1846 by Kitson & Co and a number of generally similar ones were afterwards obtained from other builders, but the type won no real favour from Kirtley. The long-boiler engine had a superficial advantage in that the long tubes seemed to promise a high boiler-efficiency by extracting a lot of heat from the hot flue-gases, but this was illusory. The relevant factor is not the mere length of the tubes, but the ratio

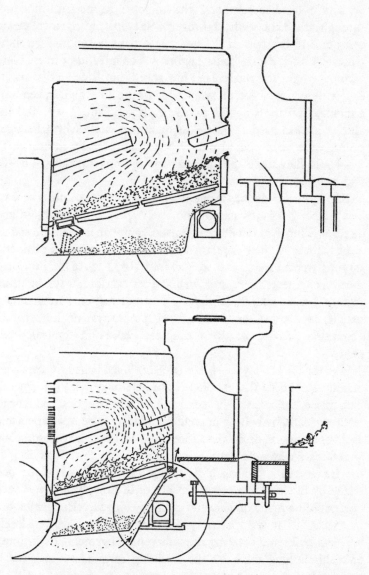

(*above*) Firebox of Johnson compound (m32) with drop-grate; (*below*) firebox
of Class 4F 0—6—0 (m52) showing how ash could reach the cab

of length to diameter, and the increase in heat-transmission through the tube-walls, however achieved, means increase in resistance to the flow of the hot gas to the smokebox. The short wheelbase of the long-boiler engine was an advantage in enabling it to get round sharp curves at low speed, but it was a disadvantage in inducing a lot of sway if anything like high speed was attempted on the straight. So the early Midland 2—4—0s, unable to pull so hard as 0—6—0s or to run safely with passenger trains, were soon phased out. When Kirtley really got down to 2—4—0s they were the counterparts of conventional 0—6—0s and were not long-boiler engines.

Kirtley was a double-frame man for a quarter-century at least and all his 2—4—0s except the last twenty were double-frame engines. They had detail variations in compliance with the standard practices of their different builders and there was a distinctly upward trend in size and weight from 1862 to 1871. But locomotive engineers were still feeling their various ways in using materials and fixing dimensions in locomotives; only fragmentary details have come down to us and (as always) no information about the relative worth of different classes in ton-miles per penny.

The earlier Kirtley 2—4—0s (m9, m10, m11) had tie-bars connecting the horns that embraced the axle-boxes and (in general) had raised fireboxes. The connections between ties and horns, whether made by bolting or welding, tended to be weak spots and a change was made in the '156 class' (m12). Each frame-plate started as a rectangle (with or without humps on top) as deep as the frame and it was made to approximate in shape to the tied frame by having large pieces cut out of it. Forty years later such cuts could be made quickly and easily by oxy-acetylene flame, but in the 1860s it was probably done by drilling lines of closely adjacent holes and severing the intervening ligaments by hammer and chisel. Smoothing off the resulting serrated profiles was a weary job that could be left to the lads.

Next came the '170 class' (m13) of thirty engines built by Beyer

Peacock & Co, and exhibiting a touch of elegance that distinguished the products of that company in Victorian times. In these, a high sweep of the top edge of the frame over each coupled axle-box, in conjunction with substantial hornstays, gave such strength that the frame-plate did not need to be so deep as to justify lightening by being cut away. In distinction from the Midland (and common) practice of conveying motion from expansion-link to valve-spindle by a sliding bar, the corresponding connection in a '170' was by a rod suspended on a swinging link near its rear end, and pinned to the valve-spindle at the other end.

E. L. Ahrons expressed in writing a warm regard for Kirtley's '800 class' (m14), and one specific reason for this was probably the feat of No 815 in hauling a 130-ton train from Carlisle to Aisgill ($48\frac{1}{2}$ miles horizontally and some 1,100ft vertically) in 59 minutes. The '800s' were basically similar to the Beyer Peacock 2—4—0 (m13). An obvious external difference was that the bent-over weather-board extended a few inches further backward and another was that the flared chimney-rim, although not exceptional for 1870, looked a shade coarse compared with the Beyer Peacock chimney.

Some of the Neilson-built engines of this class had reversing gear worked by a vertical screw in the cab and this was something very strange to Midland enginemen at that time. (It was never very numerously applied in Britain till Gresley began to multiply Pacifics and 2—6—0s on the LNER). There were many occasions when engine drivers operating unfamiliar reversing gear contrived to get going in the wrong direction after dealing with a bout of slipping in a tunnel. On one occasion, unintended backward running and a consequent collision followed a signal stop at Kibworth by a night train being taken from St Pancras towards Leicester by No 809 with the Neilson vertical screw. A frequently-quoted account of this incident partially excuses the driver by mentioning a tunnel, but in more recent years there was no sign of any such thing on the Midland main line at Kibworth. Perhaps it was a dark night when the mistake was made.

The fact that Kirtley built forty-eight engines of the '800' class inclines one to believe that he had found its performance to be satisfactory. It was a generously-proportioned 2—4—0 with the top edge of each frame-plate highly swept up and over each driving axle in the manner demonstrated in the '170 class' (m13) 2—4—0s built by Beyer Peacock, and giving in full measure the impression of battleship strength that is characteristic of double-frame engines. At the rear it looked a bit empty because there was no safety-valve where one could be expected on the raised seating on the firebox and there was no cab. Each rear splasher was rectangular and that kept side-winds off enginemen's legs, but above waist height only a bent weatherboard protected them from rain and speed-created wind. (A little rebuilding by Johnson eventually improved matters in this respect.)

But before the forty-eighth '800' had been completed, Kirtley had ordered from Neilson 2—4—0s of generally similar dimensions but with no outside axle-boxes for the coupled wheels, and therefore with outside frame-plates in the form of a shallow strip extended downwards only to carry hornblocks for outside boxes on the leading axle. These locomotives constituted the '890' class (m15) of which twenty were built between 1870 and 1876. They differed from '800s' in providing a little more weather-protection for the enginemen. Without going so far as to call the footplate superstructure a cab, one could see that it was a move in the right direction and nothing more sumptuous was provided for enginemen on the Midland (or on most other British railways) for a quarter of a century.

It was reported about the '890' class that they were less troublesome than the '800s' in respect of breakages of crank-axles, and inevitably one wonders why the change from double-frame to single-frame (for the crank-axle) should produce such a result. After some reflection one realises that these things are not necessarily effect and cause. One of the advantages of double-frames is that breakage of a crank-axle is not necessarily followed by derailment of any wheel. But even though it be accepted that every crank-axle would break eventually if allowed to run long enough, breakage could (in the ordinary way) be avoided by proper regular inspection because it resulted from extension of a crack during the running of tens of thousands of miles. Thus, with experience in watching the progress of cracks, it was possible to keep the risk of crank-axle breakage down to a negligible amount and thus to do without the advantage of double axle-boxes in minimising danger from breakages. At all events, the only double-frame engines built for the Midland after 1875 were the Johnson singles in which double-frames did not demand the fly-cranks that were the fascinating (but expensive) accompaniment of double-frames for coupled engines.

Johnson had built 2—4—0s for the Great Eastern before he came to Derby and he continued to do so on the Midland until by 1882 he had added to the stock some one hundred and fifty 2—4—0s in four classes. These were hardly distinguishable from each other in the usually quoted dimensions, apart from driving wheel diameter; there were four sizes ranging from $74\frac{1}{2}$in to 84in. The uncritical student of the subject may assume from this that Johnson was trying to discover a magic diameter that would lift performance into a new plane. The actual reasons for trying small differences in wheel diameter seem never to have been set on paper. There seems now to be no valid reason why three appropriately-spaced wheel diameters should not have sufficed for the whole gamut of steam locomotive operation from hump-pushing to 120mph maxima, but some designers were still playing with piffling differences at least as late as 1939.

The 2—4—0 wheel arrangement was successfully used in a great many British locomotives, but in the larger sizes the leading axle was taking heavy loads and there were occasional troubles on that account. Partly for this reason, the Great Western rebuilt their largest 2—2—2s to the 4—2—2 wheel arrangement in the early 1890s. Some fifteen years earlier, Johnson had perceived a possible need to develop in that direction and he was trying 4—4—0s on the Midland as early as 1876.

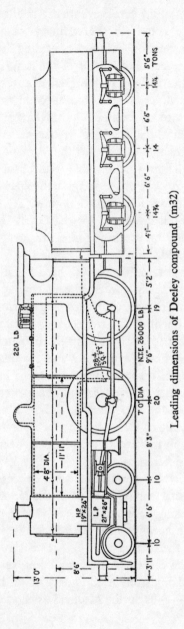

Leading dimensions of Deeley compound (m32)

82

In appearance at least the early Midland 4—4—0s were pitiable weaklings, and it is easy to see why. The later Midland 2—4—0s looked sturdy enough and their performance was well up to contemporary standards. But when the same engine was placed on a 4—4—0 chassis, with the bogie jutting ahead of the smokebox under about 30sq ft of platform doing nothing useful, the guts of the 2—4—0 was diluted; one obtained the impression of a lot of wheels with not much of a boiler to keep them going. On a railway dominated by 0—6—0s, 2—4—0s and 0—4—4Ts, each covering all its wheelbase with functional components, the appearance of a locomotive that sprawled over any unnecessary length of track was not impressive; it looked lost among all those scattered wheels. This was not, of course, peculiar to the Midland; the majority of the early British 4—4—0s, with tall chimney and narrow smokebox over a wide-spread bogie, produced the same visual impression of a firmly based lighthouse tower that would not be moved by all the forces of nature. 'Here I am, and here I stick', it seemed to say. When in later years 4—4—0s acquired fatter boilers, short chimneys and extended smokeboxes, the vertical column effect disappeared; the emphasis was horizontal, and the front of the engine looked prepared and indeed even eager to go. On the Midland this change became very marked, and 4—4—0s rebuilt with more highly pitched boilers and well-extended smokeboxes looked quite aggressively powerful. (See No 1563 on p36 and No 386 on p53.)

There was no reason why a 4—4—0 should be able to pull harder or to run faster than the corresponding 2—4—0, and no one expected it to do so. So why use eight wheels where six would suffice? Simply because a leading bogie enabled the locomotive to strike and to traverse curves less stressfully than did a single guiding axle. The bogie could pivot about its vertical axis so that two wheel-flanges could bear on the side of a curved outer rail and so share the horizontal centripetal force on the leading end of the engine. Both wheels and rails were happier with the smaller flange-forces that the bogie offered and adoption of the

4—4—0 wheel arrangement could be justified on that account.

This lines up with an objection that the Lancashire & Yorkshire was said to have raised to the running of Midland 2—4—0s over its lines between Hellifield and Liverpool and between Hellifield and Manchester in accordance with an arrangement that began in 1888; 4—4—0s were permitted but not 2—4—0s and this rule persisted long after the L & Y had built a large fleet of 2—4—2 tank engines that must have stressed the track quite as much as any Midland 2—4—0 was likely to do. A broad view of Midland 4—4—0s shows size rising over the years in four steps:

Building dates	Grate Area (sq ft)	Approx. number built	After 1907 Power class	Running Nos
1876-1895	17.5	120	1	
1892-1901	19.6	110	2	
1898-1901	21.1	40	2	300-562
1900-1905	25.0	80	3	700-779
1901-1909	28.4	55	4	990-1044

Over the years, engine weight increased from about 40 tons to 60 tons, boiler pressure from 140 to 200psi (with periods at higher pressures up to 220psi in certain classes) and cylinder diameter from $17\frac{1}{2}$ to $20\frac{1}{2}$in (21in compound LP). Piston stroke remained constant at 26in, and driving wheel diameter was 78, 81 or 84in. Stephenson valve gear was used throughout except that Joy gear was tried in a class (m23) of ten engines built in 1884. With flat valves above the cylinders, there was room to give them 19in diameter and this was one of the advantages of Joy gear. It did not, however, prove successful in this Midland application and the engines were rebuilt after two years' service to have the conventional Stephenson gear and flat valves between small cylinders. In 1896 piston valves appeared (below the cylinders) and this left room for diameters up to 21in if required.

Advantage was taken of this when superheating was adopted by Fowler.

Until the year 1900, driving wheel splashers were made with conjoining reverse curves all edged with brass. Salter safety valves were carried on the dome and a direct-loaded safety valve was hidden in a graceful brass casing on the firebox. An abrupt change came with the 'Class 3' (m31) introduced in 1900. The boiler was distinctly larger in diameter, fairly highly pitched and had a Belpaire firebox. The driving wheel splashers were separated and Salter safety valves abandoned in favour of Ramsbottom valves on the firebox, which also carried an additional directly loaded safety valve corresponding to the firebox-mounted one in the Johnson style. The rear splashers were rectangular and above them was a 'cab', a shade more generous than Johnson had previously conceded. The 'Class 3' was an engine with distinctly more guts (George Stephenson could always find the right word) than its predecessors and marked a dignified entrance into the twentieth century by abandoning prominent Victoriana in Midland practice.

The styling of the first five compound 4—4—0s (m32) introduced in 1901 was however a little florid. Deeley did good work in simplifying these engines, inside and out, and made them into the most impressive-looking locomotives the Midland ever had. The last entirely new Midland 4—4—0 design (m33), the Deeley '999', was perhaps a disappointment. It could have been expected to equal the compound in performance and at lower cost. That it failed to do so is suggested by the fact that the LMS built 200 compounds with only slight departures from the Deeley design, but made no addition to the '999' class.

Both Deeley and Fowler went in for extensive re-boilering of Johnson 4—4—0s, making them look much more powerful, but not raising them above Power Class 2. The nominal power limitation was no serious disadvantage as the Paget traffic organisation provided plenty of work within Class 2 capacity and plenty of spare engines and men to 'double-head' any train too heavy for the engine booked to take it. One result was that post-Paget performance of any class of locomotive rarely approached its pre-Paget peak. Rebuilding of any old Midland 4—4—0 might include a boiler with either a round-topped firebox or a Belpaire firebox. The former type of boiler usually had a normally narrow smokebox whereas Belpaire boilers usually had extended smokeboxes, but there were exceptions. Driving-wheel splashers might be joined or separated, running boards might be flat or be raised to clear coupling-rods, and rebuilding after 1910 might, or might not, include a superheater. Variety in Midland rebuilds did not reach Great Western heights, but it provided enough oddities to delight those who revel in such things. In 1913 Fowler rebuilt a 4—4—0 with a Belpaire boiler, extended smokebox, superheater, piston valves and mechanical lubricator and this engine (No 483) was the first of a new standard Class 2 4—4—0 (m34). All subsequent rebuilds of 4—4—0s were substantially of this form and there were some one hundred and fifty of them. In 1928 the LMS adopted this design (with small modifications in wheel diameter, cylinder diameter, and constructional details) for a standard locomotive able to go anywhere on its extensive system, and 138 (Nos 563-700) were eventually built.

No 483 as rebuilt in 1913 had 'everything that opens and shuts' but a number of the special frills were soon abandoned. Brakes on bogie wheels were a little late in 1913 as that craze was just dying out. The Fowler-Anderson by-pass valves, offering a direct connection between the two ends of a cylinder when the regulator was closed, were only a more elaborate and less satisfactory alternative to an anti-vacuum (snifting) valve anywhere between the regulator and the steam-chests. A superheater damper was generally assumed, in the early days of superheating, to be necessary to safeguard the superheater elements when no steam was in them, but this was found not to be the case and by about 1916 everyone was beginning to abandon them.

The outstanding locomotive design on the Midland originated in a straight copy from the North Eastern. From 1885 to 1890

T. W. Worsdell was the Locomotive Superintendent of that railway, and during that short period he provided it with a large number of very good locomotives besides a large number of two-cylinder compounds. These last were converted to simples, or to scrap, as quickly as possible by his brother, who took over the job and held it till 1910.

Any two-cylinder compound locomotive was bound to be a bit of an atrocity, and young Wilson was right in putting the North Eastern ones out of the way. He can be excused for having an antipathy towards compounds. He had seen what a mess three-cylinder compounds had made on the London & North Western Railway, where he had over six years of varied experience, and he must have decided, before he took up the North Eastern headship, that scrapping of compounds or conversion to simples would have to be a top priority job. All the same, he did complete a two-cylinder compound 4—4—0 (No 1619) from parts which were made to his brother's designs and got the usual amount of two-cylinder compound despondency out of it.

On the North Eastern design staff, however, was W. M. Smith, who had recognised that what Webb and T. W. Worsdell had done with compounding on locomotives had not really given it a chance of showing what slight advantage it might have over simple (one-stage) expansion. He was able to see that of the two main ways of designing a three-cylinder compound, Webb had concentrated exclusively on the wrong one and that the other might get by. The sensible course was to pass boiler-steam to a single (high-pressure) cylinder inside the frame and to lead the exhaust from that cylinder through a receiver to two (low-pressure) cylinders outside the frame. So Smith worked hard on Wilson Worsdell and with such high-pressure persuasion that in 1898 No 1619 was converted, not to a 'simple', but to a three-cylinder compound. There were one or two oddities in this engine, but in broad principle it was sensible enough and it was usefully employed on the North Eastern for many years. But it seemed that Wilson Worsdell saw no special virtue in No 1619, as he built no other locomotive like it.

Nevertheless W. M. Smith had achieved something in getting Worsdell to tolerate a three-cylinder compound at all and to keep it running. It produced a factual story that Smith could tell his friend S. W. Johnson on the Midland as a help in convincing him that there really was something worth trying in a three-cylinder compound.

A familiar fable is that a compound locomotive engine expands the steam so much that it cannot produce a strong blast or a strong draught, and therefore to get the real benefit of compounding you must use a thin fire on a large grate. There is no truth in this (as anyone who ever heard a Midland compound must know) but it sounds well. Smith probably produced this tale when Johnson's interest in compounding had developed to the point of contemplating the building of one that might run in competition with his largest existing 4—4—0s (m31), which became the Class 3 700s in the Deeley classification. So the first five Midland compounds were given 26sq ft grates; later ones had 28.4sq ft of grate, nearly 14 per cent more than that of the 700s. This difference was in itself sufficient to show a saving in coal in any comparative test at a common power output, whether compounding produced any gain or not, if only because the lower combustion-rate would mean less loss in sparks.

One must feel happy for W. M. Smith in thus being able to persuade the head man on a 'foreign' railway to give a trial to a type of compound that had failed to win Wilson Worsdell over to the cause, and actually seeing five Midland locomotives built to a design that was virtually his. It is true that they were usually known as Johnson or Midland compounds rather than Smith compounds but he might feel sure that the discerning were not deceived. It is less easy to imagine his reactions to Deeley's ruthless simplification and external cleaning up of the design to produce forty otherwise very similar engines known as Deeley compounds. Small changes in diameters

Page 89 (above) No 1214 (m38) with Fowler chimney in LMS service. Boiler carries sandbox for backward running. No side-sheet in upper part of cab; *(centre)* No 1262 (m40). After 50 years' service running virtually as built except for chimney and coal-rails; *(below)* No 1636 (m41) as built. Re-numbered 1290 in 1907

Page 90 (above) No 204 (m42). Bought by the Midland from Beyer, Peacock & Co for working trains on the Metropolitan Railway and used elsewhere after electrification of that railway. Chimney-rim slightly battered; *(centre)* No 2121 (m44). Built by Nasmyth, Wilson & Co in 1925 to LT & S design with LMS modifications. Power class 3P. Guard-irons attached to buffer-beam; *(below)* No 2385 (m47). Kirtley engine with Johnson boiler and Fowler chimney

of cylinders and of driving wheels caused a batch built by the LMS at Derby in 1924 to be called LMS compounds or (more rarely) Fowler compounds. Colloquially these later engines were sometimes 'Crimson Ramblers' and more colloquial than that it is better not to get.

With the twentieth century nigh three-quarters spent and industrial secrecy a big factor in big business, it may seem odd that a technical man highly placed on one railway should be allowed to hob-nob with a technical man still more highly placed on a larger railway. It is true that the North Eastern and the Midland were not in extensive direct competition with one another (it was hard to be competitive with the North Eastern as it had its own private sector of Great Britain), but Wilson Worsdell might nevertheless have chafed at the transmission of knowledge and experience for which the North Eastern had paid as part of Smith's salary. Smith would hardly have discussed North Eastern practice with Johnson without specific permission from Worsdell, who may well have given that permission with the knowledge that benefit from technical discussion is rarely restricted to one direction. Even though Smith were better versed in compounding than was Johnson, he might well pick up some useful tips from him on other aspects of locomotive engineering. A hint of this was shown in Smith's adoption of the Belpaire firebox in a couple of four-cylinder compounds built by the North Eastern in 1906. So there was probably complete co-operation between Worsdell and Johnson in the matter of compounding, a subject about which Worsdell had never become enthusiastic. Drawings of components of No 1619 were probably taken to Derby so that Johnson might get some first-hand information on such matters as how to fix outside cylinders on big engines.

It was perhaps natural for a designer to think that if he were going to complicate a locomotive by giving it compound expansion he might as well add further complication by providing separate reversing gears for the high and low-pressure cylinders so that, at any time, the cut-off points in the two groups could

91

F

be different in any way that the driver might choose. It might indeed be a good let-out for the designer. If there was any combination of cut-offs that was noticeably better than any other for any particular running condition, he himself might not know what it was, but perhaps an interested driver could discover it by repeated trial. Such an attitude would never have been tolerated by Brunel (to name only one engineer) as he held very firmly that anything that unnecessarily diverted a driver's attention from where he was going was a menace. He preferred that drivers should not get interested in any of the academic questions that could arise from examination of the thermodynamic or kinematic happenings in a running locomotive; the driver's specific job was far more important.

A designer enthusiastic about compounding was not deterred by any practical consideration of that kind. His attitude tended to be the common one that operators should be trained to give to up-to-date sophisticated machinery all the technical attention that it needed if it were to demonstrate its advantage over the old stuff. It is an attitude that could arise in locomotive designers only because some of them had never even ridden on a locomotive and seemed to know little of the practical realities of driving and firing. So some early compound locomotives were built so that high-pressure and low-pressure cut-offs were separately adjustable and drivers were either left to sort things out on their own, or told that they should open the regulator wide and adjust the cut-offs to obtain some specified steam pressure in the receiver between the high- and low-pressure cylinders. A driver might try such an instruction, but he would not persist in it if the engine did not feel right to him. He would find the settings that seemed most comfortable for the engine, and use them whenever they would produce the power required. The North Western three-cylinder compounds were almost invariably worked with the low-pressure valves in full gear; on the best of them no other setting was possible.

The first two Johnson compounds were built with means of

separate adjustment of cut-off in high-pressure and low-pressure cylinders. The weigh-shaft, extending across the frame under the boiler, had two arms for the valve gears for the low-pressure cylinders; the shaft was encircled by a separately rotatable sleeve similarly serving the high-pressure cylinder. The weigh-shaft and sleeve each had a vertical arm connected by a horizontal rod to a nut on a horizontal screw in the cab. One of the screws was cut on a sleeve encircling the shaft that carried the other screw. At the rear was a two-handle arm capable of axial movement so that it might be connected by dogs to either screw or to both at once. By this means the high-pressure and low-pressure valve gears could be adjusted independently or simultaneously; the latter was convenient for reversing if the driver was strong enough.

There were two regulator handles on a common axis in the usual position. One of them controlled admission of steam to the high-pressure cylinder and this was used for normal running. The other handle admitted steam through a pressure-reducing valve to the common steam-chest of the low-pressure cylinders; from there steam had access, through small pipes and past non-return valves, to both ends of the high-pressure cylinder. This equalised the pressures on the two sides of the high-pressure piston and thus prevented it from opposing the driving effort of the low-pressure pistons.

To start the engine from rest, the first operation was to set both sets of reversing gear in full forward gear and to open the main regulator. If this caused the engine to start, well and good. If not, the second regulator was opened and, with steam controlled by the reducing valve to a maximum of 170psi acting on the low-pressure pistons, the engine would then start (or refuse to start) in the ordinary way. In case of refusal, the regulators were closed, the cylinder-cocks opened to let steam out and then closed again, the reversing handle set to move both screws and the engine reversed to set back into a position in which the cranks were better placed for starting forward. When the driving wheels had made a few revolutions in the right direction, the second

93

regulator was closed and the main one was opened more widely to feed steam from the boiler only to the high-pressure cylinder. The engine was then working as a compound.

Flat valves of conventional type were provided for the low-pressure cylinders; the high-pressure cylinder had a piston valve mounted in the odd fashion of the time underneath it and, if published sectional drawings are to be believed, exactly underneath it. This feature demanded an offsetting arm in the valve gear as the central crank compelled the eccentrics to be mounted well off the longitudinal central plane of the locomotive. The reducing-valve setting of 170psi was so close to the boiler-pressure of 195psi that the valve might just as well have been omitted altogether and Deeley did afterwards omit it.

At the front (bottom) end of the sloping grate (p77) a separate section could be swung about a horizontal axis to leave an opening through which the remains of the fire could be pushed onto the track or into a pit between the rails. The operational convenience of this was far more valuable than compounding but it did not persist beyond the first five compounds; it may be presumed that it was unsatisfactory in service. A drop-gate that jammed in the up position was irritating enough; one that jammed when down was a menace that might indeed stop the locomotive from taking its intended train. Until special heat-resisting steels became available it was difficult to make such a device that was proof against the distorting effect of the heat of the fire.

Where the floor of the ash-pan was arched over the rear axle, it was close to the fire-bars and there was no air inlet at the back. So the rear of the fire tended to be starved of air at the best of times, and with the pocket filled with ash, two or three square feet of grate were effectively blanketed off and so could make no perceptible contribution to combustion.

The Johnson compounds appeared in much the same external style as the Class 3 4—4—0s that immediately preceded them. The boiler had the same twentieth-century stature and setting, the chimney was a bit stumpy with an aggressively projecting

94

wind-deflector, and the rear splasher was extended rectangularly to form a side-sheet for the footplate. The upper part of the cab looked apologetic, almost as if Johnson had wished to say to the men, 'I know you are tough boys who can stand any weather God sends, but do have a bit of protection, just to please me.'

The big ends of the outside connecting rods were placed right against the driving-wheel bosses so that the outside cylinders could be tucked closely to the frame-plates, and the coupling-rods were outside the connecting rods. The space between the inside cylinder and the crank-axle was rather cluttered with three sets of valve gear, and six eccentrics on the crank axle looked rather much, but of course you can't have progress without disadvantages and the men would soon get used to coping with the congestion when examining the mechanism and oiling round. At least there was only one connecting rod big-end inside the frame and, if the engine was set with that at the top, the two outside ones were at a handy height for attention. If, on the other hand, the inside big-end were set in its lowest position, which was best for attention from a pit, the outside big-ends were out of sight and out of reach.

Each piston was provided with a tail-rod projecting through a gland in the front cylinder-cover. This was in compliance with a new twentieth-century fashion based on the belief that any piston bigger than 20 inches in diameter could not be properly carried by the cylinder and that the extra support of a tail-rod was valuable. Among the North Eastern-inspired details in the Johnson compounds were a petticoat pipe between the blast-pipe and the chimney and clasp brakes on the coupled wheels. Deeley abandoned the petticoat pipe but clasp brakes were used in all the compounds built by the Midland and by the LMS. On each side of the engine a steam-energisable cylinder hung horizontally near rail-level between two brake-levers which it pushed toward the wheels. Long horizontal links attached to these levers pulled into action a brake-lever in front of the leading coupled wheel and another one behind the trailing coupled wheel.

Purists believed that a compound ought to have two sets of reversing gear and that drivers ought to be urged to persevere in educating themselves in the handling of compounds so that they could recognise and employ the best combination of cut-offs for any particular running condition. Only in this way, said the purists, can a compound do its best stuff. As a technical matter this view does not survive critical examination but, as it happened, it found superficial justification in a comparison between the earliest exploits of Midland compounds and their general running in later years.

After describing some performances by the first two Johnson compounds over Aisgill, Charles Rous-Marten justifiably remarked that no such running had previously been seen on the Midland. It may be added that neither was such running (by Midland compounds) subsequently seen on the Midland. Some may be tempted to believe that this falling-off might be explained by the abandonment of the double reversing gear; of the Midland compounds only the first two ever had it. There may or may not be something in this, but what is more important is to remember that in early trials of a new and expensive machine which must justify itself by demonstrated deeds, everything is brought to concert-pitch in a way that is not to be expected in normal service. Firemen would assiduously fire little and often to maintain a uniformly thin fire that they were assured the compounds must have, and drivers would snatch seconds by keeping some steam working right down the banks and so getting nineties now and again. None of this was needed or produced in normal service.

An early effort of No 2631 was to run from Hellifield to Carlisle (76.8 miles) in 79 minutes start-to-stop at an average of 58.3mph. The load was quoted as '13½ vehicles' weighing some 210 tons. Later on No 2632 averaged 57mph over this length with 250 tons. Up to Aisgill the average was 46mph, thence to Appleby 74.3 and from there to the Carlisle stop 65.9mph. A speed of 88mph is said to have been averaged over three miles somewhere between Aisgill and Appleby. It was remarked that a side-gale was blowing at the time but that, even so, the lowest speed noted on the way was 35mph on an adverse gradient of 1 in 92. No published gradient profile shows anything steeper than a very short length at 1 in 96 on the rise to Blea Moor; on the rise in the southbound direction there is nothing steeper than 1 in 100 except for a bit of 1 in 88 on Aisgill Viaduct. With a 240-ton load the same engine averaged 53.3mph from Carlisle to passing Appleby, and 45.5mph thence to passing Aisgill (48.3 miles) in 57 minutes 38 seconds from Carlisle. Down from Blea Moor speed rose to 92mph in the vicinity of Settle.

Some very detailed observations were made on the running of certain Johnson compounds between Carlisle and Hellifield in October 1902 and were extensively reported in *Engineering* in the early part of 1903. A good many indicator diagrams were reproduced and elicited an editorial remark that 'the shape and adjustment of some of the diagrams could no doubt be improved by slightly altering the valves'. Where power, speed and coal-consumption were recorded it seems odd to be bothering about the shape of the diagrams. While wondering what kind of improvement may have been desired one may remember Ivatt's remark about diagrams looking like a leg of mutton. To the writer the diagrams reproduced seem to be of about the shape one might expect with the cut-offs used which were between 55 and 65 per cent. The indicated power ranged up to about 965ihp and this was notable in 1902 for a wet steam locomotive with a grate area of 26sq ft. Coal consumption was quoted as about 26lb per mile but this was not expressed in terms of work done. It referred to the whole mileage of the engine from lighting up to returning to the shed and therefore included many miles run without steam.

As a child I read of Midland compound engines with two regulators and two reversing gears, and I thought that this represented superb refinement. I pictured a driver adjusting four controls to make the engine fly and to cause the fireman to wonder why she was burning hardly any coal. To the immature, complication tends to be more impressive than simplicity.

97

The improved compound engines introduced by Deeley in 1905 included the following departures from the original Smith-Johnson design:

1 Grate area enlarged to 28.4sq ft.
2 Only one regulator.
3 No reducing valve.
4 Only one reversing gear.
5 No petticoat pipe.
6 The biped blastpipe mounting was on two flat faces in one horizontal plane.
7 The diameter of the HP piston valve was increased from 8.75 to 10in.
8 Between the ashpan and the rear axle was interposed a sheet extended forwards and downwards to scoop a current of air into contact with the rear end of the ashpan, and thus to diminish transmission of heat to the rear axleboxes.
9 Flat smokebox door secured by six dogs equally spaced round the edge.
10 Longer smokebox.
11 Running board raised so that rod-ends were accessible in all positions of the cranks.
12 Omission of the third safety-valve.
13 Cab with extended roof.
14 Six-wheel tender.
15 Running number in large figures on the tender and in small figures on the smokebox-door.

With the regulator handle of a Deeley compound moved from the 'shut' stop into the first quarter of its range to 'open', steam was being admitted to the HP steam chest and also to the LP steam chests with no intermediate reducing valve. Auxiliary pipes made sure that a common steam-pressure was applied to both sides of the HP piston, which was therefore impotent and the engine worked as an ordinary outside-cylinder simple. Further movement of the regulator-handle gave more boiler-steam to the

HP steam-chest and suppressed the direct feed of boiler-steam to the low-pressure cylinders, and in that condition the engine worked as a compound. A single weigh-shaft controlled all three sets of valve-gear and so a Deeley compound was reversed and 'notched up' just as if it were a conventional locomotive. In short, a Deeley compound was driven as if it were not a compound at all.

With his fifteen simplifications and modifications of the Johnson compound, Deeley made out of it a simple unflorid locomotive with an austere dignity that was new to the Midland. The large figures that came later onto tenders were an American-style blemish but they had a practical value as Midland methods required signalmen to identify trains by the engine-numbers. The large figures obviously helped and so (after dark) did the large concave-mirrored lights mounted specially for the purpose below the windows of Midland signal-boxes. A Deeley compound with a train of the latest Midland coaches was a beautiful combination, unsurpassed in Britain in respect of technical excellence in 1905, apart from the advantages that Churchward was building into new Great Western locomotives. A Midland main-line train even looked a little too brilliantly refined and civilised to venture over the grim Pennine heights that barred its way to Scotland.

Fowler's application of superheating to some Deeley compounds was the last development in Midland steam. It was done slowly and spasmodically as if there were reluctance to admit that the Midland's adoption of compounding left anything better to be attained, but it was eventually shown quite clearly that superheating improved compounds as much as it improved simples. The superheated Midland compound was distinctive in British locomotive practice, only the four Great Central Atlantics and the North Eastern No 1619 being closely comparable. The Midland design arose in well-defined stages of development associated with the names of Smith, Johnson, Deeley and Fowler. Midland men thought that there was nothing to touch it for refinement and economy, however much bigger other railways' engines might be.

The LMS compounds (1045-1064) built in 1924 differed from superheated Deeley compounds in having 81in driving wheels instead of 84, and in having larger cylinders. The next lot (1065-1084), also built in 1924, had cylinders of intermediate size and the chimney was shortened by about 3in (without reducing the height of the dome) to make the engine look bigger. LMS compounds built after 1924 had left-hand drive (as was becoming standard for all new British locomotives except those of the Great Western) instead of the Midland's standard right-hand drive.

Although Deeley had developed a highly satisfactory design of compound locomotive, he would naturally wish to know just how much the compounding principle was contributing to its success. The only way of obtaining any approximation to reliable information on this point was to run a compound engine under close supervision in competition with a single-expansion locomotive of otherwise identical design. The easiest way to have done this was to rebuild a compound with two outside cylinders of the original size but fed by piston valves appropriately dimensioned to take the full boiler-output at about 20 per cent cut-off at the highest speed at which full power was normally required. (The steam must be given equal opportunities for pushing pistons in both engines and so the cylinders from which it escapes to the blast-pipe must have equal volumes in the competing designs.) The valve-dimensions used by Churchward would have suggested that for the 21 x 26in cylinders of the compound, piston valves 12in in diameter with $1\frac{1}{2}$in lap were appropriate. A valve-diameter of 12in would have made Derby pause, but unless the simple had valves large enough for early cut-off working, the compound/simple comparison would be invalidated. Deeley did not adopt this artifice, but the comparison between Churchward locomotives and Midland compounds gives a good idea of what the result would have been if he had really set out to find what a simple could do.

An alternative plan was to build a 4—4—0 with inside cylinders, and with the standard boiler, and to test it against the compounds. The building of Deeley 4—4—0 No 999 in 1907 was in line with this concept, but neither cylinders nor valves were big enough for a true comparison. No 999 had boiler and axle-spacing similar to those of the compounds, but the driving wheels were 6in smaller in diameter. This difference was in accordance with an intention to limit the engine to the part of the Midland main line between Leeds and Carlisle where a good deal of the work was done on steep gradients. The intention was largely realised; the engines of the 999 class were only rarely seen in service elsewhere.

With allowance for the difference in wheel-diameter, the 999s should preferably have had 20in cylinders and, for adequate port-opening when well notched-up, the product of valve-diameter and valve lap would have had to be about 17. It was actually about 10 to $11\frac{1}{2}$, as the valve-diameter was $8\frac{3}{4}$ or 10in. On a drawing in *The Locomotive* for 15 January 1910, the diameter measures $8\frac{3}{4}$in. The inscription is $8\frac{3}{4}$in at the front valve-head but 10in at the back one; perhaps the meaning is that the original design used $8\frac{3}{4}$in valves but that the later engines had 10in valves. From the same page it is interesting to read:

> The small end of the connecting-rod merits attention. It is fitted with a ball-and-socket joint, so that any side-play of the crank-axle will not strain the various joints of the valve-motion. This device also prevents any possible strain caused by the centres cf the two driving crank-pins which are 1ft $11\frac{1}{2}$in centre to centre being out of line with the centre-lines of the cylinders, the latter being 2ft centre to centre.

No reason is given for the half-inch discrepancy between dimensions that should obviously be equal; the most probable one is that it was due to an error in drawing or in manufacture and that the ball-and-socket joint was used to accommodate it. Its effect was easily correctable by setting each big-end brass a quarter of an inch off centre in relation to the connecting-rod. The second sentence in the quotation is specially obscure as the type of valve-gear used in the 999s is the one, above all others,

101

that is absolutely unaffected by side-play in the crank-axle. It was Walschaerts valve-gear modified in a style, used years earlier by Stévart, that avoided need for eccentrics or auxiliary cranks.

In general mechanical detail, the 999s were similar to the compounds. No 999 was originally fitted with a MacAllan cap for the blast-pipe. The cap was mounted on a shaft that extended across the smokebox and projected on the left-hand side where it carried an arm. This was linked to the hand-rail which was axially slidable by pressure on a handle in the cab. The cap was normally clear of the blast-pipe but, when adverse conditions in the boiler were making it difficult to maintain a satisfactorily high boiler-pressure, the cap could be placed on the blast-pipe. This reduced the effective cross-sectional area, thus increasing the speed of the issuing steam and intensifying the draught on the fire. It was an official alternative, nicely mechanised, to the drivers' unofficial 'Jimmy', which was a piece of wire fastened onto the blast-pipe when no one else was looking.

The smokebox rested on a saddle in accordance with the excellent American practice standardised on the Great Western by Churchward and adopted by other British railways at about this time. A noticeable difference between the 999s and the compounds was the anti-vacuum (snifting) valve on each side of the smokebox saddle. This provision for air to be drawn into the steam-chests when the engine was drifting was common with piston valves. (The HP steam-chest of a Johnson compound got by with a Furness lubricator.) The maximum working pressure of the boiler was 220psi to match that of the later compound engines but this did not persist.

No 999 ran for some years before any similar engine was built, but the complete class of ten engines were in service by the end of 1909. Differences from No 999 were not noticeable and the 999 class, superheated in due course, had a long life on the best trains between Leeds and Carlisle. The Stévart valve gear was retained but, in conjunction with rather small piston valves, it showed no advantage great enough to inspire its application to any other Midland engines. The 999s had some odd, and not advantageous features. In them, as in the compounds, Deeley followed the current fashion of applying tail-rods to pistons. Moreover he used valves with outside admission and so the valve-spindle glands were subjected to boiler-pressure. So each engine had eight fully-pressured glands whereas there was no need for more than two.

It is sad to realise that, after appreciating what Churchward was doing on the Great Western and what George Hughes did in superheating an Aspinall 4—4—0 and fitting it with big piston valves, Deeley might have built the 999s as economical flyers that could put the Midland compounds quite in the shade. But perhaps he did not really want to do that! They were Deeley compounds, better than anything else on the Midland, so why try to supersede them? In doing so one might run into trouble, as indeed did Hughes because the mechanism of rebuilt Aspinall 4—4—0s could not stand up for very long to the energy that big piston valves admitted to the cylinders at high speed. The 999s were big 4—4—0s and much might have been expected of them. More of them might have been built had not Deeley resigned in 1909. They did not intrude much on the public eye as they spent most of their working hours in the sparsely inhabited region between Skipton and Carlisle. There they did not beat the compounds, but they were not markedly inferior to them and they certainly earned their keep.

At the opposite end of the range of size of four-coupled engines, the Midland had some four-wheel tank engines. Most British railways found a need for a few such locomotives, able to get round any curve that did not derail the ordinary four-wheel wagon. As no high speed need be demanded of an engine intended primarily for rather special low-speed service, overhang ahead of the leading wheels was not specially objectionable and so outside cylinders could be used. This left the rear axle free from cranks and so the firebox could be placed close to it. Absence of eccentrics would help still further and so outside valve gear was worth consideration. On the other hand, nineteenth-century British practice was based on the use of inside cylinders and this could dissuade designers from outside cylinders even where they were specially advantageous. So inside-cylinder 0—4—0 tank engines, though rare, were not unknown.

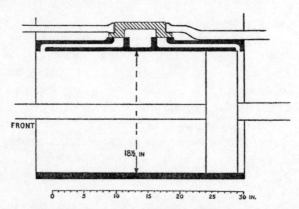

Sectional plan view of left-hand cylinder of flat-iron 0—6—4T (m56)

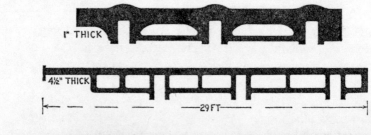

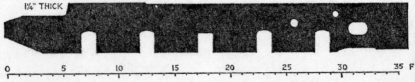

(above) Frame-plate of Midland double-frame 0—6—0 (m48); (centre) bar frame of Schenectady 2—6—0 (m60); (below) frame-plate of Lickey banker (m58)

Johnson built 28 such engines (m35) over a period of twenty years. No 1516 of this class remained in service for 58 years. They were rather quaint-looking engines (as inside cylinder 0—4—0s are apt to be) cut down to a maximum height of 11ft. The corresponding Deeley engines (m36) were considerably tanks go naturally together and Walschaerts valve-gear appeared sensible for an 0—4—0T. Outside valve-gear and full-length tanks go naturally together and Walschaerts valve-gear appeared for the first time on a Midland locomotive. The plain stove-pipe chimney was evidently a repetition of what Johnson had provided on the 1500s rather than a premonition of what Deeley had in mind for future Midland engines. 'Pop' safety valves were an innovation that did not persist on the Midland. An all-over cab was used, but it was left to Fowler to arrange a ventilator in the roof. Cylinders with flat valves fitted nicely under the running board and a Furness lubricator was mounted on the front of each side-tank. These were neat-looking engines with no special place for carrying coal; most of it had to be dumped on the side tanks and double-handled before it reached the fire. In the intermediate stage, the enginemen might have to stand on some of it.

Kirtley's 2—4—0 tank engines built for running Midland trains on the Metropolitan line did not quite meet the requirements of the civil engineer of that line and recourse was had, in 1868, to locomotives of a design already in use by the Metropolitan. Kirtley then took another look at the problem and selected the 0—4—4 wheel arrangement for a locomotive that carried its water supply in a tank over the bogie. This was called a 'back-tank' engine, or a well-tank (m38).

The 0—4—4 wheel arrangement leaves for the firebox a space unencumbered with mechanism and not limited by any consideration of length of coupling-rod. Kirtley produced what was an impressively long locomotive for the period, and this was especially notable as it might have been expected that Metropolitan restrictions would have demanded rather short engines. It had outside frame-plates with wavy top edges over the axleboxes for the coupled wheels. The main springs were above the running board and their adjacent ends were linked to a proportioning lever that placed about 45 per cent more weight on the leading wheels than on the driving wheels. Prominent on each side was a horizontal exhaust steam-pipe extending from smokebox to firebox and then, after a concealed drop to below running board, horizontally to the tank, where exhaust steam could be condensed. There were Salter spring-loaded safety valves on a tall dome, and a weatherboard above a footplate on which the men stood abreast of the entrances and so had to be careful not to be thrown off.

Judged by length of life, these engines (m38; six built by Beyer Peacock & Co and twenty by Dübs & Co) were very successful, as they worked in the London district for over fifty years. During that period, however, they were rebuilt by Johnson who made the following alterations:

1 Addition of rear weatherboard and roof to make a 'cab' that offered no resistance to side-winds.
2 Reduction in heights of chimney and dome.
3 Provision of front and rear sanding for all coupled wheels in place of the original arrangement which sanded only the driving wheels.
4 Elimination of the proportioning levers between springs.
5 Addition of rails round the coal-space on top of the tank.
6 Addition of direct-loaded safety valves on the firebox.

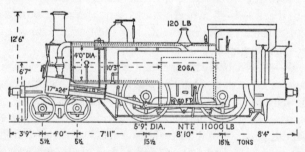

Leading dimensions of m42, condensing tank locomotive built by Beyer, Peacock & Co for Midland trains on the Metropolitan Railway

Page 107 No 648 (m48). As built by Dübs & Co in 1868. Re-numbered 2566 in 1907. Survived with some re-boilerings till 1932

Page 108 (above) No 2856 (m48). Lack of cleaning late in life left dirt clearly shown here; *(centre)* No 1433 (m49). Cleaned to look as if just built; *(below)* No 3014 (m49) as rebuilt by Fowler with Belpaire boiler and Deeley cab

In 1875 Johnson introduced his own design of 0—4—4T (m39), already established by him on the Great Eastern, and 10 engines were built to it. Soon afterwards, Neilson & Co built 30 generally similar engines (m40) with 5ft 6in wheels, but in the very numerous Midland 0—4—4Ts (m41) produced in later years the nominal wheel diameter was 5ft 3in.

Of the 26 Kirtley engines, 25 were still at work in 1923 together with 201 of the 205 Johnson 0—4—4Ts. The latter ran short distance passenger trains on most parts of the Midland Railway; here and there they handled main-line trains, notably between Leeds and Bradford by way of Shipley. In later years they were so overshadowed by the high and wide coaches as to be almost invisible in an oblique rear view of the train. On the favourable gradients between Shipley and Leeds they could work a ten-coach train up to 65mph.

In the opposite direction progress was more deliberate, even though the engine was (generally) running chimney first. In setting the valves in a steam locomotive the usual aim was to achieve the best results for forward running and to accept any consequent imperfections in the setting for backward running. For that reason tank engines that did not use any turntable in a normal day were set so that they ran chimney-first in the uphill direction and this would suffice to explain the normal practice with Midland tank engines between Leeds and Bradford. When snow was on the ground, however, the 0—4—4Ts were run the other way round, not because snow affected the valve-setting, but simply because it usually came with east winds and enginemen found it warmer to have the boiler in front of them when running fast towards the east from Shipley. In an entirely different part of Midland territory, 0—4—4Ts replaced 0—6—0Ts on passenger trains from Brecon over the hill to Colbren Junction and down to Swansea, although there were times when drivers would have been glad of the extra adhesion of the six-coupled engines if not of their backless cabs.

Goods traffic provided the main income of most British rail-

G

ways and the majority of locomotives spent the greater part of their time with goods trains. The Midland was typical in this respect and for nearly eighty years it built nothing but 0—6—0s for goods traffic. There was a gradual increase in size over this period, but only one change in general design. The 0—6—0s built before 1875 had double-frames; those built after 1874 had single-frames. Another development at or about this time was the placing of something like a roof over the enginemen's heads.

There was no marked increase in size in the 0—6—0s (m46 to m48) built up to about 1874 and this justified their common grouping in Class 1 when classification by power was introduced in Deeley's time. The step from 15.5 to 17.5sq ft of grate area crossed the boundary between Class 1 and Class 2. A jump in 1903 to 21.1sq ft marked the beginning of Class 3, but thirteen years had to elapse before a superheater and bigger cylinders produced the Midland Class 4F; its boiler was 4in larger in diameter than those mounted on Kirtley double-frame 0—6—0s sixty years earlier, but its grate area was the same as that of Class 3 engines.

The foregoing remarks indicate the general trend in development of Midland 0—6—0s. Presentation of their meticulously recorded history is not attempted here, firstly because it has so many details and secondly because it lacks so many significant ones. A long serial in the *Journal of the Stephenson Locomotive Society*, although giving running numbers, works numbers, building dates, piston stroke, cylinder diameter and wheel diameter of individual locomotives, includes few other details of technical importance. Furthermore, many of the older engines were re-boilered, re-cylindered, rebuilt and renumbered to the extent that each could provide material for a history of its own, still without providing a significant technical picture of itself.

The Midland never matched the North Western in independence of outside manufacturers and this is some reason why Midland 0—6—0s were never built with such standardisation as Ramsbottom achieved at Crewe in the 943 0—6—0s of Class

DX. So the Midland 0—6—0s had many variations in detail. There was, however, one common feature in all the Midland 0—6—0s built in many places over a period of some eighty years after about 1860 and that was the wheel-spacing. Matthew Kirtley selected 8ft 0in and 8ft 6in for 0—6—0s and these dimensions sufficed for the whole history of Midland steam and its descendants.

All these engines had steam brakes and many of them were fitted for working trains with vacuum (colloquially 'vaccum') brakes. Those employed on main-line goods trains had to work pretty strenuously at times, but on the branches the daily miles were in many cases few and unstressed. Away from the pressures of competitive train services, there was a good deal of gentle pottering in unchanging conditions. There were instances of 0—6—0s stationed at the same shed for some fifty years without ever being away from home at night except during periodic visits to Derby for general repairs.

There appears to be no record of any striking vivacity of a 0—6—0 on any Midland passenger train but an LMS-built 0—6—0 of the Midland 4F design was said to have touched 80mph on an occasion in 1963 when in an emergency it took the 300-ton Waverley express from Appleby to Carlisle.

The Midland single-frame 0—6—0s were conventionally average; even the Midland 'big goods' (Class 4F, m52) was mediocre compared with the contemporary Great Eastern 'big goods' (Class 1270 0—6—0) which was 25 per cent bigger in grate area and 15 per cent bigger in nominal tractive effort.

The Midland Class 4F 0—6—0 nevertheless merits some special examination here. Not only was it the latest and largest Midland 0—6—0, of which 192 examples were built between 1910 and 1923, but it was adopted as a standard design by the LMS, whch built examples of it as late as 1941, to a total of 772, consecutively numbered from 3835 to 4606. There were, of course, some modifications in detail over thirty years, but the main elements remained unchanged.

111

As built in 1911, the Class 4F was Henry Fowler's first Midland design and it was natural for him to include in it the more worthy of current refinements.

The boiler was the Belpaire version of the one standardised in 1903, but fitted with a superheater and more highly pitched than those of earlier Midland 0—6—0s in order to clear the piston valves above the cylinders. Each cylinder-end had a relief valve intended to save it from destruction by excessive pressure from trapped water, but this artifice did not always succeed.

Superheating was tried very cautiously by British railways in the first decade of the twentieth century and the Midland was not one of the leaders in this development. The first 4F had a Schmidt superheater and the second a Swindon superheater. These were of the common fire-tube type; the different names given to superheaters in those early days were usually associated only with different methods of fixing the superheater tubes in the headers. This was, of course, a vital feature because leakage of steam into the smokebox could noticeably spoil the draught on the fire. It was generally accepted at the time that superheated steam affected lubrication so seriously that flat valves could not be expected to work reliably with it. So the 4Fs were given piston valves placed directly over the cylinders and worked by Stephenson gear through rocking levers and rocking shafts. Similarly it was deemed essential to use a mechanical lubricator for valves and pistons on a superheater-fittted engine, and the 4F included such a lubricator on the left-hand frame-plate just ahead of the middle splasher.

Each piston had a tail-rod working in a tube that had to be so long as to extend through the front buffer-beam just above what would normally have been the upper edge. To avoid this, and to keep the front platform free from obstruction by the tubes, the buffer-beam was heightened in the middle third of its length, and the platform raised to match. Tail-rods for pistons were a current craze and many British pistons over 19in in diameter were provided with them. Tail-rods were all eventually abandoned as being valueless reciprocating masses and as adding two wear-and-leakage points to the engine. Steam reversing gear was another (dying) craze followed in the 4Fs, but conventional screw-gear began to replace it a year or two before the merging of the Midland in the LMS at the beginning of 1923. If steam reversers had been provided with positive mechanical locking instead of the unreliable hydraulic locking afforded by a cataract cylinder, they might well have survived more impressively on British railways.

Under the sloping grate was a large ash-pan (p77) unprovided with any air-inlet at the back. Behind the sloping rear wall of the ashpan was a heat-shield which, projecting below the bottom of the ashpan, guided the relative wind of the engine's movement up and back to form a wall of cold air between the ashpan and the rear axleboxes. This protected the axleboxes from undesired heat, but unhappily the air-stream continued past the firebox foundation ring to emerge as a cold upward draught between the boiler and the footboards in the cab. Still more unhappily, ash that dropped out of the front opening of the ashpan could be caught up by this draught, and so on a wet day enginemen on a 4F could be assailed at one and the same time by water leaking through the roof and ash blowing up between the boiler and the floor.

An oddity was the original arrangement for working the superheater damper. It could be done in either of two ways at the driver's discretion which he exercised by setting a control valve on the side of the smokebox. One setting had the effect of keeping the damper shut except when the regulator was opened to make the engine pull, whereupon a feed of steam would open the damper. The other setting left the damper open, unless the blower was set to work briskly, and then a steam feed would close the damper. The first condition reflected the current opinion that, when no steam was passing through the superheater elements, hot gas should be kept away from them lest they should be overheated. The second condition reflected the idea that the elements would not be overheated, unless the fire was being

113

strongly urged by the blower, while no steam was passing through them. The finally accepted opinion was that there was no need to bother at all, because the gas surrounding the elements was never hot enough to harm them, except when the engine was working pretty hard, and at that time the current of steam through them protected them from being burned. Fowler-Anderson by-pass valves were fitted instead of plain anti-vacuum valves applied to the steam-chests.

The footplate of the 4F was miserably small, less than 4ft from the boiler-back to the hinge of the fall-plate. The distance of about 6ft from the fire-hole to the front plate of the tender was a little longer than the ideal. There would have been no difficulty in extending the cabfloor backwards over the front end of the frame of the tender so that the fireman could work with both feet on the same floor, as was the case on Great Eastern engines, but of course it had never been designers' custom to bother about enginemen's convenience and Fowler made no exception in the Midland 4F. On the other hand, it is pleasant to note that the term 'footplate' was a misleading one. Enginemen's feet did not in fact usually stand on a plate but on boards which, even though of hard wood, were gentler than steel. ('Don't sit on that granite', said the cave-dwelling hermit to his visitor, 'Come on to this limestone, it's softer'.)

As the 0—6—0 tank engine was the simplest kind of steam locomotive that could pull and run, it was early on the British scene. It was used extensively by nearly every one of the larger British railways and on the Great Western it worked—with saddle tanks, and later pannier tanks—in very large numbers. On the Midland the 0—6—0T was a side-tank engine in three main varieties totalling some 350 locomotives built from 1871 to 1902 and surviving long enough to become LMS locomotives in 1923. The first class (m53) had no cab, the second class (m54) had backless cabs and the third lot (m55) had cabs with backs and fronts and roofs. Some 422 locomotives, differing only in detail from m55, were built by or for the LMS in 1924 to 1931. It is rather surprising that the modest increase in size between m54 and m55 was held to justify the difference in power classification between 1F and 3F. All the Midland 0—6—0Ts were built with round-top fire-boxes, Salter-type safety valves on the dome and a direct-loaded safety valve inside a Johnson brass casing on the firebox. They were ordinary elemental two-cylinder engines with flat valves and Stephenson valve-gear.

They were typical all-purpose locomotives, widely spread in function and geography and nearly every Midland shed had some of them. While they were obviously goods tank engines, they were useful as shunters at large passenger stations and as haulers of both passenger trains and goods trains on branch lines. For many years the standard 1F engine (m54) worked all Midland trains, passenger and goods, in that Midland 'island' in the neighbourhood of Swansea and also all the trains that reached the area from Hereford. The contrasts between the industrial scene at the extreme south-west, the unfenced mountain road between Colbren Junction and Brecon, and the lush countryside on to Hereford, were very noticeable. They emphasised the impression that 0—6—0Ts could be at home anywhere. As an 'all-adhesion' locomotive the 0—6—0T was ideal for steep gradients and so it was natural to use it from Swansea to Brecon and to Brynamman. The first twenty standard 1Fs (Nos 1620 to 1639) were stationed at Upper Bank (Swansea) as soon as they were placed in service in 1874-5; six of them were still working in that area right up until they were withdrawn from service in 1923 to 1928. Two of them had been fitted for pull-and-push passenger train services from Swansea.

Perhaps in deference to northern rigours, Nos 1725-9 were built in 1883 with all-over cabs and vacuum brakes for working passenger trains in the Worth Valley between Keighley and Oxenhope. Some of the 1Fs were still in service as late as 1964 in the Staveley Ironworks near Chesterfield, and their shed was a special one inside the works boundary. Both 1Fs and 3Fs (m55) were in their turn bankers on the Lickey incline right through

115

into the British Railways period. Although challenged there in that period by Great Western 9400s, the LMS 0—6—0Ts continued on the Lickey until diesels took over.

Some replacement boilers for 0—6—0Ts were of a standard design with Belpaire firebox and most chimneys were replaced by others of current standard design. All-over cabs were fitted on some 0—6—0Ts that originally lacked them, but these visible changes were about the only significant ones made even to the oldest Johnson 0—6—0Ts. They were built primarily for menial jobs that hardly changed over the years and, even after steam had been replaced by oil-spray into compressed air, the 0—6—0T remained the best form of locomotive for such work.

The same might be said of the 0—6—0 tender engine in respect of long distance goods trains that did not need to run fast, and indeed many British railways made some use of such engines on the slower passenger trains that did however, here and there, run up to the mile-a-minute rate. The 0—6—0 was not kind on the track at such speeds, but it was not so bad as to call urgently for an alternative. Indeed, when force of circumstance caused an alternative to be used in some numbers on the Midland, the authorities did not recognise it as such, and the Midland never had a specific mixed traffic locomotive.

The Midland was one of the British railways that bought locomotives from America in 1899 because no British manufacturer could meet the immediate need for more power. It was an emergency situation and the American purchase was a stop-gap measure; nobody expected any American machine to last for very long and so nobody was surprised or disappointed by the performance of the American 2—6—0s. The Midland bought forty altogether, and only one of them survived until 1915. Thirty of these engines were built by Baldwin and ten by Schenectady. They were comparable in size, not so big as most of the Midland 0—6—0s at the time, but they could do a good job when new.

The Baldwin engines with bogie tenders were (probably) of

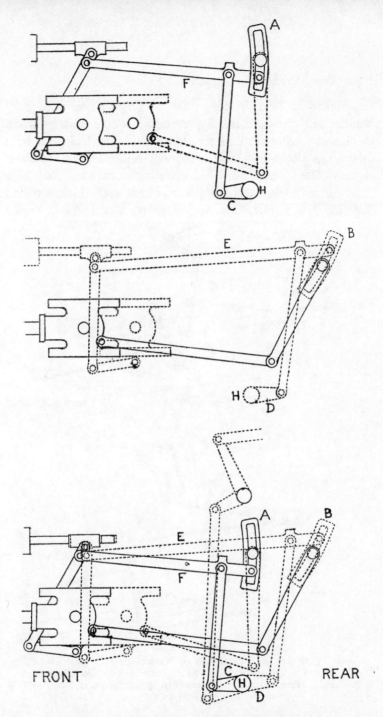

Stévart valve-gear in 999 class 4—4—0 (m33). (*above*) Motion for left-hand valve; (*centre*) motion for right-hand valve; (*below*) complete assembly. Components in the right-hand half of the locomotive are shown by dotted lines

some standard Baldwin design and to English eyes were a bit ramshackle. The Schenectady engines, however, had six-wheel tenders and other features suggesting that they had been built to a design devised to make them look something like Midland engines. The writer hazards the opinion that they may well have been the most elegant-looking locomotives ever to come out of America. For a time, Churchward on the Great Western used

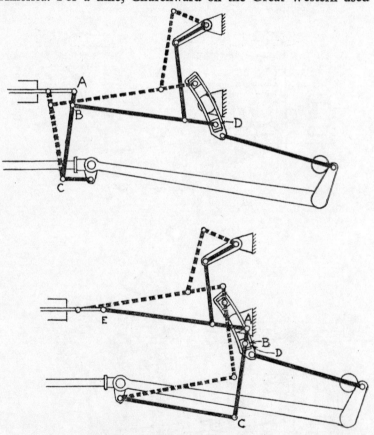

(*above*) Conventional arrangement of Walschaerts valve-gear; (*below*) Walschaerts valve-gear modified in accordance with Deeley's patent No 16372. Dotted lines show mechanism in 'full backward gear'; solid lines show 'full forward gear'

their external design of chimney. In all forty locomotives the most markedly un-British feature was the double-side-window cab with extended roof. The contrast with the unsheltered crudity of Johnson footplates must have impressed even the most hard-favoured enginemen but it did not beguile Johnson into emulation. Each American cab contained quite a lot of boiler and so could be too hot for comfort in warmish weather.

The Railway Magazine was extremely critical of British purchase of foreign-built locomotives and rather contemptuous of the engines themselves. Unrest on the subject was evidently sustained and as late as mid 1901 a daily newspaper secured an interview with the chairman of the Midland Railway. He made a statement on the matter, and so did the Locomotive Superintendent Johnson, in these terms:

To begin with, these American engines are heavier in fuel, oil and repairs than our own. The orders were given in February 1899 and the engines were delivered in the second half of the same year. Now these engines were not at all English engines built in America. We laid it down that they were to be of the same power as the Midland standard goods engine, and there were a few small details to which the manufacturers had to conform; but, generally speaking, the Americans had a free hand, and the engines were for the most part of their own design and pattern, and made in their own way. When they arrived, we put them on to our mineral trains running between Toton sidings, Wellingborough and London, and set them to do the same work as our own standard engines are doing. In January of last year we commenced a six months' comparative test, terminating at the end of June, between these Americans and our standard Midland goods engines, built by Messrs Neilson, Reid & Co of Glasgow and Messrs Kitson & Co of Leeds. The two types were set to draw similar mineral trains under the same conditions, and a careful account was kept of the total mileage covered by each, the total coal consumed, and the charges for repair which belonged to each engine. The result was conclusive and is briefly as follows—

119

Extra working cost of American engine over English engine
Fuel 20-25 per cent
Oil 50 per cent
Repairs 60 per cent

It must be said for the foreign engines that they worked their trains satisfactorily, but their inferiority on the three points named is, on the above showing, incontestable. I never had any doubt in my own mind as to which was the better engine of the two. As to the possibility of repeat orders, I can say nothing beyond referring you to the result of the test. Each American engine costs us £400 less than did those for which contracts were given to British firms immediately in front, and at such a reduction the American engines were put free on our rails just as English engines were. Then there is another point. As I have shown, the Americans were delivered here within a few months of the order being given, yet some contracts which we let out to British firms in 1897 were not completed until February 1900. Of course, this was largely the fault of the engineering strike which caused us to put our work out to America.

It may be gathered from the foregoing that the American 2—6—0s did not make a very favourable impression on the Midland, but nevertheless their designs had features that were worth studying. Each cab, for example, contained a forward facing seat and a back-rest for each man. Absence of inside cylinders left plenty of room for access to the inside mechanism which was limited to two widely separated sets of Stephenson valve-gear. Above each cylinder was its balanced valve, readily laid open for inspection by removing the cover-plate from the steam-chest. The Baldwin engines had bar-frames $4\frac{1}{2}$in wide and the smokebox, of plain cylindrical form, was supported on a saddle and stayed to the buffer-beam. The loading of the swing-link type pony-truck was equalised with that of the leading coupled axle, and the driving axle and the trailing coupled axle were similarly equalised. Knife-edge pivots were used throughout the equalising mechanism. The water spaces round the firebox were at least $3\frac{1}{2}$in wide except near the foundation ring where the width was

120

3in. Inner fireboxes were of copper, 33in wide inside, and 6ft long.

Partly because of the general belief that American machines were not made to last, and that these engines had many features unfamiliar to Midland staff, it is unlikely that they were accorded the very best treatment. If they were not, repair costs would tend to be heavy on that account. If, on the other hand, the adverse figures quoted by Johnson truly represented the comparison, what were the reasons?

Inferior materials might explain higher rates of wear, higher repair cost and shorter life. An extra pair of axle-boxes and extra pairs of sliding surfaces in the rocker-shaft valve gear would account for higher consumption of oil. Greater leakage-rates past valves and pistons could explain why more coal was burned. The most marked shortcoming of the American engines was in shortness of life; the similar ones bought by the Great Northern and the Great Central at the same time had the same failing.

Within their limitations of size and wheel-arrangement the Midland 0—6—0Ts and 0—4—4Ts were very satisfactory locomotives but by the time Deeley had taken charge at Derby there was a need—or at least a field—for a tank engine faster than a 0—6—0T and more powerful than a 0—4—4T. An obvious development of the later was the 0—6—4T, and when Deeley considered this he no doubt took into account the fact that there were very few examples of that wheel arrangement in Great Britain and none of them regularly running fast. This circumstance might have counselled caution, but in fact Deeley completed a design, went straight into production, and Derby turned out forty locomotives to that design in the year 1907. They remained in service for an average period of about thirty years and, although this was rather below normal expectation in Britain, it was not bad, and does not suggest that the design was seriously defective. On the other hand, there is no evidence that the performance of these engines was more than adequate and this is rather sad as their appearance was very impressive.

With 0—6—2Ts well established in passenger train service on the North Western, and others used on short distance goods trains on the North Eastern, Deeley evidently saw no great difficulty with a 0—6—4T and proceeded to build a batch in the form of a standard Midland 0—6—0 extended over a standard bogie. The side-tanks reached to the front of the smokebox and were cut away to give topside access to the motion. The top of the bunker was higher than the top of the tanks and looked austerely dignified without coal-rails. With the outer sheets of tanks and bunker apparently in one piece with the sides and roof of the cab, the general impression was very smooth and neat and inspired the name 'Flat-iron'. A cab-roof ventilator suggested some consideration for the enginemen.

Surprisingly for the Midland in 1907, a round-top firebox was used and the Midland's favourite third safety valve appeared as a pop valve behind shrouded Ramsbottom valves. The leading axle had controlled side-play on the Cortazzi principle so that the wheel arrangement tended to be 2—4—4T so far as riding was concerned, and coupling-rod bushes were spherically formed to suit. The leading axleboxes received weight through twin helical springs, but elsewhere in the engine laminated springs were used, those of the bogie being applied to equalising beams. (Helical springs were usually confined to driving axleboxes where even momentary reduction of wheel-grip on the rail might allow a slip to start, but reduction of load on a leading wheel might bring worse results than a slip.)

These engines were first applied to suburban trains from Manchester and from Birmingham and a few of them retained their first shed-allocations throughout their lives. Some were used on fast passenger trains in the Leicester–Derby–Nottingham area, but this practice did not persist. In 1913-14 half a dozen of the 2000s were fitted with Westinghouse brake equipment and tried on the Tilbury section of the Midland, but they did no better than the native engines. In 1911, No 2023 had been tried on the Somerset & Dorset line with the same result.

A common belief is that the 2000s did not ride very comfortably when running chimney-first at high speed, and of course no engineman likes to run fast and far, however smoothly, with the bunker leading because of the coal-dust. Perhaps on account of unhappiness of the 2000s at speed, the tendency of the LMS was to use them more particularly on goods trains than had formerly been the case, and it was not until 1935 that their dubious reputation for riding received specific support from destructive derailments. A speed limit of 45mph was then imposed on them and within four years they had all been taken out of service.

They had all been fitted with Belpaire boilers, extended smokeboxes and superheaters between 1919 and 1927, but retained their flat valves between the cylinders. This last remark may well raise the question as to how it was possible to accommodate valves between 18½in cylinders, and pursuit of this point leads to the dismal conclusion that the 2000s were perhaps the most port-strangled locomotives to be built in the twentieth century. The drawing on p104 gives some details. The openings in the port face were 15½in long; the one leading to the blastpipe was 3½in wide, while those leading to the cylinders were only 1½in wide. But between the port-face and the cylinder-ends the passages were less than 0.6in wide. So the cross-sectional area was less than 10sq in and in passing from valve to cylinder-end, the steam had to travel 10in between two sharp right-angle bends.

The Great Western outside-cylinder 2—6—2 tank engines, comparable in size with the Midland 2000s, had cylinders and valves like those of the Saints; the cross-sectional area of the passage was 55sq in and the mean steam-path was about 7in long with no bend at all. This numerical comparison would rouse reluctance to accept any suggestion that the 2000s were flyers and explains a difference in voice. Where a Saint would bark, a Flat-iron wuffled. It may seem obvious that, in order to avoid severe restriction of the width of steam passages, the valves should be placed above the cylinders. Webb on the North Western had done this as far back as 1879, when he tried Joy valve gear on the 'Cauliflower' 0—6—0s. After that, Joy valve gear gradually became the standard valve gear on the North Western and on the Lancashire & Yorkshire. It was the simplest means of working valves above cylinders, but no one else liked it very much; Johnson tried it and rejected it. Stephenson valve gear with rocking shafts would have sufficed for the 2000s, but these additions to the mechanism may have been deemed by Deeley to be more objectionable than strangled steam passages in an engine that would not be required to run fast. Certainly there were enough Midland jobs within the unsparkling speed-range of the 2000s to keep the forty of them occupied for a great many years, but they were not fast enough to do the top jobs of the Tilbury tanks.

Perhaps the most notable feature of the 2000s was that, by dint of special attention to lubrication, their flat valves were made to give satisfactory service with superheated steam which came to their steam-chests after re-boilering by the LMS. In the 2000s, the tail-rod for each valve bridle was offset by about an inch from the valve spindle. Each piston rod was offset by half an inch from the centre of the associated crank-pin, and so each connecting rod worked in a skewed manner accommodated at the small-end by spherical shaping of the gudgeon-pin while the big end managed as best it could. *Engineering* for 31 May 1907 made the comment (apparently with Midland inspiration) that the object of this arrangement was to enable the connecting rods 'to adapt themselves freely to the side-play of the driving axle'. This might explain the spherical pin, but it cannot explain the 1in difference in spacing between the cylinders and the crank pins. The corresponding discrepancy of half an inch in the 999-class 4—4—0s was tentatively ascribed (p101) to an error in drawing or in manufacture. Can the same explanation be reasonably suggested for the 2000s? Surely Derby would not make two mistakes of this character in one year? Or did Deeley really believe that there was some advantage in the offset?

The 2000 class is a typical example of a locomotive that was

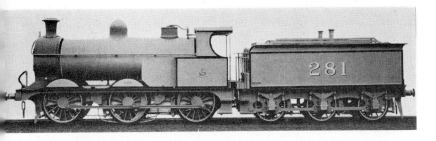

Page 125 (above) No 281 (m51) as built by Deeley. Sanding effective on only four wheels in either direction of running. Re-numbered 3811 in 1907; *(centre)* No 3938 (m52). The 'big goods' as modified by the LMS. Superheater-fitted. Snifting valve at bottom of smokebox. Mechanical lubricator for valves and pistons. Second one for axleboxes. Piston tail-rod covers project above buffer-beam; *(below)* No 4252 (m52) as built by the LMS with left-hand drive and short chimney

Page 126 (above) No 1413 (m54) as built in the nineteenth century. Sand-pipes front and back are a long way from the wheels. Re-numbered 1703 in 1907; *(centre)* No 1753 (m54). Rebuilt with Belpaire boiler and pop safety-valves. Tool-box near smokebox. Fire-irons on side-tank; *(below)* No 1925 (m55). Awaiting re-painting after heavy repair. Fitted with condenser. Near the bottom of the smokebox is an arm that controls the steam-diverting valve

not quite conventional and yet was not so unconventional as to suggest that it might have unusual difficulties or that it might be expensive in repairs. The 2000s were never employed for any length of time in a type of service in which members of the public might expect to have a chance of recording exceptionally energetic work by them. The story of the 2000s is undistinguished and undramatic and to that extent they were typical British locomotives. They were good enough to keep but not to be built in very large numbers, and only a very exceptional exercise in cost-accounting and mechanical testing could establish whether the Midland might have got on just as well without them. A review of British locomotive practice with the 2000s specially in mind may suggest that perhaps the 0—6—4T was a type of locomotive that was best left alone, even though it be admitted that there is no quantitative evidence on the point.

OPERATIONS IN THE SOUTH-EAST

The Metropolitan Railway, with its Circle, was a very useful connection between all sorts of unlikely places and all sorts of other unlikely places, and moreover was a means of connecting some of them with stations on the main railway lines. The Great Western, the Great Northern and the Midland saw value in running some of their trains onto the Metropolitan line instead of stopping them in the main line termini. One snag was that a great deal of the Metropolitan line was underground with very little ventilation, and so the outpourings of steam locomotives were not welcome in its territory. After unsuccessful experiments with a fireless steam locomotive, the Metropolitan acquired locomotives provided with condensers so that, when working underground and using its condenser, a locomotive need not discharge much, if any, steam. If no coal had recently been added to its fire, it need not discharge any smoke, but nothing could be done about the sulphurous constituents of the gases from the fire. By careful firing to minimise smoke, visibility in underground stations could

127

H

be kept no worse than it was in the streets; by suppressing exhaust steam, passengers would be kept free from damp, and if sulphur dioxide could have been suppressed, they would have had no special reason to cough. These ideals were not in fact invariably realised. Still, the Circle was faster than the horse-buses, the passengers continued to come and the trains were pulled by ungainly-looking 4—4—0 tank engines built by Beyer Peacock & Co in 1864. They remained in this service for over thirty years.

When it had been agreed that the Midland should run some trains on the Metropolitan line, Kirtley proceeded to develop a double-frame 2—4—0 tank engine (m37) on the basis of his '170 class' 2—4—0 (m13) and to fit it with condensing equipment in the Beyer Peacock mode. Ten of these engines were built and tried, but the Metropolitan engineer complained about their effect on his track. With keen discernment and commonsense, Kirtley recognised that this Metropolitan man would find something to grumble about whatever Midland engine ran on his track, and so he recommended the Midland management to buy some Metropolitan tanks from Beyer Peacock and to use them on the Metropolitan line with the implied question 'What about these?' Kirtley did not live to see the full extent of his sagacity on this point; over thirty years after his death, the Metropolitan was still complaining (this time to the Great Northern) about locomotives sent into its tunnels.

By some juggling with locomotives already partly built, Beyer Peacock were able to supply the Midland with a few Metropolitan tanks (m42) quite quickly and they were in service by October 1868. They had Midland livery with chimneys of Beyer Peacock profile (but without the usual copper cap) and Salter safety valves on the domes. These features were reproduced on most Midland engines built in the subsequent thirty years.

The basic design of these Metropolitan tanks was that of eight smaller engines supplied by the same builders to the Tudela & Bilbao Railway in 1862. The Metropolitan engines were fitted with pipes through which the exhaust steam could be directed

128

into the side-tanks instead of into the blast-pipe. When this was being done, the blower was kept going to maintain a brisk draught on the fire and the engine made blastless progress that was eerie when first noticed by any interested observer. Station stops gave the engine frequent opportunities for some recovery of boiler-pressure. Condensing was fairly effective until the water in the side-tanks became too hot, when the discharge of steam from the escape-pipes showed that they had not been put there for nothing.

The most striking feature of the Metropolitan tanks was the leading truck with four wheels packed together on a four-foot wheel-base. Lateral movement of the truck relative to the main frame was under the guidance of an arm projecting horizontally backwards to a vertical pivot-pin some six feet behind the centre of the truck. The arrangement has been called a Bissel truck, although that name is usually taken to imply lateral control by swing-link suspension, whereas vertical load was placed on the truck through flat horizontal sliding surfaces. According to Ahrons, this truck, whatever its exact nature, was not very satisfactory, but nevertheless it was allowed to soldier on for some seven years, after which it was replaced by an Adams centre-pivot bogie. This, in view of the short wheel-base of the bogie, looked like asking for trouble, but the Metropolitan tanks dominated the Metropolitan line as long as steam lasted on it.

Two years after the Midland had got its Metropolitan tanks going, it deemed it politic to remain a victim of a bit of horseplay by the Great Eastern Railway. In 1864 the two of them had taken over the Tottenham & Hampstead Railway without much profit for either, but in January 1870 the Midland built a new access to it by a flyover beyond Kentish Town and this opened a useful route for goods traffic to Stratford and the Thames docks. In March 1870, the Great Eastern built across the line at Stepney a footbridge too low to admit standard Midland locomotives. Instead of following such old-time tactics as fitting an engine with a chimney strong enough to dislodge the footbridge (there would have been little technical difficulty about this), the

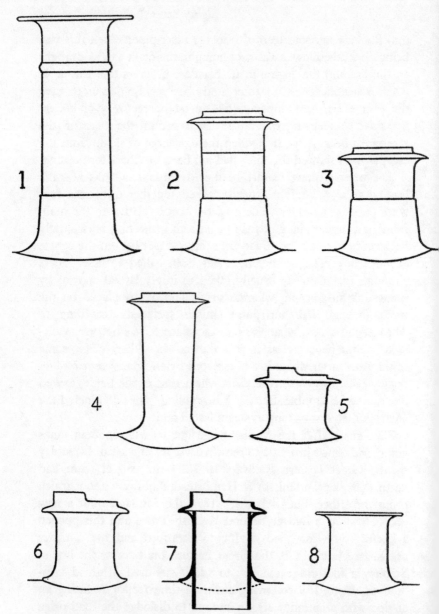

Chimneys: 1 Kirtley, 2 Johnson, 3 Johnson cut down on m53 to clear Stepney bridge, 4 Schenectady 2—6—0, 5 typical Deeley, 6 Fowler standard, 7 section of Fowler standard, 8 Fowler standard reduced by loss of top rim

Midland meekly cut down a number (sixty eventually) of goods engines low enough to clear the obstruction.

A class (m53) of 0—6—0 tank engines was built in this way, and in accordance with current Midland practice for low-speed tank engines, there was no roof over the footplate. Tall enginemen had to remember to make themselves small at Stepney. The height of the dome above the top of the boiler was too small to admit standard Salter safety-valve springs in the usual position directly behind the dome. The arms were therefore set sideways (in plan view) to position their ends sufficiently off-centre for standard springs to be inserted. A short chimney of excruciating ugliness was produced by inserting a standard chimney-top in the tall standard chimney-bottom. It looked like a man's head projecting from a collar wide and high enough to encircle his chin.

The Great Eastern, like elephants and the Metropolitan, never forgot. Over forty years after the Stepney nonsense, it announced to the Midland that, contrary to what it had implied to the original designer, some 4—6—4 tank engines under construction by Beyer Peacock for the Tilbury section of the Midland would not after all be allowed to work into Fenchurch Street station. The engines were thus debarred from handling the heavy trains for which they had been particularly intended, and so they were normally used on trains into and out of St Pancras.

TILBURY TANKS (m43, m44, m57)

In 1912 the Midland acquired the London, Tilbury & Southend Railway, concerned almost entirely with suburban passenger traffic. Of its 82 locomotives at the time of the take-over, 70 were of the 4—4—2T type and the others were six-coupled engines engaged on goods trains. Under construction were six 0—6—2Ts and eight 4—6—4Ts, the latter to be 94-ton engines of an untried design. Tilbury locomotives had been in the care of T. Whitelegg from 1880 to 1910 when his son, R. H. Whitelegg, took over the job.

With an overall length of about 46 miles (Fenchurch Street to Shoeburyness), this was obviously a very small railway compared with the Midland. It was perhaps natural for Derby to believe that it could cope with any Tilbury problem without noticing it, and indeed improve on anything that they were doing there. Such, however, was not the case. The Tilbury had concentrated on commuter traffic and worked it at an intensity not surpassed even by the Great Eastern. It did so, moreover, with locomotives of the 4—4—2T type, which few locomotive engineers would have regarded as first-choice for that sort of service. Perhaps it was not ideal, but specialisation on it for many years had enabled Tilbury staff to get the very best out of it and that was good enough to take the Midland by surprise. Clearly, said Derby, what is wanted for heavy short distance passenger traffic is a six-coupled tank engine, just try this! With that they sent a Deeley 0—6—4T down to Plaistow and instructions that it be tried out on the hardest Tilbury passenger jobs, and five more were moved in 1913-14.

It is reasonable to doubt whether the Tilbury drivers would make any special effort to get the very best out of strangers, and especially strangers sent by unwanted overlords, and no doubt Derby took such action as it could to offset reluctance to co-operate. But the action did not work very well, nor did the engines either on passenger trains or goods trains. Derby had to accept the verdict that the Deeley engines simply could not do the hardest work of the Tilbury tanks, nor in fact did any other locomotive sent to the Tilbury line from the Midland. The local staff were naturally gleeful about this and their satisfaction was vindicated after the grouping of 1923. The 4—4—2Ts were reaching the ends of their economic lives and new engines were required to replace them. The best that the LMS could think of was to build, over a period of seven years, thirty-five locomotives that were simply Tilbury tanks Midlandised in certain details. They did not even have Belpaire fireboxes (whereas the Midland had hardly used any other form in new construction for some twenty years) nor did they have superheaters. The LMS would not face the risks of novelty in this wasps' nest.

A number of constituent companies of the LMS had vigorously insisted that the classes of locomotives they used were the only ones that could possibly do the work demanded on their lines. In principle, this is nonsense, and the central design authority in the LMS could not, would not and did not accept it. But the Tilbury line looked like an exception. There might be some loco-motive other than the Tilbury 4—4—2T that could do its work, but at short notice (seven years) the LMS failed to find one.

All the Tilbury 4—4—2Ts were virtually of one design in two readily distinguishable sizes (m43 and m44). The larger size was built in three batches in 1897-8, 1900-03 and 1909. The first and third of these were given the Midland power classification 3, while the intermediate one, with only small differences, was in Class 2 until re-boilering qualified it for Class 3. The dimensions of the smaller size (m43) suggested Class 2, but this may never have been officially allotted as by 1912 these engines were largely restricted to goods traffic and were not first-rank passen-ger train engines.

The most noticeable feature of the Tilbury tanks was that their cylinders were *not* very noticeable. Tucked close to the frame-plates and below deep running-board valances, they did not stand out. Each crosshead was guided by a single slide-bar hidden by the valance, and as the coupling-rod was outside the connecting rod it more readily caught the eye. The flat valves were inside the frame, but the exhaust passages from them were outside. The small casing that extended from the lower part of the smokebox to the running board concealed an outside steam pipe, although not in the latter-day sense as it was an *exhaust* steam pipe. There were splashers over the bogie wheels and the guard-irons were attached to the front of the buffer beam in line with the frame-plates. This was in the style of the Great Eastern with which the Tilbury had many early associations. The cab-roof was well rounded in the manner that suggests building to the maximum

133

height of gangway consistent with clearing a tight tunnel.

Examination of dimensions and drawings of the Tilbury tanks reveals nothing that might suggest why the engines should be exceptionally powerful for their size or highly efficient in getting power out of coal. It is possible that they were better than average in these respects because they were specially well maintained. There was certainly more time for this on the Tilbury before 1912 than there was on the LMS in general after 1923. The imposition of Midland standardisation in details and procedure made it impossible to keep operating efficiency up to Tilbury standards and so the harder haulage jobs were eased by reducing train lengths; this was easier on the engines but applied more lateral pressure on the passengers. As our subject is Midland steam, we need not say much here about the colouring of Tilbury tanks before 1912. It was perhaps a shade too colourful for some tastes and an unbiassed observer might well regard its replacement by Midland red as no backward step.

Tilbury chimneys were curvaceous in a slightly aggressive way and the front-raised rim, wind-deflector, or *capuchon* on the later ones seemed a little out of place on a tank engine which might be expected to run as far with bunker leading as with chimney leading. This was not entirely the case on the Tilbury as turntables were employed so that the harder turns could be run with chimney first, but nevertheless it is not easy to repress the reflection that if the deflector is a good thing for forward running it is probably bad for the other way. It is said that the designer of the Tilbury 4—4—2Ts was once questioned on this point and admitted that the deflector was added primarily because it gave a purposeful air to the appearance of the engine. The deflector appeared on the 4—6—4Ts (m57) which, by reason of their symmetrical wheel arrangement, were deemed not to justify the trouble of turning. Bunker-first running did, however, have the rarely mentioned disadvantage that illumination of the back plate of the cab by fire-light at night made it hard to see signal lights through the look-out windows.

134

The 'Baltic' tank engines were very much longer and heavier than any others on the Tilbury and they had many teething troubles. It is unlikely that Derby would take any keen interest in getting them going and the Tilbury staff may have been a little indifferent about engines that were prevented by Great Eastern civil engineer's restrictions from running into Fenchurch Street station which received and despatched the Tilbury trains that were hardest to work. These long engines were apt to sway about a vertical axis at speed and this could be alarming at times. It was tolerable when all clearances were at their minima and this was probably the case when one of the 'Baltics' was tried out for maximum speed without a train. A top rate of about 94mph is said to have been attained but the sway was rather bad at that speed. On no other occasion (so far as is known) did a Tilbury tank exceed 90mph, although a 4—4—2T was urged up to about 83mph on a special occasion when an employee who was travelling as a passenger wanted to catch the last train of the day at a connecting station.

THE LICKEY BANKER (m58)

The appearance, soon after World War I, of a ten-coupled locomotive of Midland design and construction was an event of great interest for British railway engineers and railway enthusiasts. The engine was announced as intended for banking duty on the Lickey incline and it certainly looked as if it might be good at slow slogging, but why the tender? How could a tender be justified for an engine that was not normally to go more than two miles from home? Why should not all the weight of the engine and its coal and water be on coupled wheels? What design philosophy had given rise to this strange giant?

Production at Derby had been for so long limited to six-wheel and eight-wheel locomotives that the building of 2—8—0s for the Somerset & Dorset Railway just before World War I was an epoch-making event; it set Derby designers sighing for fresh

135

worlds to conquer. So Henry Fowler took another look at the Lickey. For sixty years, banking there had been done by six-wheel engines, and they met all requirements. If any particular job looked like being too hard for one banker, they simply used two, three or four; there were plenty of them ready with steam and men, all the time. Each engine had to slog a bit, but even slogging at ten miles an hour for twelve minutes with a 16sq ft grate was not exactly a killing job for an adult fireman. For the driver, it was hardly a job at all. It was quite nonsensical to have four men on two little engines buffered up behind a slowly moving train with another driver finding the way on another engine at the leading end.

As by 1910 it was accepted practice for one man to run a locomotive at quite high speed behind a coach or coaches with the driver at the front end of the leading coach, there was no excuse for having four men on two Lickey bankers. There could, of course, be objection to having only one man on one engine coming down the Lickey bank on its own, because he might be taken ill, or fall off, or something, but two men on two engines coupled together was no more risky than two men on one engine for such a short trip as that. So an easy way to save on wages in Lickey banking was to couple two 0—6—0Ts to form from standard components a 0—6+6—0 two-man super-banker with about 98 tons of adhesion weight and 32sq-ft of grate area.

Such an arrangement would have been a triumph for the operating department but would bring no special credit to the design department. As it was not adopted, the designers were left with an opportunity of devising an alternative in the form of a single big engine that might perhaps be as effective as two 0—6—0Ts. One way of achieving such a result would have been to sling a big boiler, Garratt-fashion, on a frame resting on two 0—6—0 chassis or shortened versions of them. Mr H. W. Garratt would have had to be paid a very handsome royalty to make this scheme more expensive than what was actually done.

Nothing in fact materialised on this subject during World

War I, but shortly afterwards The Banker was completed at Derby in the form of a four-cylinder 0—10—0, and after local trials early in 1920 it began duty at Bromsgrove as MR No 2290. It was withdrawn from that service in May 1956 as BR No 58100, having worked continuously up and down the Lickey through all the intervening years. It visited Derby Works at approximately annual intervals for general repairs which did not take long as, after 1922, a spare boiler was substituted for the worn one. There were also spare cylinder-blocks, but only one was ever used.

In grate area (31.5sq ft) No 2290 was practically equal to two 0—6—0Ts, but in adhesion weight (73.7 tons) it was more than 20 per cent 'down'. In nominal tractive effort (43,000lb) there was only a few per cent difference, and of non-paying load the 0—10—0 had about 6 tons more to lift up the bank. There was no great difference between the alternatives except in the vital matter of adhesion weight, where twin 0—6—0Ts scored heavily with 98 tons against 74. The essential fact was that the 32-ton tender behind No 2290 could make no useful tractive grip on the rails. It is melancholy to reflect that with no very marked modification in design, No 2290 might have saved quite a lot of coal if anyone had considered this possibility. As the big engine took the place of two 0—6—0Ts, it certainly halved the wages bill and perhaps that was regarded as a highly satisfactory achievement without trying to win anything more. It is a pity that, having decided to build a four-cylinder banker, Derby did not design it in a way that would have enabled the four-cylinder principle to give the advantage of which it is peculiarly capable (see p172). That No 2290 failed to beat the twin tank engine combination may be deduced from the fact that no similar banker was built.

No 2290 was fitted with steam reversing gear, and this was far less detrimental here than it was on the average British locomotive because it had little chance of demonstrating its perpetual fault, which was that of gradually (or suddenly) dropping into full gear whether the driver wanted it or **not**. The only driver's order that steam reversing gear could be relied upon to obey was to move from full gear in one direction to full gear in the other direction. In Lickey-banking service that was all it had to do, but even so it caused more bother in maintenance than it could ever have been worth. Nevertheless it lasted for eighteen years before being replaced by screw reversing gear. Why the handle of the screw reversing gear was made to work in the opposite direction to that of reversing handles on other Midland engines could be explained by an indisposition to ask Derby Works to cut left-hand threads. Design staff may also have been reluctant to believe that it mattered which way a reversing screw worked if a defining arrow were displayed near the reversing handle. The facts are, however, that drivers did not normally look for arrows when working the reversing handle, and that non-uniformity of 'handing' of reversing screws on locomotives of any one railway was not only asking for trouble, but many times caused it.

Unusual features of No 2290 were the provision of a handbrake additional to that on the tender and the fitting (in 1922) of a large electric headlight to help the driver to find the rear of any train that the engine was to push in the dark. It is said that some drivers preferred not to use this light, because it announced to the men on the train-engine that No 2290 was the helper, and therefore that they need not work their own engine particularly hard. This at least is one of the stories about The Banker. It is not very convincing as any driver who approached Bromsgrove from the south with the idea that he was not going to help the bankers, unless it turned out that they simply could not get the train up on their own, would take good care to see what engines were in the lay-by as he passed, and to judge which would come out and give his train a push at the back. But as everyone knew that No 2290 was rated as equal to two of the 0—6—0Ts, why should any driver expect to get more assistance from the one than from the other?

During thirty-six years' service on the Lickey Bank, the Midland 0—10—0 covered some 840,000 miles, an average of 64 per day. Even though half the mileage was idle in coming down back to Bromsgrove, the loaded mileage per day was 32, distinctly more than the mean for Midland engines in 1921. So although the Lickey Banker unavoidably spent more time in standing still than in running, the average Midland engine was no better in this respect.

CHAPTER FOUR

Some Details

When, after the railway grouping of 1923, Midland locomotive design was scrutinised by engineers from other members of the LMS group, some features were criticised, but on the whole it was accepted as representing good average British practice, strong and reliable, but not outstanding except in having produced over forty compound locomotives that were not at all bad. Although nearly all steam locomotives were fundamentally identical, every large railway had some distinction in its way of dealing with the details and those of the Midland engines may be studied with advantage. A legend associated with the special valve-gear used by Deeley in his 999 class 4—4—0s has long needed elucidation on a particular point.

DEELEY AND THE STÉVART VALVE-GEAR

The vast majority of British locomotives in the nineteenth century had valves worked by link motion, the so-called Stephenson valve-gear (fewer than 1 per cent of Midland engines had anything else), and if no alternative mechanism had ever been devised, it could have served the steam locomotive to the end of its days with little detriment to anyone. But the almost equally old Walschaerts valve-gear was more convenient than link motion for a valve above an outside cylinder because it required only one return crank whereas link motion needed two eccentrics.

Deeley was moved by this convenience of Walschaerts gear to

140

try it in his 0—4—0Ts (m36), and then it was natural to consider whether it might be worthwhile to apply it to a new 4—4—0 *inside* the frame. There it would need only one eccentric for each cylinder and indeed the proximity of the two crossheads, plus a bit of scheming, might enable the engine to work without any eccentric at all. That would be excellent.

In the ordinary Walschaerts valvegear applied to a two-cylinder engine, the expansion link associated with a particular cylinder is oscillated by an auxiliary crank (or eccentric) at right-angles to the main crank worked by the cylinder, and therefore either in line with the other main crank or exactly opposed to it. It is therefore possible, as an alternative, to oscillate each expansion link by a connection with the crosshead of the other cylinder. This was done (for example) by Stévart in Belgium in some sixty eight-coupled locomotives built in 1873. A bit of ingenuity and thought is required to design the 'crossover' connections so that they miss each other in all conditions.

In 1905-6 Churchward on the Great Western worked out a scheme of this sort and it was applied in a four-cylinder 4—4—2, No 40. In 1906, Deeley on the Midland was granted a British patent on something to do with valve-gear and there is a story that he sent to Churchward a letter in complaining terms about infringing patents. Because of its prior use, the Stévart gear itself was not patentable and, unless the Patent Office had made a mistake, Deeley's patent could not have been in respect of the conventional Stévart gear. Examination of the specification of patent No 16372, granted on 28 June 1906, shows that it referred to a modification of Walschaerts gear, and that what Churchward did was no infringement of the Deeley patent. So restriction of Great Western Stévart valve-gear to the one example in No 40 cannot have been due to any threat of patent litigation, and may indeed have no connection with any of the contents of the alleged letter.

Deeley's 999 class used Stévart valve-gear but not with the special feature that justified Patent No 16372. This feature was not peculiar to the Stévart modification of the Walschaerts gear. It was the pivotting of the combination-lever on the pin in the die-block instead of on a pin in or near the valve spindle. Viewed transversely this was perhaps a slight simplification, but viewed vertically it is a complication because the combination-lever and the forked end of the valve-rod must lie between the two halves of the expansion link which is consequently wide and bulky. Mechanically it is no improvement on the conventional Walschaerts gear and in fact Deeley did not use it in the 999 class nor (so far as the writer is aware) was it used at all. The significant parts of a Patent Specification are the 'Claims', and those of No 16372 read:

1. In valve gear for two-cylinder coupled engines in which the opening of the inlet port of each cylinder is determined by the movement of the crosshead of the other engine and the lap and lead of the valve by movement derived from its own crosshead, the herein-described arrangement of parts in which the 'floating' levers are fulcrummed directly in the rocking links or quadrants and the driving shafts of the latter are ranged out of line, substantially as described.

2. In valve gear of the character described, the arrangement of reversing gear in which the weights of the linkage connecting the valves of the two engines with the shaft of the reversing lever are balanced against each other substantially as described.

3. A valve gear for two cylinder coupled engines constructed and arranged substantially as herein described and illustrated.

Claim 1 is incorrectly worded in so marked a manner as to make one wonder whether anyone had taken the patent application seriously. If the 'floating' (combination) levers had been fulcrummed on the rocking links, the cut-off could not have been altered, nor the engine reversed. What is meant (and what the drawing in the specification can be interpreted to mean) is that the combination levers are fulcrummed on pins in the die-blocks or (using less precise wording) on the die blocks. Claim 2 is not really valid because, in the conventional Stévart mechanism,

Page 143 (*above*) No 2000 (m56). Deeley 'Flat-iron' as built. Cab side-sheets skimpy. Later rebuilt with Belpaire boiler and superheater; (*centre*) No 2101 (m57). Note Great Western-style chimney. Splashers over bogie-wheels; (*below*) No 2516 (m60). Schenectady 2—6—0 new in 1899. Much of the lower part of the firebox visible through large openings in the bag-frame. Cab well warmed by inclusion of about $2\frac{1}{2}$ft of boiler

Page 144 (*above*) No 2704 (m48) with coal train at Nottingham; (*centre*) No 1021 (m32). Deeley compound with up express on Midland main line; (*below*) No 1000 (m32). Original Midland compound restored to its condition in 1914, being tested on British Rail in 1959 before preservation as a 'runner'

operation of the reversing gear causes the die-blocks to have equal and opposite movements in the expansion links. This means that the weights of the two movable sets of mechanism are automatically balanced against each other by any form of mechanism that correctly connects them and is not specifically designed to be unbalanced. (The novelty in claim 1 is illustrated on p118.)

The Stévart gear used in the 999 class is shown on p117. Because one expansion link (A) was mounted ahead of the other (B), the weigh shaft (H) could be placed in an intermediate position with one lifting arm (C) projecting forward and the other (D) backward. This enabled rotation of the weigh shaft to lift one radius rod (F) while it lowered the other (E) as is necessary in the Stévart gear. The weigh shaft was normally placed above the valve-gear, but in the 999s it was placed below (possibly to find space for longer support links for the radius rods) and this involved a bit more complication in the shape of an additional rocker shaft and connecting arms and a link. The fore-and-aft staggering of the expansion links made it less difficult to provide the crossover connections between the crossheads and the link-trunnions.

Churchward's arrangement of the Stévart gear in GW No 40 did not use the combination-lever-mounting described in Deeley's Claim 1 nor did it have expansion-links out of line, as described in that Claim. So Churchward had not infringed Deeley's patent in any way. Because No 40's expansion link trunnions were in line, neither of them could be extended into the other half of the engine. The levers mounted on them had therefore to be shaped to do this and to miss each other in all positions of the cranks. In consequence, their action looked something like that of a pair of scissors and so the mechanism was sometimes called the 'scissors gear'. There was nothing comparable in the Deeley mechanism, and there would have been no justification for calling it a scissors gear.

The Churchward arrangement, although much neater than Deeley's, hindered access to some of the other mechanism to an

145

J

extent that could hardly be justified by mere freedom from eccentrics, and this is probably why it was limited to a single locomotive on the Great Western. Walschaerts gear required only two eccentrics and there was plenty of room for them on the crank-axle in the space that commonly took four eccentrics for Stephenson valve-gear.

BRAKES

It is startling to reflect that railways had been extending very rapidly, and passenger train speeds rising very noticeably, for forty years before a Royal Commission was set up to investigate facts and figures about the generally very poor methods of braking British passenger trains. Comparative tests were arranged and the Midland co-operated most notably by permitting the famous Newark brake trials of 1875 to take place on its Newark–Nottingham line. The Midland participated actively in the trials by sending three 2—4—0s and trains for test, one with Westinghouse brakes, one with Barker's hydraulic brakes and one with Clark's hydraulic brakes. Westinghouse brakes gave the best results in the Newark trials and the Midland for a time bade fair to adopt the Westinghouse system. In the end, however, the Midland settled for vacuum brakes, which were eventually fitted to the vast majority of English passenger vehicles.

By 1875 steam brakes were widely employed on British locomotives, and the Midland so used them throughout the rest of its existence. During this period some other railways (eg Great Western and North Western) went over to vacuum brakes on engines, but the Midland did not, nor did the LMS or British Railways.

The Midland made early and sustained use of a brake application valve of what became a familiar type. Movement of one handle applied both the vacuum brakes on the train and the steam brake on the engine. Moreover, application of the train brakes by any means (eg by parting of pipe connections when any

146

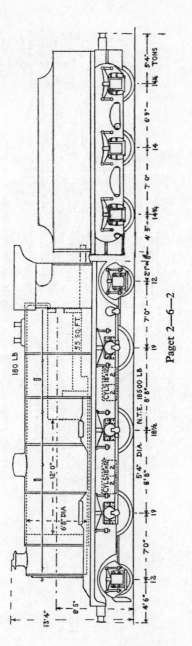

Paget 2—6—2

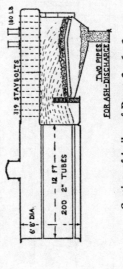

Section of boiler of Paget 2—6—2

147

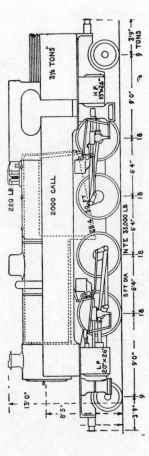

Deeley proposal for 4-cylinder compound 2—4—4—2 tank engine

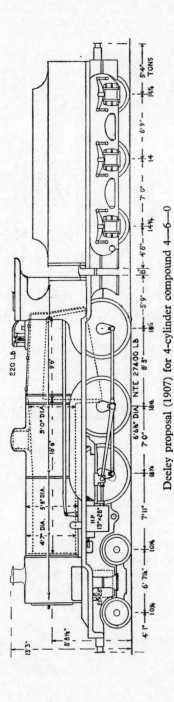

Deeley proposal (1907) for 4-cylinder compound 4—6—0

148

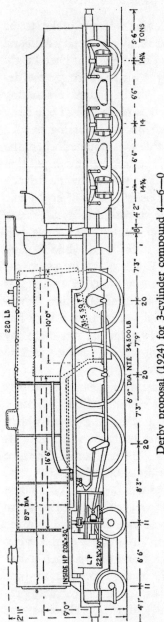

Derby proposal (1924) for 3-cylinder compound 4—6—0

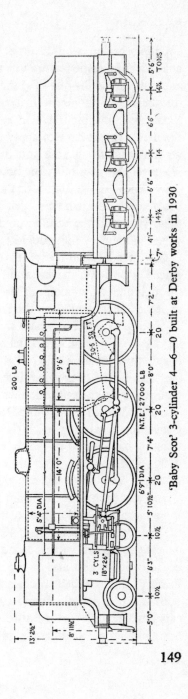

'Baby Scot' 3-cylinder 4—6—0 built at Derby works in 1930

coupling broke) would cause the engine's steam brake to be applied. A fantastic feature was that on many pre-Deeley Midland engines (eg the 0—4—4Ts) the brake handle was at knee height for the driver in his normal running position. Perhaps the designer had imagined that in some unusually intensive shunting the driver might have to apply the brakes while he had one hand on the regulator handle and the other on the reversing handle. To cover this possibility the brake handle was mounted where the driver could move it with one knee. It remained only to position the sanding gear handle so that it could be worked by the driver's other knee and the result would have been a piece of ergonomic one-man-bandery that could hardly be surpassed today.

On later Midland engines the brake application valve was placed where the driver could work it by hand while looking through the front look-out or while leaning out to watch the approach of the tender to the front of a train that the engine was about to pick up. This was a multiply-repeated operation requiring clear vision and great delicacy, and yet on only a very few locomotives in the whole of British railway history was there any hint that it had been taken into account when deciding where to mount the brake-application handle.

In the Midland brake-application assembly, steam flowed past a mushroom valve to reach the engine's brake cylinder. When a vacuum was created in the train pipe it acted on a piston which, with spindles and a lever, forced the mushroom valve onto its seat in opposition to boiler pressure. In this position of the valve a port was open to allow steam in the brake cylinder to escape to the atmosphere, and so the steam brake was therefore 'off'. When the train pipe vacuum was sufficiently weakened, steam pressure on the mushroom valve opened it and steam went past it to the brake cylinder and also to a piston on the spindle of the valve. Pressure there tended to close the valve and did so when it had built up to a predetermined multiple of the drop in train-pipe vacuum. Steam brake pressure was therefore approximately proportional to vacuum brake pressure and the mechanism was known as a proportional valve. A brass cam-plate was nevertheless provided to open the steam valve when the brake handle was moved to 'on' in case friction were too strong for the steam.

Release of the vacuum brake was effected by use of a separate handle connected to the right-hand hand rail, because the ejector was mounted on the boiler and near to the smokebox. This position was adopted to minimise the length of exhaust-pipe from the ejector as its efficiency was affected by drag in the pipe. It was obviously inconvenient for drivers to have separate handles for application and release of brakes, but they got used to it on the Midland and on the Great Western. A third handle near the brake handle admitted steam to the small ejector which was more efficient than the large ejector in balancing the constant, but normally small, leakage of air into the train-pipe at couplings and elsewhere. A hand-brake was provided on every tank-engine and on every tender; it was used to secure the engine when it was left unattended and also to help in restraining unbraked goods trains on downgrades.

To the 483 class 4—4—0s (m34) Fowler fitted brakes for the bogie wheels, but this was only in belated compliance with a craze that was already dying. Every locomotive engineer who tried bogie brakes soon found that they were far more trouble than they were worth and Fowler was no exception.

CABS AND CAB-FITTINGS

A formal historian of Midland locomotives would no doubt perk up a little at mention of the subject of cabs, because a reasonable interpretation of the word 'cab' would enable him to say that no Midland engine had such a thing in the nineteenth century and therefore to appreciate with some satisfaction that his labours were lightened on that account. Designers of early Midland locomotives, and indeed of many other contemporary ones, understood very clearly that the Stephensons' *Rocket* scored a substantial and significant victory even though it carried no hint or semblance of a cab. Obviously then there was no need for a cab and even by the year 1844 very few cabs had been seen on British locomotives. Some were in use in North America where the average winter was much colder than the worst over here, but in Britain there was just no call for cabs. Stage-coach drivers never had any, so why should engine drivers want any?

This was put as a purely rhetorical question, but after weatherboards had become common an unrhetorical answer was found for it. This was, 'because stage-coaches never ran under bridges with small boys dropping bricks on drivers' heads'. Those who may have the impression that sex and vandalism are twentieth-century inventions may be surprised to be told that such is not the case; the Victorians were not so backward as all that. Actuated solely by technical interest in the question as to what would happen to a locomotive if you dropped a brick down its chimney, some of the numerous offspring of our Victorian forbears sought an answer by actual trial, and faulty timing could put the engine-men at risk. This was recognised, especially by enginemen, but the general feeling of those not personally involved was that the little chaps should be allowed a bit of fun now and then, until a Midland driver was 'beaned' by a brick. Kirtley, at least, recognised a trouble-sign in the episode. If this kind of thing went on, the Midland was going to be faced with enginemen's demands for danger-money and labour costs were high enough already. Possible remedies were to arm enginemen with machine-guns, to build up bridge parapets so that no one could reach over them or to put a shield over each footplate. Kirtley tried the latter. He extended the upper part of a steel weatherboard further backward over the footplate to receive some support from slender pillars at the back. Here then was some inkling of a cab, although conceived and executed as a bomb-proof shelter.

Now mark well the sequel, as it has a bearing on the long and laboured history of locomotive cabs in Great Britain. The combined roof and weatherboard acted as a powerful amplifier of sound from vibration (just as was found in the tinny cabs of BR engines in the 1950s), while the pillar-fastenings came loose and jangled like the metal luggage-racks in the BR diesel multiple-unit coaches in the 1960s. Tough though Victorian enginemen were, they had their feelings and they just would not take the row from these flapping bent plates. 'Give us Barrabas', they implied in kindly reference to the bridge-infesting guttersnipes. The pillars were therefore removed and the roof shortened so that it would not flap too much, although remaining useful in keeping bricks off the men. There was no corresponding protection when running tender first, but of course there was then less danger because the little fellows were aiming to get the chimney and not the men. Anyone who did get hit could rest assured that it was the result of simple error of judgement and not of malice or horseplay. Many young railway enthusiasts must have noticed the rarity of overbridges that offered any good view of trains passing under them. This was not a sign of ill-will by the railway company but, generally, the result of providing enginemen with reasonable static protection against potential droppers of bricks.

In reviewing what was built over the footplates of Midland locomotives and of other British locomotives one is led to wonder how the word 'cab' should be defined. In 1885 the North Eastern began to provide each new tender engine with a six-windowed house covering the footplate and the fall-plate between it and the tender. This kept rain off enginemen not only when the engine was running forward but also when it was standing. It became a standard feature of North Eastern locomotives and (later) of Great Eastern locomotives. This proving to be entirely practicable, could anything much less commodious be called a cab? If not, then no Midland engine had a cab until Deeley took a hand, if then.

Kirtley provided a bent iron weatherboard that half-formed a short roof but there was no side-sheet. Johnson put up a weatherboard and stiffened it with very narrow side-sheets and a short roof. At speed the weatherboard prevented the relative wind and rain from hitting the men directly, but vortices behind the back edges of the shelter gave them plenty of air and also water when any was falling from the sky. Side-sheets below waist height gave some protection against direct impact of side winds on legs but a gale through the gangway would provide plenty of draught about any feet on the fall-plate. When reaching back into the tender, the fireman got the full force of any side wind and coal could be swept off his shovel.

All this seems fairly dreadful and yet it was normal in Britain. One would have thought that with the North Eastern example there for all to see, enginemen on other lines would have clamoured for more protection but there seems to be no evidence that they ever did. Certainly an experimental side-window cab put on a Great Western engine was received very coldly by enginemen and was afterwards replaced by the skimpy Great Western standard. With this in mind, one can hardly criticise Midland policy in leaving enginemen virtually shelterless. It is sometimes suggested that enginemen prided themselves on being tough and resented any suggestion, by protective measures, that the locomotive superintendent was not convinced of this.

But just think of what incongruity there could be on a single train. Take a bad case, such as that of a goods train going from Settle to Carlisle with a westerly gale and heavy rain. The 25 miles to Aisgill occupy an hour or more with the wind and rain roaring across the cab and the fireman pretty continuously occupied in getting coal on the fire. The driver is in his front corner as close as he can get to the weatherboard but nevertheless unable to escape the wind and wet. The fireman stands (if he can) with his back to the roaring rain and is disgusted to see how much of the coal he picks up is simply blown off the shovel onto the track. On Ribblehead viaduct he may indeed have a respite from shovelling coal because if he tried it the wind would take the lot. Long before the engine may cease pulling (at Aisgill) the enginemen are as wet and buffeted as if they had been through a carriage-washing plant. During this ordeal, did they ever think

154

that at the back of the train, in the van with all crevices stuffed with newspaper, was the guard, nice and close to a warm stove, cracking his 'bacca', with absolutely nothing else to do for a solid hour? Did they really reject the suggestion that in a proper side-window cab with a long roof and side-doors they could be nearly as well off as he?

Neither side-doors nor side-window cab ever appeared on any Midland tender-engine, although Deeley, with wider upper side-sheets and an extended roof, did improve things a little for engine-men. The curves of the 'cutaways' were in an elegant style and on 4—4—0s each side sheet was extended forward in quarter-circle form to hide the top part of the rear wheel. Fowler later started fitting Deeley cabs with ventilators in the form of a bevel-edged rectangular plate over a similar but smaller opening in the roof. This positive provision for ventilation suggested great refinement in design and an assurance that the men really could be warm enough at times on a Midland engine. Running tender-first (and some goods engines had to do a lot of it) was always extremely cold and uncomfortable. To mitigate this, a number of Midland tenders were fitted with weatherboards with top sheets and side sheets so substantial as to cause the term tender-cabs to be applied to them. Protection of this kind was a feature of the tenders attached to the 2—8—0s built at Derby for the Somerset & Dorset Railway in 1914 and the Lickey banker also had one.

It has to be recorded, however, that enginemen raised objection to these tender-cabs and that some of them were afterwards removed. The writer does not know what particular feature was claimed to give offence (and in cases of this sort the specified objection is not always the real one), but unless a tender-cab is appropriately designed it can make handling of long fire-irons difficult or impossible. The back-plate should have a large opening that can be closed by a door when it is not needed. There was obvious value in some such provision on any tank-engine with an all-over cab but not every such engine had it. Firemen might make-do by manoeuvring the back ends of long fire-irons through an opening made by moving the window from a back look-out. If the construction did not permit of this, the glass was in danger during fire-cleaning.

A Midland practice was to place the blower-handle on the middle of the back-plate of the boiler, over the fire-door, and this can be criticised. The blower projected steam from the top of the blast-pipe into the chimney in order to induce a draught through the fire when there was no exhaust-steam from the cylinders. As draught on the fire was the fireman's concern, the blower-handle should be within easy reach of the fireman, but as it was the driver who decided when the flow of exhaust-steam should cease, the blower-handle should be mounted where the driver could reach it. Central mounting of the handle would therefore seem to be appropriate.

In most circumstances a long engine-chimney created enough natural draught to make it unnecessary to use the blower when the engine was not using any steam. In other circumstances that might not be the case and flames might come out of the firehole into the cab to the danger of the enginemen. To turn on the blower was the remedy, but it was not easy with flames licking its handle, unless the handle was of a form that could be moved by a blow from the shovel, though that could not be picked up instantaneously. With this in mind, central mounting of the blower-handle is seen not to be ideal. The driver's side was the safer, because it was easier for him to turn the blower on immediately before he closed the regulator and this action became second nature, so much so that very early schemes for connecting the blower-handle to the regulator-handle were found to be superfluous.

On a locomotive with large rear wheels the splashers over them took up a lot of room in the cab. In many cases the splasher was made with a flat horizontal top surface and this could form a rudimentary seat extending from front to back of the cab. The narrow space between the splashers did not seem to leave much room for the fireman to work in, but in actual fact the narrowness was not entirely disadvantageous as he could lean on the splasher on the left, if the driver was on the right-hand side as he was on Midland engines. On the Midland compounds, the inside splashers did not extend right to the back of the cab and so the fireman might not merely lean on the splasher but could rather vaguely sit on it, although the corner where these flat surfaces met did not in fact make for the most comfortable sitting. Nevertheless it is not too much to say that when everything was favourable and no big push was being made, you could fire a compound while sitting down, or at least not absolutely standing up. On Midland 4—4—0s the reversing screw was mounted in bearings carried on the horizontal surface that might otherwise have formed a seat for the driver. To compensate for this, a horizontal board was mounted above the screw and this formed a seat cut away to expose the cut-off indicator.

Noticeable on Midland engines with Belpaire fire-boxes was the extensive total area of glass in the front sheet of the cab. This type of outer fire-box bulged into the space normally occupied by circular front windows on engines with round-top fire-boxes. Narrow rectangular look-outs were therefore provided alongside the vertical walls of the firebox, and to forestall any grumble that the Belpaire firebox restricted the look-out, two additional windows were provided above the horizontal roof of the outer firebox.

CHIMNEYS (see p130)

The chimney of a locomotive tends to be its face. No other part of it dominates its appearance in any comparable way and so it is natural to comment on the various chimneys used on the locomotives of any particular railway. Midland chimneys were characterised in styles associated with the chief mechanical engineers. Kirtley chimneys were markedly flared at the top in a common early Victorian style which, by comparison with what came later, looked vulgar. Johnson chimneys were more nearly elegant in having a smaller flare and (in some cases) a refined taper outwards toward the base. Some had the appearance of being built from three separate pieces and, to the writer's eye, this was very regrettable. Within the visible cast-iron chimney on each of the early compounds was an inner steel chimney, but it did not extend so high as the rim which was hollow. Gas-flow through the chimney therefore induced a toroidal vortex in the annular cavity of the rim.

Deeley's first change was to a functional chimney with external taper inwards towards the base in conformity with the usual shape of the inner chimney proper. Later he went to a parallel formation, inside and outside, with a rim and a raised lip (capuchon) to act as wind-deflector. The rim was hollow so that the whole chimney might have a uniform thickness of metal as is desirable in the interest of producing a sound casting. Fowler retained the general form of the later Deeley chimney, but slightly altered thicknesses and fillets.

The form of any chimney, and perhaps particularly of its rim, conveys (to some observers at least) an expression of character and mood. The Kirtley chimney looked happy in a barmaid style. The Johnson chimney might have a smile or a pout according to the particular shape of the rim. Some rims looked remarkably like those of the chimneys that Robinson used later on the Great Central and were a bit surly. Deeley chimneys looked moderately benign, but the Fowler pattern tended rather to scowl.

British locomotive chimneys in general had a shaped external part enclosing a liner filled with the outcoming gas and therefore subject to wear by the grit that scraped through it. In many cases the liner was renewable and so the decorative outer cylinder might last for the whole life of the locomotive. Fowler used no liner within the chimney proper and, as the 'as cast' surface of the inside was pretty good at resisting wear, it is unlikely that maintenance cost exceeded that of successive steel liners.

The vortex of gas and grit generated inside the rim was in no way advantageous and occasionally the abrasive effort was

158

enough, if sufficiently prolonged, to wear through the outermost part of the rim. The result was that the top half of the rim fell off and was perhaps never found even if anyone looked for it. It was rare for a Midland engine to be allowed to run for very long with such a decapitated chimney, because it was grotesquely ugly. It was very noticeable and anyone who saw it and listened could confirm that loss of the vortex in the rim made no difference to the slightly booming woof of the exhaust sound of the larger Midland engines; it was obviously associated with resonance in a very much larger cavity than the annulus of the chimney rim.

TUBE-PLATE, SMOKEBOX AND DOOR

Very odd things were done at times by the Midland about the support of the boiler at its front end. Common British practice was to make the front tube-plate of the boiler with a downward extension to be bolted to the cylinder-casting, and with a forward-pressed flange extending all round its edge except at the bottom. The front plate of the smokebox was generally similar to the tube-plate, but with the flange bent backwards. The smokebox was formed by bending a plate to match the flanges and bolting or rivetting it to them. The plate was wrapped round the flanges and on that account was called a wrapper plate.

It was never easy to make air-tight joints between the three plates and the cylinder casting. Because of the heat of the smokebox gases and vibratory stresses in running, the joints eventually worked loose enough to permit appreciable leakage of air into the smokebox. The steaming of the engine was then spoilt and it ran at well below top efficiency until the next general repair; the leakage had usually to be accepted till then.

An alternative was to use the drum-head tube-plate in the form of a circle with a flanged edge. This was fitted inside the boiler barrel. The front wall of the smokebox was also a flanged circle and the smokebox was formed by wrapping a plate round the

159

cylindrical forms of the front end of the boiler barrel and the flange on the front plate. The smokebox was thus of the very simple cylindrical shape and it rested on a similarly shaped saddle which was an upward extension of the cylinder casting.

In the Johnson compounds the smokebox was a positive horror of purposeless complexity. Johnson and Smith between them contrived to combine the drumhead tube-plate with a wrapper type smokebox *and* a wrapper type outer smokebox, and for good measure added an outer chimney, an inner chimney and a petti-coat pipe. They gave to Deeley, in his role of simplifier, plenty to work on; he went right back to the outdated wrapper type smokebox and was satisfied with one chimney and no petticoat pipe.

The cylindrical smokebox was adopted by Deeley for the 999 class 4—4—0s (m33). It was said (many years later) that Derby failed to make a success of this construction, simple though it is, and did not persist with it. Why they should have been discon-certed by what everyone else found to be advantageously simple was probably the common revolt against anything new, but what-ever it was it left Midland designers and their successors thoroughly frightened off. As late as 1927 the LMS introduced in the 'Royal Scot' 4—6—0 a Derby design spoiled by its wrapper-type smokebox.

Deeley decided that when you want the edge of a circular door to make an air-tight joint with a flat surface it was more sensible to clip the two together at points close to the joint than to anchor the middle of the plate to a cross-bar. So six dogs held the Deeley door and there was no need to make it domed.

A feature of many of the rebuilt forms of 4—4—0s was a smokebox markedly extended ahead of the chimney. This, com-bined with a raising of the centre-line of the boiler, transformed the appearance of the engine from one of wilting weakness to one of aggressive punch and power. In the writer's view this was entirely admirable but some contemporary critics expressed aes-thetic dissatisfaction. The technical advantage of the extended

160

smokebox lay in its space for a lot of 'char' to accumulate before beginning to obstruct gas-flow from the lower tubes. Not until World War II was any British front-end announced to have been designed to chuck the char out of the chimney, though every engine did it in some degree.

LUBRICATION

A noticeable feature of a great many Midland locomotives was a distinctively-shaped brass fitting at the base of each side of the smokebox. This was a Furness lubricator periodically re-charged with oil which was drawn slowly by partial vacuum into the cylinders when the engine was running without steam. It was not applied to engines with superheaters as they had mechanical lubricators which pumped oil slowly to valves and cylinders so long as the engine was running—with or without steam. For lubrication of valves and pistons when a wet steam engine was running with the regulator open, the Midland used a conventional type of sight-feed lubricator mounted inside the cab.

Sliding surfaces in the mechanism were lubricated by oil lifted from oil-boxes by worsted trimmings and conveyed to site by pipes in the usual way. The Midland was also conventional in leading oil to axle-journals in the wrong place. The right way is to apply oil to the underside of the journal where there is no load on it, and whence it is drawn into the loaded region by rotation of the axle. There should be no groove in the loaded area of the axlebox. Deeley must have known this, and yet even in and after his time at Derby, Midland axleboxes continued to be conventionally inferior to what they might have been. For years after the grouping of 1923 poor axlebox design continued as a feature of Derby practice. The LMS applied mechanical lubricators to the driving axleboxes of Class 4F 0—6—0s in trying to get out of trouble that sensible axleboxes would never have suffered if the cranks had been set so as to minimise horizontal forces.

Among the numerous irrelevancies examined in the evidence

161

K

about the circumstances of the Aisgill collision in 1913 was a reference to the drivers' practice of walking round the running board while the engine was in motion in order to put a bit more oil on somewhere. This may have suggested an imperfection in Midland locomotive lubrication, but there was in fact nothing in it. Midland 4—4—0s regularly ran non-stop over the 99 miles between London and Leicester, and even over the 196 miles London to Leeds, without any need for either engineman to leave the footplate. So there can have been no justification for going round the engine before it had run 50 miles. Less highly developed locomotives half a century earlier might have needed a bit of coddling, but British locomotives in the twentieth century were long past such weakness.

TENDERS

The tender was a very undramatic companion for any loco-motive, vital but not vivid, passive rather than active and perhaps only one in ten of enthusiastic engine-watchers would spare a glance for it. Midland history is, however, somewhat distinctive here, as it was one of the few British railways to make much use of tenders on more than six wheels. The vast majority of Midland tenders were, however, six-wheelers.

Weight was placed on the axleboxes under tenders by lami-nated springs. In Kirtley's practice these springs were placed over the running board close to the side-sheets of the tender. S. W. Johnson brought to Derby some ideas he had used on the Great Eastern, and a bad one among them was that of hiding the springs for the tender between inner and outer frame-plates. Perhaps it was an upsurge of enthusiasm for the current Vic-torian love of concealing things, but technically it was just one of the bits of idiocy dotted about the history of nineteenth-century locomotive design. Johnson was soon over it and adopted what became the conventional layout in which springs below the run-ning board conveyed weight to axleboxes in hornblocks attached

162

to the outside of outside frame plates. By 1881 he had finalised his design of six-wheel tenders and for a long time there was no need for anything different.

But as the nineteenth century ran to its close, more luxurious provisions for passengers led to heavier coaches, faster running also called for more power, and longer non-stop runs made still further demands for more water in tenders. So in 1900 eight-wheel tenders appeared on the Midland and, moreover, were attached to single-driver locomotives (m8) which in that year appeared in their largest Midland form. Even at 51 tons, however, those engines were outweighed by their tenders.

Dignified and majestic were the big Midland tenders with sturdy-looking outside frame bogies and axleboxes. It was left to Drummond on the South Western to demonstrate in metal how hideous a tender could look when mounted on two ordinary locomotive bogies with inside frames and fully exposed wheels. The locomotive enthusiast with an eye for looks was not displeased to learn that inside frame bogies for tenders not only looked bad but were bad, as their axleboxes, in the hot wake of the ash-dribbling ash-pan, could be troublesome. Stroudley had much earlier started the visual horror of wheel-exposure in six-wheel tenders, but Drummond pressed the point home with eight-wheelers and the cult ended with them.

Most of the Midland Class 3 4—4—0s (m31) were provided with eight-wheel tenders, and many of them must have run many miles for which six-wheelers would have sufficed. It may have been reflection on this that suggested to the Midland that there were such things as water-troughs. In 1903 troughs were laid near Oakley, near Loughborough and near Melton Mowbray, but an order for eight-wheel tenders was already in progress and so some were built as late as 1904. The water troughs near Hawes Junction were not installed till 1907.

Deeley dignified tenders no less than locomotives by extending the side-sheets upwards to form coal-restraining plates instead of using the conventional coal-rails. He also used the large

163

vertical areas as sites for the engine number in 18in figures. This was fine, but because of difference between repairing-times for engine and tender, 50 engines could be kept going with 48 tenders. The tender was therefore not really a good place for displaying the number of the engine, but this realisation reached Derby only after some years of contact with other members of the LMS group.

COLOUR

Because the writer is aware from the printed word that statements about what is sometimes called the livery of locomotives can arouse emotional outbursts of wave-length splitting denial, he hesitates before making even the barest statement about colour of Midland locomotives. In Kirtley's time it was green. In 1873 Johnson tried a rather different green and in 1874 still another. In 1880 he turned to red and in 1883 to another red that persisted for forty years as Midland red. During Deeley's time, black was adopted for goods engines instead of red.

Midland coaches had been red long before the engines were, and perhaps right back to the beginning of the Midland in 1844. It was a dignified red and it majestically beautified locomotive and coaches of every Midland passenger train. It contrasted sharply with the predominant green of rural scenery and it suggested an aggressive quality that the Midland had always needed if it were to expand or indeed to survive.

CHAPTER FIVE

Some Unfulfilled Projects

In the following pages are some notes about locomotive designs that were developed at Derby at least to the stage of outline drawings. There were, of course, other projects and Radford's 'Derby Works and Midland Locomotives' (Bib Ref 4) refers to a 0—8—0, a 2—6—6—2T (Garratt), and a 0—12—0T with a tapered boiler barrel. The latter feature suggests that Derby was taking some notice of Churchward practice on the Great Western, at least in respect of an externally obvious feature. Sad to say, the really significant characteristic—provision of valves large enough to work well at high speed—was rejected for a long time in Britain by everyone not brought up at Swindon. Deeley's addiction to outside admission for piston valves is hard to explain.

COMPOUND 2—4—4—2T

An extraordinary Deeley doodle (p148) was essentially a 2—8—2 tank engine with compound expansion. Its distinction seems to have arisen from a desire to avoid inside cylinders and so two low-pressure outside cylinders were proposed in the normal position, while two high-pressure cylinders were to be placed behind the coupled wheels in a position where the plate supporting the cab-steps would have prohibited any convenient access to the piston-rod gland and the valve-spindle gland. The low-pressure pistons worked cranks on the third axle; the high-pressure pistons similarly worked the fourth axle. Coupling rods

165

connected the second and third axles; other coupling rods connected the fourth and fifth axles. Coupling-rods between the third and fourth axles were evidently deemed superfluous and none was proposed. Steam had a long horizontal journey from the boiler to the high-pressure cylinders and another long one forward to reach the low-pressure cylinders. Pipes lagged well enough to avoid excessive loss of heat would have cut deeply into space that could have been used to carry water in the tanks.

This design would have made a visually acceptable engine apart from the single slide-bars and crossheads which tend to look elemental rather than elegant and are great grit-gatherers. Their positions abreast of the leading and trailing coupled wheels would impose a severe restraint on the side play that the axles might have been given as a means of alleviating possible difficulties with what would otherwise have been a rigid wheel-base of 19ft. The locomotive would be a poor starter from rest unless it were provided with starting valves that would divert exhaust from the high-pressure cylinders to the blast-pipe, so that all four cylinders might use boiler steam for starting. With this provision, with bunker extended upwards to hold 5 tons of coal, and with plenty of facilities for refilling water tanks, a locomotive of this kind might have done well in short distance suburban passenger train service. This engine could not be a flyer as, traditionally, the low-pressure cylinders had flat valves where there was plenty of room for piston-valves. Moreover the piston-valves for the high-pressure cylinders had outside admission. The boiler was to be that used on Deeley compounds and Deeley 999s.

2—6—2 No 2299 (PAGET) (see p147)

After about 1870, every now and then someone would examine steam locomotives and declare, 'Why!—these things are just like George Stephenson's *Rocket*, they're years out of date. We can do a lot better than this if we really get down to it in the light of modern developments'. This happened at Derby soon after

Deeley took charge and as a result there was built an outside-frame 2—6—2 numbered 2299. Deeley was not responsible, and although built in the Midland Works at Derby it was not at their expense. The idea was C. W. Paget's, then works manager there, and the story is that he paid for it himself.

Every ordinary steam locomotive had hundreds of firebox-stays which held the inner and outer firebox walls at their designed spacing in spite of the steam pressure. Each stay was simple enough, being a bar of metal (usually copper or steel) with a screw-thread at each end. Stays could be very troublesome at times and every locomotive engineer would have liked to use boilers that did not need to have stays. Lots of people designed stayless boilers (and some were made) but did not seem to realise the enormous advantage that the conventional 'water-wall' firebox had in catching all the heat the fire threw at it and passing it into the water to make steam; it did this with water spaces generally not more than 4in wide. Even the inner wall of the firebox did not get much hotter than the water in the boiler. Anyone who eliminated stays had to sacrifice water walls and to substitute firebrick which, when the engine worked hard (if it ever did), would become white-hot at its inner surface and not much cooler at its outer surface unless it were bricked out to a thickness much greater than the 6 or 7in which was as much as space allowed on a locomotive with a reasonable width of grate. So a stay-less locomotive boiler was bound to lose a lot of heat through the walls of the firebox.

The boiler of No 2299 was a barrel some $6\frac{1}{2}$ft in diameter and 12ft long, with a backward projection of its upper part for 12ft in the cross-sectional form of a segment 6ft wide and 2ft deep. Under this projection was the firebox, built of about 7 tons of bricks and containing a horizontal firegrate about $8\frac{1}{2}$ft by $6\frac{1}{2}$ft over a shallow ash pan. This had a slightly sloping bottom on which no ash would slide unless forcefully pushed by water jets for which nozzles were provided. There were two fire doors with bottom edges only about 5in above the fire-bars and, with a 9ft throw slightly uphill from the nearly red-hot backplate to the front, there would have been need of two firemen. The design was good in that it had only about nine dozen stays 2ft long, but the firebox, grate and ashpan were astonishingly unpractical, wasteful of heat, hard to fire and liable to be choked with ash. This was not strongly demonstrated because trouble with valves prevented the locomotive from doing any sustained hard work. Good points were pipes for discharging ash and smokebox char directly into a pit between the rails.

The development of the steam turbine after about 1897 imbued many engineers with the idea that rotary motion was the modern thing in an engine and that reciprocating motion should not be tolerated where it could be avoided. So many people had a go at rotary valves and most of them were glad to abandon them. The essential fact is that in valves the despised reciprocating motion works quite well, while rotary motion is less happy. The general use in high-speed steam engines and internal combustion engines of 'trunk' pistons (which carry their own gudgeon pins and act as their own crossheads) inspired Paget to use them in No 2299 which had eight single-acting cylinders and eight inside cranks, besides those used with the coupling-rods. There were two crank-pins on the first and last coupled axles and four on the middle one. There were four cylinders in front of the middle coupled axle and four behind it. Steam that leaked past pistons formed a white cloud near the ground on the leeward side of the locomotive. The corresponding leakage in a conventional locomotive is unnoticeable in the discharge from the chimney.

The valves for all cylinders had a common axis in the central longitudinal plane of the locomotive. They were rotated by a shaft connected by bevel gears to a cross-shaft under the rear wall of the fire-box. This shaft was connected by spur gears to a parallel one (at coupled-axle height) with outside fly-cranks coupled to the main coupling rods. Reversing was effected with steam assistance by the use of a planetary assembly of bevel gears on the upper cross-shaft. Cut-off was changed by the partial rotation of the ported liners in which the valves rotated.

By comparison with the conventional steam locomotive, No 2299 was a 'box of tricks' even with everything worked properly, but the valves were liable to leak badly or to seize up solid. After the latter had caused the engine to block a main line for some hours—even though on a Sunday—further testing was strongly discouraged. There are other versions of what actually happened, but there is no doubt that the project was abandoned because of difficulties with the valves and cylinders. There was also a bit of bother with the brickwork and a good deal more could have been expected if the engine had run very far. The general pattern of the story of No 2299 was pretty closely repeated in that of Bulleid's 0—6—6—0 'Leader' on the Southern Region of British Railways some fifty years later. There were too many new things being tried at once and far too much optimism about the endurance of very hot brick walls on a hard-riding rail vehicle, about their reluctance to transmit heat and about the physique of firemen.

Some dimensions of No 2299

Grate area	55sq ft
Boiler barrel diameter	80in
„ „ length	145in
Nominal tractive eff.	19,000lb
Adhesion wt.	56 tons
Total „	80 tons
Tender „	43 tons
Boiler pressure	180psi
Cylinder diameter	18in
Piston stroke	12in
Driving wheel dia	64in

Eight single-acting cylinders with diameter greater than piston stroke (motor-car engine designers call this 'better than square').
The tubes were of the Serve type, $2\frac{1}{2}$in diameter each with seven radial-axial internal fins.

OTHER TEN-WHEELERS (see pp148, 149)

The Midland never had a 4—6—0, but in 1907 Deeley sketched out a design for a four-cylinder compound 4—6—0. Enough has been published about it to enable some comments to be added to the one that it was sad to see Deeley belatedly simulating the Northern of France style of four-cylinder compound, already found wanting by Churchward on the Great Western.

To the extent that the design was that of a tapered-boiler 4-cylinder 4—6—0 with inside valve-gear and outside cylinders well behind the others, it was similar to that of the Great Western 'Stars'. The barrel of the Deeley boiler was, however, about 6in smaller in diameter and its tapered character was to be concealed by its enclosure in lagging sheets in cylindrical form about 5ft 7in in diameter. With inside (low-pressure) cylinders above the bogie-centre, there was no possibility of providing access to their glands or crossheads through holes in the frame. The outside cylinders were to be immediately to the rear of the rear bogie wheels and so the inter-frame bracing and the Stévart valve-gear would have obstructed access to anything inside the frame in a very marked manner. Piston-valves of 8.75in diameter were proposed for both the high-pressure cylinders (13in x 28in) and the low-pressure cylinders (21in x 26in). The outside valves were to be driven by rocking levers from the inside valve-spindles. An alternative story is that the valve-gear (presumably Walschaerts) was to be applied to the outside valves and this would have been very much superior in minimising the mechanism inside the frame.

Steam sanding was to be provided in front of all six coupled wheels; it is interesting to remember that the LMS Royal Scots were given this feature when they were about twenty years old. No back sanding was shown on the Deeley 4—6—0; this was a common optimistic omission from many British main-line passenger train engines. It seems to have been judged that, as they would never need to run very far tender first, it didn't matter about sand for that direction.

It is said that Deeley was prohibited from building any locomotive to this design by the lack of a need for anything larger than the Smith-Johnson-Deeley compound for the light loadings to which Paget policy limited passenger trains on the Midland, but something of the kind might well have eliminated the need for double-heading passenger trains on the Leeds–Carlisle line.

More convincing than Deeley's contemplated 4—6—0 was a design prepared by the LMS for a three-cylinder compound 4—6—0, very much in the form of an extended Midland compound but with piston valves above the cylinders. For the engine to be a flyer in the Great Western style the product of the diameter and lap of the valves for the low-pressure cylinders would have needed to be about 22; for example, 12in valves would require 1.8in lap but, as those dimensions were very much outside Derby practice at the time, it is unlikely that the engine would have been given them. It would probably have been a 'miner's friend', like the Gresley Pacifics before their valves were put right.

The front wall of the firebox was sloped to reach ahead of the middle coupled axle. With a boiler pressure of 220psi, 6ft 9in driving wheels and low-pressure cylinders 22.25 x 30in, the nominal tractive effort was over 34,000lb. With details right, such a locomotive could have been a winner but even at that, unlikely to have been superior to a three-cylinder simple with 20in cylinders using steam at 180psi through steam-tight piston valves dimensioned for economical power-development at full speed. Derby might not have been convinced of that in 1924, but British experience in the following three or four years made it clear to everyone prepared to take critical notice of what was going on.

IMPROVED LICKEY BANKER

Trains were assisted up steep gradients by banking engines only where the train engine alone could not have made the climb with any certainty. So even banked trains usually ran quite slowly and every banking engine usually pushed as hard as it could up the grade. When any ordinary steam locomotive was exerting its maximum pull (or push) its cylinder efficiency was very low, and this was accepted because normal duties required maximum pull for only a small fraction of its total mileage. But a locomotive specifically produced for banking, and not intended to do anything else, should clearly be designed for high cylinder-efficiency when pushing at the slipping limit of its adhesion weight.

The highest cylinder-efficiency in any steam locomotive was attained when the valve-gear was notched up so that the actual tractive effort was about 30 per cent of the nominal tractive effort; in that condition the cylinder efficiency was about 80 per cent higher than it was in full gear with the engine exerting its full nominal tractive effort. To get that efficiency in a banking engine pushing hard almost at the slipping limit defined by the adhesion weight, the nominal tractive effort would have to be about 3.3 times that at slip, or about 3.3 times the nominal tractive effort normally provided. Such a high nominal tractive effort would be troublesome in operation, because when set in full gear (as is often necessary to be sure of getting away from rest) the engine would be excessively prone to slipping.

But a four cylinder engine might well be made with nominal tractive effort equal to twice (even if not 3.3 times) the tractive effort at slip, because it could be easily arranged so that when set in full gear for starting, application of steam could be limited to two cylinders. In that condition, it would be no more (or less) prone to slip than was the average steam locomotive. Once on the move, it could be notched up to about 30 per cent and steam admitted to all four cylinders. Tractive effort near to the slipping limit would then be available with cylinder efficiency about 50 per cent higher than that in full gear. In other words, coal consumption could be expected to be down to about 67 per cent of that required when producing the same propulsive effort in full gear. So by giving a four-cylinder engine a nominal tractive effort of about half the adhesion weight, and a starting valve that fed only two cylinders, it could exert its maximum pull in running at 30 per cent cut-off instead of 75 per cent and thus save some 33 per cent in coal.

The nominal tractive effort of the Lickey banker No 2290 was just over a quarter of the adhesion weight. To raise it to half the adhesion weight, the cylinder volume would have needed to be doubled, for example by increasing the cylinder diameter from 16.75 to 23.7in. This, however, is too big to be accommodated in the British loading gauge. What else might be done? The working pressure of steam might be raised from 180 to 200psi (the boiler was in fact made to take this), the piston-stroke lengthened to 30in, and the wheel-diameter reduced to 4ft 3in. With these changes, a cylinder-diameter of 21in suffices to produce a nominal tractive effort of 88,000lb instead of 43,300lb and this scheme is just practicable.

In the actual engine Derby had not found it easy to accommodate four cylinders. The inside ones had to be set high enough for the lower slide-bars to clear the leading axle. The pistons drove cranks on the middle axle, while the second axle had also to be cranked to clear the inside connecting-rods. The outside cylinders were set at the same height and inclination as the inside cylinders. To avoid any necessity for valves or valve-gear between the frame-plates, long 'crossed ports' were provided whereby piston valves above the outside cylinders controlled movements of steam to and from the inside cylinders as well as serving the outside cylinders in the ordinary way. This is not an arrangement that could be tolerated in a high-speed locomotive, and it makes for a very large clearance volume for the inside cylinders, but this is not a serious disadvantage in a locomotive that does most of its work in full gear at low speed. Its use in No 2290 suffices to explain why the engine made a sorry showing when tried on main-line goods train work in 1924. This was no discredit to it; no locomotive intended to do its best at about 12mph is to be criticised merely because it is unimpressive at 30mph.

Four valves would be essential in the 88,000lb tractive effort engine because the inside pair of cylinders and the outside pair would have to be able to be worked independently of each other. The outside cylinders would be used for all movements of the engine; the inside ones would be brought into action only after the engine had got under way on a banking run. Because of this restricted use of the inside cylinders, each of their valves could be work by a slip-eccentric set to give 30 per cent cut-off in forward or in backward gear, according to the direction of motion; the inside valve-gear could thus be very simple.

Use of three-bar crossheads would enable the inside cylinders to be set lower than those of No 2290 and there would be enough room above them for the 8in piston valves that would suffice for banking speeds. Because of the independence of the two pairs of cylinders, the cranks could be set, without detriment, to give eight exhaust beats per revolution of the wheels instead of only four, and this would be advantageous

(a) in reducing cyclic pulsation in tractive effort during each revolution of the wheels, and

(b) in reducing cyclic pulsation of draught on the fire. (This is valuable at low speed although it makes no difference at high speed.)

As usual in steam locomotives, these gains in working efficiency would make the engine rather less impressive to the listening observers. They would hear, instead of four full-strength beats per revolution, eight half-strength ones. At 12mph there would be 10 beats per second, leaving little chance for perceptible pulsation of draught.

CHAPTER SIX

Midland Speed, Power and Performance

In the following pages some indication is given of Midland steam at work by figures relating to the running of a number of express passenger trains on several of the Midland main lines. On the more undulating routes, the downhill maximum speeds were at least as high as contemporary ones on other Briish railways and it is clear that to this extent Midland engines were free-running. Many of the loads quoted are smaller than those commonly found on other British main lines at the time. The Midland ran its rather light expresses very gaily over its ups and downs and gave Midland enthusiasts no reason to believe that the daily work of main-line passenger train locomotives on other British railways was any better. The North Western ran heavier trains over its less heavily graded main line and so did the Great Western between Paddington and Taunton via Bristol but, off the main lines, it was usual to make less strenuous demands on the locomotves.

The dedicated student of railway working may wish that authentic details had been recorded of the running of pre-1914 British trains of all types; instead he must be glad that some of the express train-timing records of a few energetic observers were published in that period and are therefore still available. They were made, not with any technical object in mind, but as a means of paying a little written homage to objects of admiration and affection. They earn the thanks of truth-seekers three generations later.

It was very easy for any traveller on a train to note the passing-times at as many stations and signal-boxes as he cared to select from those on the route, and British railway enthusiasts are fortunate in that many of their number became painstakingly industrious in this pursuit. This was largely due to the articles contributed to the *Railway Magazine* by C. Rous-Marten and C. J. Allen. They themselves provided the bulk of the timings before World War I; later on, timings by correspondents became more numerously published with the result that there is now a very great deal of readily available information about the running of British main-line passenger trains in normal service. On this basis, at least, it is possible to quote figures that enable Midland fast running to be compared with what was done on other British railways. There is no similar information in respect of the running of the goods trains that made most of the money for the Midland.

On pp246-52 are gathered together figures gleaned mostly from *Railway Magazine* articles on 'British Locomotive Practice and Performance' in the early years of the twentieth century. They have been selected to represent a range of locomotives and loads. For every undelayed run, the times reported by the observer are reproduced here. Wherever there was a delay (apart from those imposed by permanent speed-restrictions) a time-allowance has been made for it, on the basis of observed undelayed running in the vicinity, and the figures given here are the times that would (or could) have been made with no delay. This is done so that figures in adjacent columns may be directly comparable.

Train-timing enthusiasts before 1923 were fewer than they later became, and so the published records were not sufficiently numerous to show whether it was unusual for locomotives to run much faster than the published time-table promised or to suggest whether any of the recorded runs was specially meritorious. What the figures given here do show, however, is that Midland running on some routes at least was as fast as anything scheduled over them by the LMS for many years after the grouping of 1923. The times quoted for the Leeds–Rotherham route may well seem unbelievably fast to those whose experience of that route is entirely post-1940. Notes made by C. Rous-Marten suggest that on the St Pancras–Leicester road in the late 1890s, Midland singles not unusually reached speeds well above 80mph, but that a full 90mph was rare. It was in 1906-7 that the Midland began to indicate the tonnage of each coach by a number exhibited on it. Weights quoted for Midland trains in earlier days are necessarily somewhat speculative. The figures given here are estimates of the loaded weights of the trains.

Run 1 was non-stop to Nottingham (123½ miles) reached in 129min 52sec from St Pancras, some four minutes early, and so the driver cannot be criticised for sloth. Rous-Marten was disappointed that speed fell to 35mph at mile post 59¾, but it is clear from what happened later that no useful purpose would have been served by running any harder at that point.

Run 2, non-stop to Leicester, was not so fast as Run 1, although 77mph was touched between Ampthill and Bedford. Minimum speeds were 34mph at mile post 59¾, 40 at Desborough and 43 at Kibworth. The scheduled allowance of time to Leicester was 112min and this run suggests that it was generous.

Run 3 was very lively right from the start but was badly delayed—to the extent of a dead stand—beyond St Albans, and the actual times to stations beyond that point were about 3½min longer than those quoted in the table. An average of 77½mph from Luton to Bedford was notable (but Rous-Marten quotes no maximum figure) as was the minimum of 55mph beyond Sharnbrook. At Desborough the minimum was 50mph and the report particularly mentions that the driver slowed right down to this, the prescribed figure, in running through Market Harborough. This suggests that such precision was not common in those days, nor was it at Market Harborough fifty years later. After one has ridden through at 77mph without disaster, one is inclined to think that restriction to 50 is a bit severe.

177

L

Run 4 shows what a compound did in taking a modest load to stops at Luton and Leicester before carrying on to cover the next 97 miles to Leeds (Run 12) in a nett time of 106min. The minimum speeds at Elstree, mile post $59\frac{3}{4}$ and Desborough were 54, $49\frac{1}{2}$ and 53mph and the time of 13min 25sec for the thirteen markedly rising miles from Wellingborough to Desborough was unusually fast. Maxima at Radlett, below Ampthill, below Irchester and below Desborough were 71, 79, 72 and 72mph.

There is little to add about Run 5 beyond a note that a maximum of 81mph was reached near Bedford and that the minimum beyond Sharnbrook was 41mph.

Rous-Marten remarked that Run 6 was made with 'a furious gale blowing right across the track, with frequent showers which, drying intermediately, kept the rail always "greasy"'. There seems to be a little confusion here because a rail washed by rain water that then evaporates is about as clean as it is ever likely to be. Rails are made greasy by condensation on a layer of the very fine dust that is normal nearly everywhere after a calm dry spell. Maxima were 72mph at Radlett and 78 in the approach to Bedford where the train stopped just before reaching the station.

The load of 350 tons on Run 7 was considerably greater than the 'special limit' of 240 tons imposed some years later on Midland compounds running to Leicester on a non-stop schedule of 105min. Rous-Marten estimated the performance of No 2634 on this occasion to be equivalent to a non-stop run in $105\frac{1}{2}$min. Minimum speeds at Elstree, beyond St Albans, beyond Sharnbrook, at Desborough and at Kibworth were 47, 50, 39, 42 and 48mph. Maxima approaching Bedford and approaching Wellingborough were 80mph.

In the up direction, Run 8 was not so notable as the circumstances that preceded it. Starting from Wellingborough, a rebuilt 4—4—0 had whirled the 100-ton load gaily over the brow above Irchester and had swept down to a quick stop at Sharnbrook in just over 11min for the slightly more than 8 miles. After getting away again very fast and passing Oakley, 3.8 miles, in less than

178

5min, something went wrong with the engine. The driver decided she wasn't fit to go to London and stopped abreast of the Bedford engine shed in less than 9min from leaving Sharnbrook 7 miles back. Then followed some lightning work of a kind at which the Midland was quite unapproachable. An explanation was made to the appropriate authority, an engine and crew were alerted while the 4—4—0 was being got out of the way, the replacement engine was backed on, coupled up, brake-vacuum checked and the guard's green flag waved in 2min 25sec (ie in less than 2½min after stopping). The writer can recollect nothing remotely comparable with this in anything he has seen or in any story he has ever read, or been told, about any railway operation in Great Britain. It is very hard to believe, even if advance notice had been given by way of a whistle-code sounded by the driver of the 4—4—0 as he passed Oakley Junction or Bromham. One may muse for some time also about the nature of the defect that enabled the driver to decide almost immediately (without consulting Bedford shed) that the engine should not try to get to London, yet did not preclude him from running at top speed to Bedford.

The report states that the replacement engine was taken to London by the Bedford driver who brought it onto the train. The driver of the failed 4—4—0 would therefore remain at Bedford for some time. Had he some personal reason for wanting to do that? It must have been Midland custom at the time to compel the crew of a failed engine to stay with it. General practice after engine failure was for the original crew to take the train on with the engine that replaced the one they had brought. Anything that followed the fire-brigade motions at Bedford was bound to be anti-climax but No 642 did very well. To cover 19.6 mostly uphill miles to Luton in 22½min start-to-stop was excellent; the train came over the top at Toddington (north of Leagrave) at 55mph and touched 64 before the stop at Luton. Very lively too was the run from there to St Pancras with 71mph at St Albans, 80 at Radlett, 64 minimum at Elstree and 77 maximum at Hendon.

Runs 9, 10 and 11 compare the running of a Class 2 4—4—0 with that of compounds with heavier loads. Run 11 shows a non-superheated compound with a big train. No details of running are available beyond what can be learned from the table, apart from the fact that a maximum speed of 80mph was attained at Radlett. Here was a non-superheated compound, beating the 105-minute schedule with a load 35 per cent greater than the 240-ton special limit load that applied to superheater-fitted compounds.

Run 10 (the continuation of Run 13) was non-stop over the 196 miles from Leeds to London in a nett time of 209min against an allowance of 213min.

Run 12 followed Run 4 after a normal station-stop at Leicester. It was very brisk in the first stage with a maximum of nearly 74mph at Loughborough and only 21min for the 20.8 miles from the start to a slow passage of Trent Junction. After that speed was worked up to 60mph on the gently rising gradients to Stanton Gate. The highest recorded speed in subsequent running was 65mph at Killamarsh and the average from there over the $30\frac{1}{2}$ miles to Normanton was 61mph in spite of the usual speed-restriction at Rotherham (Masborough).

Run 13 was the preamble to Run 10, Leicester being passed at about 30mph after averaging 54.3mph from Leeds and before averaging 58.3mph on to London. Such an average as 53.3mph from starting from Leeds and slowing through Normanton to passing Rotherham at reduced speed is not remarkable as a haulage feat on gentle gradients but is very different from the usual running over that route in the 1960s.

Run 14 was an excellent effort by a non-superheated 999, the average of 45.8mph from Settle to Blea Moor being specially notable. The time of $28\frac{1}{2}$min for the 30.8 miles from Appleby to the stop at Carlisle was also unusually brisk; it included a maximum of 83mph in the dip before Lazonby.

Runs 15, 16, 19 and 20 are not quite within the strict terms of reference of this book as they were made in the course of specially observed running of regular LMS trains purposely overweighted on particular occasions in 1923-4.

On Run 16, No 1008 climbed from Settle to Blea Moor at 38.2mph as against 35.8mph by the similarly loaded superheater-fitted No 998, but this was a long way below the 45.8mph of the wet steam No 995 with 255 tons. The compound gained 1½min on No 998 from Leeds to Blea Moor, or about 2 per cent, and so the difference in mean power output was not great. Closer examination shows, however, that the engines were practically neck and neck at Settle Junction so that No 1008 gained the 1½min in about 24min which is about 6 per cent. Moreover No 1008 dropped in speed from 66 to 33mph, whereas No 998 dropped from 72 to 29. So the compound made what was a distinctly better climb, but whether that was more sensible than spreading the effort more evenly over the Leeds–Blea Moor length is doubtful. Both engines beat schedule time (86min) to Aisgill and after that no special effort was required to get down to Carlisle in 49min. These runs show no operational superiority of the compound over the single-expansion engine but coal consumption tests did so later on.

Of the up runs, No 17 was made when, in the early days of the compounds, they showed what they really could do on the Carlisle road. The train touched 72mph on the dip near Lazonby in covering the generally adverse 30.8 miles to Appleby in 34½min, and then averaged 45.5mph up the mean gradient of about 1 in 130 to Aisgill where the minimum speed was 43mph. Down the bank past Settle, Rous-Marten noted a top speed of 92mph but in his *Railway Magazine* report of the run he quoted no time for any point between Aisgill and Hellifield and so provided no material that anyone could use to suggest that the maximum might not have been quite so high as 92.

Run 18 was much more sedate all the way and the top speed was only 72mph. This was a straight honest-to-goodness time-keeping run, the booked allowance being 95min.

Runs 19 and 20 were LMS test-runs and the load of 370 tons

was something quite unprecedented for a Midland 4—4—0 over such a hump as Aisgill or indeed anywhere else while anyone was looking. Estimated average drawbar horsepower figures from Carlisle to Aisgill are 650, 730 and 840 for runs 17, 19 and 20; from Appleby to Aisgill the corresponding figures are 710, 840 and 900 for a saturated compound, a superheated simple and a superheated compound. Run 20 shows a Midland compound at its very best in power production, but taking 26min 44sec to climb from Appleby to Aisgill. In the same series of tests the same engine with 320 tons covered that length in 24min 3sec, whereas on Run 19 No 998 with the same load took 25min 58sec.

Run 21 was a pre-1914 performance on the 5.35pm train from St Pancras to Manchester with one intermediate stop at Leicester. The average speed over the 27.3 miles of easy grades to Spondon Junction was 57.5mph but the next bit to Derby North Junction was taken with caution and at that point the average had come down to 54mph. At Rowsley, after the slow at Ambergate, it was 51.5mph and at Peak Forest, with all the climbing done, it was 48.6mph. It is interesting to note that the speed restriction at Throstle Nest Junction, and the 1 in 100 rise thence to Manchester Central, almost neutralised the gain in speed on a fast descent of 24 miles as the final average was only 48.9mph. In accordance with normal practice, brakes were used to moderate speed here and there, notably at New Mills South Junction, taken at about 50mph.

Run 22 was made with the same train as that of Run 21 but it was notable for the run-in over the last 25½ miles from Peak Forest. It was a time-keeping effort, and nothing more, as far as Millers Dale, and there was some relaxation from there to Peak Forest summit, where speed was down to about 25mph. Moreover steam was shut off as soon as the whole train was over the top and the regulator was left shut for some 23 miles. It seems unlikely that there was any reason why it should not have been opened earlier. What is more likely is that the driver was finding by actual trial how far a passenger train could get by gravity alone if it could just crawl over Peak Forest. At all events, no brake was applied until the engine reached the platform-end at Manchester Central. The most interesting moment was the passage of New Mills South Junction at 74mph, as after that the speed gradually fell to 68mph at Cheadle Heath and much more rapidly on the gentler grades to Withington. It was down to 30mph when the regulator was opened at the foot of the sharp rise to Throstle Nest Junction and it was kept at about that figure up the 1 in 100 that extends most of the way from there to the terminus. The arrival was about half a minute late.

Of the up runs, No 23 was pre-1917 with a wet-steam compound, whereas No 24 was made by an LMS compound in 1927 with a load some 45 tons heavier. This evidently more than outweighed the advantage from superheating as No 1013 had the lead all the way. This was particularly the case on the $17\frac{1}{2}$-mile climb to Peak Forest, where all the hard work is over. From there down the steep grades to Rowsley the time made depended only on the extent to which the driver was prepared to let go on that twisty track. Gravity provided all the power he could use; he decided how soon and how hard to put the brakes on. No 1013 did not exceed 64mph anywhere but No 1049 touched 76 between Monsal Dale and Longstone and 72 between Bakewell and Rowsley. On the straighter length beyond Ambergate, where steam could be used without risk of excessive speed, No 1013 reached 67mph at Duffield, and No 1049, showing some superiority at last, went through at 72.

Runs 25, 26 and 27, published in the *Railway Magazine* for June 1925, were perhaps just a little outside Midland history during which period compounds were not regularly used (if at all) between Derby and Bristol. Run 25 was made in the first week of regular running of compounds, and with a light load of 200 tons No 1057 gained nearly four minutes on the leisurely schedule time of 51min (48.5mph). Apart from the regular restriction to 45mph at Burton, speed was generally around a mile a minute against the slightly rising tendency of the road.

The Class 3 locomotive on Run 26 had not much to spare with the load of 275 tons. She touched 61mph in the dip before Repton but 60mph was not exceeded afterwards until the one-mile descent to Kingsbury produced 62mph and the slighter one beyond gave 65.

On Run 27, No 520 covered the 37.7 miles from Saltley to Pear Tree in 37.8min including a slack to 50mph through Burton and this represents the longest distance at nearly 60mph on Runs 25 to 28. Maxima were 66 before Kingsbury and 70 beyond Wichnor, with a minimum of 60 between Kingsbury and Wilnecote. But the load was light and the road downhill and so this was not hard work even for a Class 2 4—4—0.

Run 28 was timed by E. L. Ahrons in 1888 over the slightly longer route that avoided Birmingham but included Whitacre Junction. The engine was a 1282 class 2—4—0 (m17) and the load was a light one of 115 tons. The downhill start to Ashchurch was brisk; from there to Abbot's Wood the running was unhurried and thence to Bromsgrove it was adequate. The re-start from Bromsgrove in 31sec was better than normal and the 20.9mph average up to Blackwell was well removed from 'stalling', although not arduous even for one engine, let alone two. With all the uphill behind them at Blackwell, the crew of No 1295 required judgement rather than stamina to reach Derby on time. The driver did excellently to stop in Derby station 16sec early after a two-minute stop at the home signal. The time of 57min from passing Blackwell at about 20mph to the signal stop at Derby meant an average of 56mph with a very severe slowing at Whitacre Junction and the barest excess over the mile-a-minute rate anywhere. The nett time of $102\frac{1}{2}$min from Cheltenham to the Derby platform was $17\frac{1}{2}$min less than the very generous allowance of 2 hours for the 87 miles and of this No 1295 had gained $16\frac{1}{2}$min.

At the start of the Birmingham–Bristol line there is a mile up at 1 in 80 and none of the Midland engines really liked this. On Run 30, No 773 dropped over a minute on the allowance of 7min on the way up to Selly Oak and gained nothing on to Blackwell.

There was, of course, no point in running any harder as it was easy enough to pick up a minute on the cautious allowance of 5min for the 2.2 miles of steep downhill to Bromsgrove and No 773 was on time at that point. Over the 24 miles of generally favourable grades to Ashchurch (passed at 69mph) the average speed was 66mph with a maximum of 73mph at Defford. After six miles up at about 1 in 300, speed was 50mph when the regulator was shut for the stop at Cheltenham.

Run 29 was a notable one by Class 2 4—4—0 No 522 with a train of 230 tons and a schedule time of 63min to Gloucester. This was a minute or so easier than that of the succeeding run and the driver of No 522 took advantage of this up to Blackwell, but afterwards equalled the speed of No 773 from Bromsgrove to Ashchurch with similar maxima. The train stopped at Gloucester in 40sec over the hour from Birmingham, the average speed being 51.5mph.

Run 31 by another Class 2 engine, No 521, showed good work by the time of 34½min for 31.3 miles of distinctly adverse average grading to Bromsgrove. Maximum speeds were 68mph at Ashchurch and 67 at the Avon bridge before Defford; from passing Ashchurch and running against the steepening gradient to the stop at Bromsgrove, the average speed was 56.5mph. With the 0—10—0 in the rear from Bromsgrove to Blackwell, 20sec were lost on the 7min schedule and No 521 lost a further half-minute on to Birmingham.

The foregoing presents a fair picture of the running of trains on the main lines of the Midland Railway during its last quarter-century before the railway grouping of 1923. In the realm of pure speed, the Midland was perhaps the leading British railway in the first few years of the twentieth century, Johnson singles and Johnson compounds having been timed at 90 to 92mph, but there was less exuberance later and published records report few maxima higher than 83mph. This was because the engines could do what they had to do without using much steam downhill and indeed on some roads they might go a long way with none at all.

185

Midland policy, certainly in the twentieth century, was to avoid working any engine very hard because to do so inevitably increased coal consumption and repair-cost per unit of useful work done. So far as published statistics can tell us, this policy succeeded, but it tended to prevent Midland engines from delighting enthusiasts by running hard and fast with big trains.

It is a pity, perhaps, that the Midland was never involved in the type of competition that in special circumstances invited running appreciably faster than regular services required, as this might have enabled a few Midland engines to show that they could achieve start-to-stop speeds of over a mile a minute. The 'Races to the North' in 1888 and 1895 did this for the main competitors and the Plymouth–London 'Ocean Mail' competition in 1904 did it for the Great Western and the South Western, but there was nothing comparable on the Midland proper. After the 1923 grouping, however, competition between the LMS and the LNE led the former to make a couple of prestige runs that foiled an announced intention of the LNE to break a British record. This enabled what was essentially a Midland engine to win a distinction for its class.

On 27 April 1928 a notably long non-stop run was made by LMS compound No 1054, one of the batch of slightly modified Midland Deeley-Fowler compounds built in 1924. On this day, the down Royal Scot train was run in two parts, the first one being taken by 4—6—0 No 6113 non-stop from Euston to Glasgow (Central) (401.4 miles) and the second part by No 1054 from Euston to Edinburgh (Princes Street) (399.7 miles). No 1054 was just too late to establish a British record for length of non-stop run because No 6113 had stopped in Glasgow a few minutes before No 1054 stopped in Edinburgh. No other British 4—4—0 ever approached this achievement by No 1054 (Great Western runs over 261.5 miles between Paddington and Fishguard were the nearest), but the world's record non-stop run by steam on rails had been established by a Pennsylvania Rail Road 4—4—0 as far back as 1876 when the 438 miles from Jersey City to Pittsburgh were covered non-stop at an average of 43.5mph. No 1054 was provided with a tender modified to carry more coal than usual so as to give a bigger reserve margin against unusually difficult running conditions, and a third man rode on the engine to relieve either driver or fireman as need might arise. The train was of six vehicles (about 180 tons) and the running time of 8hr 11min corresponded to an average of 49mph.

Any holder of a reasonably good watch with a seconds hand can easily time any train in enough detail to produce figures such as those quoted on pp246-52. They show how quickly a loco-motive did its job on a particular occasion and one may judge that the heavier the load the harder it had to pull. One may use a train resistance formula (there are plenty to choose from) to establish how much work the engine did during any timed inter-val of a particular journey, and may thus effect some sort of a comparison between different efforts made by different loco-motives at different times. One may indeed work out the figures to as many places of decimals as one's current mood may dictate and, carried away by the ease of such calculations, may forget that a resistance formula is no more than a convenient but unjustifiable guess. On any particular occasion the resistance might have been anything up to 15 per cent greater or less than the formula sug-gests; its originating measurements of the resistance of a train in apparently identical conditions on successive days might show variations of this order. So unless the engine's pull had been measured by a dynamometer (which the Midland never did), no power output figure on any particular occasion could be more than impressionistic. It is regrettably necessary to add that even dynamometer cars could be 20 per cent in error.

It has already been mentioned that the first Midland (Smith-Johnson) compound was tested in October 1902, in the sense that indicator diagrams were taken on it while running regular trains between Leeds and Carlisle, that gauge-readings were recorded and that records were taken of consumption of coal and of water. An extensive excerpt from the results was published in

Engineering. In this one searches in vain for any information on the one vital point about a compound engine; did it get along on less coal than a simple engine would have required for the same job? Diagrams and figures are recorded in profusion but they say nothing at all about this. There could in fact have been no attempt to find anything to say about it as no dynamometer car was used, and it was therefore impossible to measure what amount of useful work the engine had done in pulling any train.

This is just one example of a phenomenon familiar to anyone who has failed to find, in a whole library of books on a particular subject, any answer to some simple, straightforward question about it. Great amounts of time, money and labour are commonly expended on investigating technical matters without reaching any answer to the associated practical questions. Voluminous reports have been made, glanced through by a few officials associated with the work, and by a few who hoped to gain information on particular points, and were then left for half a century or more till some historian sought them out for publication regardless of utility. After looking through many of the 1902 test results without discovering anything significant, one may well be struck with despondency on encountering such a figure as $1001\frac{1}{2}$ ihp. To quote, in connection with a quantity that in road-testing a steam locomotive can hardly be measured with any uncertainty less than about 10 per cent in either direction, a figure suggesting *one half of one tenth of one per cent* to be discernible was a warning that the report should be read with discretion.

In contributing to the discussion on a paper presented by Hughes to the Institution of Mechanical Engineers in 1910 on 'Compounding and superheating in Horwich locomotives', Fowler said that in a comparison between a Deeley compound and a Deeley non-compound (999 class) with an identical boiler, the former saved about $2\frac{1}{2}$ per cent in coal per ton-mile. As such a difference is within the range of uncertainty on consumption-figures unrelated to any figures for work done, it does not prove the compound consumed less coal per unit of useful work done.

The compound showed about 7 per cent economy in coal in relation to a smaller non-compound engine (700 class, m31), but as the grate area of this engine was some 12 per cent less than that of the compound, its higher combustion rate per square foot of grate could in itself explain a higher coal consumption per pound of steam produced by the boiler. So again there was no evidence that compounding was perceptibly advantageous. Midland compounds could be expected to do better than other Midland engines because they were bigger. They did not convincingly beat the equally big 4—4—0s of the 999 class in coal consumption per unit of work done.

The Midland compounds were never thoroughly tested by the Midland, but after its absorption into the LMS, Derby could borrow the L & Y dynamometer car (the Midland never had one of its own) and the effects of altering the lap of the hp valve were investigated in test-runs between Derby and Manchester. With the relative settings of hp valve-gear and lp valve-gear fixed by a common reversing shaft, the easiest way to alter the relation between the cut-offs in the hp and lp cylinders was to alter the settings of the valve-heads on the hp valve-spindle and perhaps to alter the width of the heads. The only effect of such adjustment would be to alter the relative power outputs in the hp cylinder on the one hand and the lp cylinder on the other; it could not make much difference to the maximum power obtainable from any particular steam-flow at any particular speed. The great advantage of the dynamometer car was that power output could be measured and so coal consumption could be expressed as a multiple of useful work available at the drawbar, but this does not seem to have been done. Of course it must have been a little off-putting to find that, on two runs of one locomotive in nominally identical conditions, the coal consumptions per mile differed by 25 per cent. Nevertheless coal consumptions were recorded in such figures as 0.1142lb of coal per ton-mile as if there had been some reliable means of distinguishing between 0.1141 and 0.1143.

In 1923, 1924 and 1925, dynamometer car tests were made

with trains on the 48-mile climb from Carlisle to Aisgill. With an average gradient of about 1 in 230, and no speed restrictions, this length was ideal for a good hard 'bash' with no interruptions. Whereas Midland compounds had not normally been allowed to take more than 240 tons on the fastest schedules on this route, test-loads ran up to 370 tons. The locomotives were superheated Deeley compounds, and the slightly modified compounds that may be called 'Fowler compounds' built by the LMS after 1923. A figure that has some technical significance is the weight of coal burned by a locomotive per unit of work done in pulling its train. This is usually expressed as 'pounds of coal per drawbar horsepower hour', and for a high-class superheater-fitted locomotive working to its capacity on a passenger train averaging 50 to 60mph it is about 3; for wet-steam engines, 4 is good. The lowest figure returned by a Midland engine (No 1008, superheated compound) was 3.6; in similar tests an almost identical locomotive (No 1065 built by the LMS) returned 4.3 to 4.7. The range from 3.6 to 4.7 (ratio 0.78) is disconcerting, but even so it seems clear that the Midland compound of 1902, even when simplified and superheated, was not so economical as the best single-expansion locomotives.

In 1928 it was discovered that the LMS dynamometer car was not producing reliable readings of drawbar pull. This is not to say that it could not ever be correct, but only that at times it could be wrong. Careful investigation showed that because of this the power output of a Royal Scot on test had been overestimated in the ratio of 1 to about 0.78. Inevitably, the coincidence of this figure with the ratio of coal rates of No 1065 and No 1008 makes one wonder whether No 1008 happened to have been tested in circumstances that caused the dynamometer to overestimate the pull, whereas No 1065 was tested during a more nearly veracious period. As the defect in the dynamometer mechanism was associated with friction on surfaces that might be either dry or lubricated, it could well have had sharply defined bad and good periods with 22 per cent difference in calibration.

This is more likely than that Nos 1008 and 1065, nearly identical and both brought up to concert pitch for the tests, really differed in efficiency to anything like such an extent as 1 to 0.78.

With minds aware of a proved error of 22 per cent in 1928, and a suspected error of 22 per cent in 1923 to 1925, we must hesitate before placing any reliance on any of the dynamometer car results reported for Midland compounds. We may conclude that the superheated Midland compound's coal-rate was about 4lb per drawbar horsepower at a time when the GW Castle had shown about three, the figure attained in later years by other good British superheated single-expansion engines. It is to be regretted that, on the subject of power output by Midland compounds, the results of the LMS dynamometer-car tests should have to be treated with reserve, especially because the figures for load and mean speed from Carlisle to Aisgill make it pretty clear that the compounds were working a good deal harder than they normally did. The test figures for drawbar horsepower do not in fact differ markedly from those estimated on the basis of the known resistance of gravity and of not-quite-so-reliable train resistance formulae, and so it is possible to make a few broad statements on this aspect of Midland locomotive performance.

On particular occasions Midland compounds developed about 850 drawbar horsepower for up to an hour or so continuously and about 1,000 for a few minutes. These figures were highly satisfactory in that they well exceeded any time-table demand ever made on Midland compounds, but they are not necessarily remarkable in any purely technical sense. They are not, for example, unusually high in relation to the grate area which is a basic limitation on power production by a steam locomotive. They agree in placing the Midland compound in Grade 17 in a range in which Grade 20 is a high-class standard attained by many different classes of British locomotives, some indeed reaching Grade 23. This means development of some 35 per cent more power per square foot of grate area than any Midland compound is known to have done. Against this it may properly

191

be remarked that the Midland compound was never intended to work with anything like such intensity of effort, that it was never asked to do so and therefore that it is no discredit if it never did.

In the LMS tests the superheated compounds worked harder than any had done on the Midland Railway itself, and harder than anything normally demanded of LMS compounds by the LMS. A Caledonian 4—4—0 tried at the same time was outclassed. When, after some experience with the LMS compounds, Scottish drivers bashed them along as if they were not compounds, and got out of them a good deal more power than they had normally shown in English service, some enthusiasts imagined there to be some special skill or artistry (perhaps even wizardry) in the Scottish drivers. In actual fact, nothing done by LMS compounds in Scotland substantially exceeded what Midland compounds and LMS compounds did in the Carlisle-Aisgill trials. It is useful, in the interest of economy of thought, to remember this. One might pursue Smith-Johnson-Deeley-Fowler compounds on their various jobs from Aberdeen to Euston, Carlisle to St Pancras, York to Bristol or Liverpool, and so on, without discovering any performance not decisively surpassed by the best of what was done in the tests of 1924 and 1925.

It may be added that compounds built by the LMS in 1924 differed from the superheated Midland compounds in having slightly larger cylinders and slightly smaller coupled wheels. No changes of that kind could make any perceptible difference to the abilities of a locomotive that retained its original boiler and adhesion weight. When LMS testing of Midland compounds and LMS compounds had made this clear, cylinder diameters of later LMS compounds were standardised at figures nearer to the Midland ones than to the larger ones adopted for the first series of LMS compounds. This had the solid practical advantage of leaving more metal for the repeated cylinder re-boring that was common practice with steam locomotives and changed cylinder diameters by greater amounts than the differences announced to exist between differing batches of particular designs.

After one has examined the history of the development and use of the locomotives on any particular railway, how does one judge whether they were as good as they might have been or ought to have been? First of all, did they normally keep time with their trains? If the railway concerned continued to operate and to expand its activities over a period of many years, it surely meant (among many other things) that the engines ran their trains to time or with such small losses as could be made up by saving time in other operations. By this test, at least, Midland steam did all that was required of it, but was it unduly costly? Doubt about this rather naturally arises out of reflection about the un-usually large proportion of double-headed trains on the Midland. Even if it were possible to assess quantitatively the cost of run-ning a particular train, the full story would require some account of its influence on the running of other trains. The cost perform-ance of a particular locomotive may be assessable, but it is the total cost of running all the trains that matters to the manage-ment. It is difficult to assess what may be called the true cost of any operation in any large organisation, but it is usual to attempt it, and British railways expressed train-running costs on the basis of train-miles. Moreover the figures were commonly published. A few of those for the year 1906 were 10.6d (4.4p) for the Great Northern, 11.1d (4.6p) for the Midland and the Great Western, 12.5d (5.2p) for the North Western and 14.2d (5.9p) for the North Eastern. In that year, therefore, the Midland was equal second with the Great Western, with a locomotive-running cost about 5 per cent higher than that of the Great Northern, but 11 per cent lower than that of the North Western. So if train-miles on the Midland were equal to train-miles on the other railways, the Midland was in the first three by this criterion and its loco-motives were about as economical as the best on other British railways. That Midland steam cannot have been bad is also sug-gested by the Midland's overall excellence indicated by the figures in the last line of Table 2 on p237.

Performance of Midland engines, in the statistical sense, must

193

M

have been reasonably good or the railway would not have flourished as it did. Performance of individual engines could be seen to be satisfactory in so far as they were able to keep time with their trains. But performance in any more technical sense than that is little documented apart from statements that certain engines burned some particular number of pounds of coal per mile. Such a figure is no indication of technical excellence or otherwise in the absence of quantitative information about the work done by the engine per mile.

The cost of running individual locomotives cannot even be estimated without a lot of special work and the task was probably never attempted by any large railway until the Stamp management of the LMS began to do so long after the end of the Midland proper. Of a group of classes specially examined, the Midland Class 2 4—4—0 showed the lowest repair cost per mile, but as it is certain that many other classes of LMS locomotive normally did more work per mile than did the Midland Class 2, this numerical fact had less significance than might at first have appeared. This merely emphasises that costs per mile or per train mile, while perhaps better than nothing, need considering with discrimination.

DIMENSIONS AND PERFORMANCE

In examining the literature of the nineteenth-century locomotive one finds fewer dimensions per class than those presented in much later years. Driving wheel diameter was rarely omitted. Diameter of cylinder and stroke of piston seem to have been the next most highly regarded, and after that came heating surface and working pressure of the boiler. As these were the most commonly quoted dimensions it is perhaps not surprising that some students of the locomotive began to think that nothing else mattered very much, and that differences in these dimensions should suffice to explain differences in performance. A very odd belief was that cylinders must not be too big for the heating surface or they would 'beat the boiler'. This curiosity appears to have developed from the baseless assumptions that

(1) steam production is limited by heating surface,
(2) steam consumption is determined by cylinder size.

In actual fact, steam consumption was determined by the combination of running speed, boiler pressure, regulator-opening, cylinder-size and cut-off in the cylinders. The cylinders could not take any more steam than the driver allowed them to take. Steam production was determined by the size and ferocity of the fire. Heating surface was essential as a transmitter of heat to the water in the boiler, but not critical; it did not *generate* heat. The fire's ferocity was determined by the draught applied to it and this was governed by the ferocity of flow of steam from the blast-pipe to the chimney and was affected by the layout in the smokebox.

If steam production was less than steam consumption then the boiler pressure gradually dropped and it was then said that 'she's not steaming'. When an engine was found to be unsatisfactory in this respect the fireman started to fire more carefully, to leave the firedoor open for as little time as possible, to keep the fire as thin as possible and so on. Very often these changes would get over the trouble. If not, the driver did not pray for fitters to come to his next stopping place with a pair of smaller cylinders; that would do no good even if it were practicable. He knew that what was wanted was a hotter fire and that this could be made by the stronger draught that could be created by reducing the opening of the blast nozzle. So at his next stop he did not send a wire for smaller cylinders, but fixed a wire across the blast-pipe.

The simple essential fact, not in any way connected with cylinder-size, was that in the ordinary locomotive boiler the draught required to urge the fire to produce steam at normal rates, or even higher, could be developed by allowing that steam to escape to atmosphere through a blast-pipe and smokebox properly proportioned for the purpose. What was done with the steam on the way to the blast-pipe was of no importance to steaming, provided only that the steam still was steam and not water

195

when it came to the blast-pipe. Locomotives were designed, built and adjusted to do what they had to do with reasonable coal in reasonably good conditions. But if the coal was bad, the fire tubes clogged or the boiler internally dirty, the engine might fail to steam properly. Then the easiest and quickest remedy was to pep up the blast by readjustment of the orifice of the blast-pipe.

All this is so simple and obvious that you would think it would have been known even in Kirtley's time and you would be right. Yet read below what a journalist contributed to the *Railway Magazine* in 1901 after having ridden on a Midland 4—4—0 from London to Nottingham with a start-to-stop average of 57mph over the 51.8 miles from Kettering:

> But I could not help noticing that towards the end of the trip the steam steadily went down and could not be got up again to its proper pressure of 140lb while full speed was being maintained. And it appeared a reasonable conclusion that a boiler with only 1,120sq ft of heating surface was not sufficient to maintain in steam a pair of 19in cylinders, even with a light load.

Note how he builds a boost for the cylinder diameter/heating surface myth out of nothing. The last 13 miles into Nottingham average 1 in 270 down so that a fair speed could be sustained, if need be, without using any steam at all. As the engine was to end its journey at Nottingham, a low pressure would suffice there and so the fireman let the boiler pressure fall with 13 miles still to go. But even 100lb of steam would be enough for 75mph down that gradient and so the footplate-rider saw the boiler pressure go down as the speed rose. His interpretation of this was that the pressure 'could not be got up again' whereas there was no need for it to be got up and no evidence that anyone tried to get it up. On the contrary, maximum economy demanded that it should be allowed to fall. The rider's misinterpretation of what he saw was used to provide superficial support for the legend that a locomotive could not be much good if its designer failed to find some magic relation between cylinder size and heating surface.

There is no critically vital relation between any of the usually published dimensions of a locomotive. At the most, a few of them may give some general idea of the potentialities (and limitations) of a conventional locomotive. Its maximum sustained starting pull is limited to its nominal tractive effort or to a quarter of its adhesion weight, whichever is the less. (An *instantaneous* starting pull with slack couplings may be big enough to break one of them). Its maximum sustained power may be limited in any of several ways, but the grate area is usually the significant dimension in this respect. Driving wheel diameter is only one of half a dozen dimensions that determine its maximum useful speed. Remachining to correct the effects of wear in service enlarged the cylinder diameters and reduced the wheel diameters; some types of repair, such as patching frames, caused a locomotive to gain in weight with age. These things should be remembered before attempting to base any hair-splitting comparison between different classes of locomotive on their published dimensions; they did not always include the significant ones, and they were not in every case correct.

Figures relating to dimensions of locomotives are here largely concentrated in tabular form. This procedure is not much favoured by historians in general because

(1) it does not look like a 'story'
(2) it mercilessly exposes the gaps in knowledge
(3) it makes everything so easy for the reader that he may wonder whether he's getting his money's worth.

In this book, however, the convenience of tabular concentration for author and reader alike is held to outweigh any disadvantage in it and leading dimensions of Midland locomotives are given in Table 3 beginning on p238. It is an assembly of information collected from many publications and judiciously averaged out.

This is a necessary part of any document carrying such a title as *Midland Steam*, but the full picture is very much larger. Even the locomotives themselves, carefully designed, carefully made and beautifully painted, were static objects until someone had

197

filled boilers, lit fires, oiled the works and opened regulators to get things moving. The heavy and dirty work of shed staff who brought engines from the dead into life again, and the slightly less dirty but more draughty work of the enginemen, have always tended to be taken for granted, and are considered in only a very small fraction of the total volume of published work on the steam locomotive. It is not easy to describe the unpleasantness inseparable from emptying fireboxes, ashpans and smokeboxes and from washing out boilers, and perhaps no one wants to know how depressing a dead locomotive could be.

A live locomotive running fast was a different matter and, although enginemen's work was rarely idyllic, no book on *Midland Steam* could be more than half-written if it included no account of it. Broadly it was monotonous but now and again there were incidents that enginemen would remember.

CHAPTER SEVEN

Midland Steam and Men

The following pages describe some Midland steam experiences as recounted by enginemen. No numerical details are quoted because none is known to the writer. Curiosity about names, dates, engine numbers or anything of that sort is apt to stem the flow of talk about remarkable happenings on locomotives and so one takes care not to risk all by demanding chapter and verse. A little experience convinces one that on locomotives nothing is too improbable to have happened. One finds also that what may be unquestioned regular practice on one part of a large railway may be declared to be quite impossible by workers on another part of that railway.

LIMPING HOME

It had been a funny day right from the start (said the driver) because we set out with a compound that had somehow got to London and we failed with her on the way down to Derby. She'd been all right at first, and we'd got through Leagrave well enough and were running as usual down the bank with not a care in the world except a bit of big-end knock as she worked up speed on the bottom bit. But even after we'd got past Oakley it was still there and up to Sharnbrook it had come to be quite a bit of a pound. It didn't stop her from pulling or running and we were well on time at the top, well enough in fact for me to shut off in about a mile and let her roll down to Wellingborough. By the

199

time we'd got to Kettering I was hardly noticing the knock but it did show up more on the pull up to Desborough. I listened and looked and it seemed to be the outside big end on my side that was going off a bit, but it was nothing to worry about. Every engine knocks—some more than others—and after you've ridden fifty miles with a knock you don't notice it any more.

I had a look at the big end at Leicester but there was nothing to see and it was no warmer than you could expect. It was only about thirty miles to Derby and it would do that all right and so off we went as usual. We'd got up a good speed by Loughborough and we'd just lifted a bit from the trough when she started to bang-bang-bang on my side and so I stopped quick at Hathern.

I knew where to look and found that something had gone wrong in the right big end and bits of brass had broken out. I set her in full fore gear and got my mate to open the regulator while I watched the big end. Then I signalled him to do the same in back gear, while I saw how far the big end moved on the pin. There was a good half inch of slack and that was enough to let the piston hit the cylinder covers. But I thought that we could get away with it, if we went slow and pulled her up close to midgear so that there would be plenty of cushion steam. It was going to be a lot quicker to go slow to Derby than to wait for something to give us a tow. I told the signalman that it might take us half an hour to get to Derby and that was what we were going to do unless something stopped us on the way.

It was all right. I started with the regulator only just open, notched her well up, and passed on to the second port of the regulator. We got two bangs in every revolution but they were big-end thumps and not bangs on the cylinder-covers. We picked up speed bit by bit and got up to about forty without frightening ourselves to death. We were late at Derby but at least we had not troubled anybody and we would have been later still if we had waited for help.

We got a Class 3 engine to go home with and she was not bad

but of course not as good as a compound. We did pretty well with her at first and there was nothing to grumble about, but she went off the boil a bit on the way from Ampthill up to Leagrave and we dropped a minute or two. But we didn't do so bad down past Luton and lost no more time on to Elstree.

We'd just got in the tunnel when there was a bang somewhere up in the front and fire started to blow out through the crack in the door although the regulator was open. It's a good thing the door was closed, because as it was we were both driven back into the tender and wondered what to do. I thought a bit and then decided there could be no harm in putting the blower on. So I managed to knock the valve open with the shovel and that pulled the flames down a bit but they were still coming out. I thought about it a bit more and decided that the main steam pipe joint must have gone so that there was not much steam going into the cylinders or out of the blast pipe, but what was passing the regulator was going straight into the smokebox and the blower was not strong enough to pull it all up the chimney. So we had to close the regulator somehow. The old shovel came in useful again and with a few quick stabs I managed to shut the regulator and the cab was all clear again.

We came out of the tunnel at fifty or sixty miles an hour and what were we going to do next? Well of course we would run down to Mill Hill all right without steam and even to Hendon but would we run up to Cricklewood? If so, we could stop there and get another engine.

I shut the blower down to a reasonable amount (no use wasting steam even though we daren't open the regulator) and just let her go. On we went without gaining any speed that you could notice but without losing any either and it was going to be touch and go whether we would get up to Cricklewood from the dip on the far side of Hendon. Ought we to stop at Hendon? I worried about this for a minute or two and then decided to risk running through if we *were* running well as we came to the box. In the end I did risk it, down into the dip and up the other side. We slowed down o'course, but not as much as I would have expected and we came up to Cricklewood at about twenty miles an hour and I suddenly said to myself, 'Let her go through, risk it, if we can get to West Hampstead we're home'.

So I did risk it, but in the next minute I wished I hadn't as we slowed down to about fifteen and I made sure we were going to stop. But no!—she kept going, and at West Hampstead she'd picked up again and I knew that if we got all the boards off we should run into St Pancras. As we must have lost a lot of time from Elstree they had had enough time to clear the road for us, and everything went right. We drifted down through the tunnel and past Kentish Town at quite a reasonable speed, and we ran into St Pancras as if nothing had happened, but of course we were very late as we had been doing less than thirty most of the way from Hendon. We should have been a lot later if we'd stopped anywhere for help, even alongside Cricklewood shed, and so I thought we came well out of what could have been a nasty jam.

As you can imagine, there was a hell of a fuss when I suggested that our engine should be pulled out of St Pancras with the empty stock and nobody would agree to anything as fast as that. They sent another engine from the shed to pull us in and that's how we got back to Kentish Town shed, about an hour late. I made my report but I don't know whether anybody really believed that we'd run the last twelve miles into St Pancras without steam, but we certainly did.

I had more lost time reported against me for that one day than I had in any ten years of my time as a driver and, after I had told them why I did what I did, they told me I should have done something else. That's as it always was, and always will be.

SAVING COAL

It would be dramatic, but untrue, to say that no one could travel in daylight by train from Settle to Carlisle without looking for some time at the scenery. Plenty of people have done so simply because they have not been told beforehand that it is worth looking at. There are, however, many more enlightened passengers and on one journey I was interested to note that an engineman—apparently returning home as a passenger—was viewing the passing scene with sustained absorption. I remarked on it after a time and he said, 'Yes, anybody who can come along here without looking at the country has got no romance in him'. I asked whether he was used to working trains over it and he said, 'Yes, nearly every day, and every day I find it worth looking at'. I suggested that, as it was a hard road, enginemen might not have much chance to look at anything but what they were doing.

No (said the driver), it's not as hard as you might think. There's a lot of climbing of course and a fireman has to keep at it on the uphills, but there's a lot of downhill, where a passenger train will run itself. So will a goods train if you let it, but that's a different matter. If you've got a goods engine that's not up to the mark, the uphill can be a worry, but down the big hills with a goods train is a bit of a worry whatever sort of engine you've got. But on a passenger train you usually have a reasonably good engine and the only trouble is bad coal. That doesn't happen very often, and on the whole it's not a hard road for either driver or fireman except in winter when it can be very cold and very windy. Then there can be a big drag on the train and a bad draught on the footplate. If I had to stick to one line I'd as soon work Leeds to Carlisle as anywhere. I've fired and driven all sorts of engines on all sorts of trains over it for years and so I can say I know it pretty well.

They call Settle Junction to Blea Moor the Long Drag and so it is, but Ormside Viaduct to Aisgill is longer. It's not quite as steep on average as there's an easy bit from Crosby to Smardale and another at Mallerstang, but with the extra mile it's about as hard as the other side. Of course, with a passenger train you usually get a flying start up to Settle but by the time you're passing Stainforth you're down to straight slogging. On both sides you've done thirty or forty miles mostly uphill before you get to the big hill and if you're having a rough trip it does put you off a bit when you think of what you've got in front of you. On the other hand, if things are going well you could say that you're just nicely warmed up.

Once you're over the top, either way, the fireman on a passenger express has no more shovelling to do and in fact you can say that Leeds to Carlisle or Carlisle to Leeds is only about fifty miles for a fireman. I once had a fireman who tried to make it less still. He would say that you don't need either fireman or fire once you start going down, and so you could let your fire burn down to nothing on the last two or three miles of the climb. Nothing after Ribblehead going north, he would say, and nothing after Mallerstang going south.

But it's not as easy as that, and I tried to show him. It's true that for a lot of the way down on each side the train will run itself, but on the short bits of uphill it will slow down a lot if you don't give her some steam and in a lot of places she'll keep going but not fast enough to keep time. We did a bit of experimenting on this when things were going well. When they weren't, there was no time for playing about but generally there was nothing to worry you with a passenger train on the Carlisle road. The best time for trying anything out of the ordinary was in the dark when nobody but signalmen could see what you were doing. The guard might, but I don't think guards took any interest in what went on after dark unless you actually stopped where you shouldn't have done, and even that didn't always wake them.

Now whichever way you're going, you are bound to use steam between Blea Moor and Aisgill; either way you've got some uphill before you get onto the big drop and so you have to admit that the real top is Aisgill going north and Blea Moor coming south. The question is, how far can you get without steam from there on? Well it does depend on how fast you come over the top; you could expect to be doing about fifty either way.

What happens then depends on two things, the wind and the weight of the train. The wind's generally across and this is what

204

does slow you. The engine doesn't run free like a train; the train has to push it down the hill. Coming down from Blea Moor past Settle you'll be doing a good eighty if you don't brake anywhere but after Settle Junction you've four miles of uphill past Long Preston and Hellifield to the top near the 230 mile-post. Once when we tried it we were only doing about twenty miles an hour when we got there, and we must have lost two or three minutes, but we just let her go to see what would happen. She was very slow in picking up speed and was doing forty or forty-five at the junction at Skipton. We passed the station at less than thirty, well behind time, and I decided that the experiment had gone on long enough. So I opened her out and we made good time on to Bingley and after Shipley.

So we could run from Blea Moor to Skipton without steam if we had to, and that was something to know, but we should have stopped in the next mile or two. Next time we tried, I opened her out pretty hard after Hellifield and kept her going at the same speed up to the top. We were doing nearly sixty there instead of only twenty. But we lost speed on the way down to Skipton Junction and we were doing about fifty there. So we came through the station at thirty-five or so, not much better than before, and I had to put steam on again in another mile or so to make any useful speed. So that was it! You could just get to Skipton without steam with a full load in reasonable wind if you didn't mind losing time, but if you were in trouble you would be wiser to stop at Hellifield, where you could always get some help.

It's pretty much the same down the other side. You'd be doing eighty at Ormside, but the hump to Appleby would pull you down below fifty and you'd pick up again on the way down to Long Marton. But by Newbiggin you'd have slowed a lot, you might be going a bit faster at Culgaith, but you would never get to Langwathby. So you could run without steam to Long Marton, but you needed it after that to keep anything like time. My mate said, 'All right, you need steam after Appleby or after Hellifield, but you don't need much, and so you can afford to run your fire right down in running between Blea Moor and Aisgill. In fact you can run it down quite a bit in the last mile or two up to the top'. And that's what he would do if we were on time and not in any sort of trouble. After a bit of experimenting he found that when you knew the engine and knew the coal you needn't put any on after Selside going to Carlisle or after Mallerstang going back. Selside is about fifty miles from Leeds and Mallerstang's about forty-five from Carlisle. So either way it needn't be more than a fifty-mile job for the fireman.

Some men will tell you that you couldn't run an engine hard up the four miles from Selside to Blea Moor without firing, and I didn't think so till my mate gradually got round to doing it. In fact the fire gets hotter as it burns down. It gets really white and if everything's all right the engine starts to blow off, but if you overdo it and the fire gets too thin, then you may get a hole in it and then the steam goes down with a run unless you slap a couple of shovelfuls on the hole. So you have to watch it, and of course that's just what a lot of men won't do. They'd sooner put plenty on the fire without bothering too much about what's happening than take a bit of care and save a couple of hundred-weights.

But this mate of mine did think it was worthwhile to save coal if only because it meant less work for him. He never came over either top with any more fire than the engine needed to get to the other top. He said he didn't mind firing for the first hour of any express train trip on the Leeds and Carlisle road, and that two hours of firing a day ought to be enough for anybody.

Going north you can take it easy from Blea Moor to Hawes Junction, but then you have to pull a bit up to Aisgill. It's just the same the other way. Aisgill to the Junction is easy, but there's a good mile up through Blea Moor tunnel before you can shut off. So you can't get by with no fire at all, but if the driver is careful you don't need a lot. After you start going down, the engine can do all you need even with a hundred pounds of steam.

The main thing to watch is that the ejector is good enough to keep the brake-vacuum up with that pressure. With a bit of care you don't need to brake anywhere except perhaps at Shipley, and with a bit of luck with signals you can run right into Carlisle or Leeds without braking till just before you stop. Once you're unhooked from the train you don't need vacuum to get to the shed as the engine has a steam brake.

An engine driver's job is pretty monotonous, but he can make it interesting for himself and his mate in finding out how far he can go in saving coal and water and brake blocks. But the Carlisle road in daylight is interesting any time. There's so much grand country to see and so much variety in light and shade from one day to another that I never get tired of it. It's better than going to the pictures, especially if you like fresh air, and it doesn't cost you anything.

WINDY NIGHT

A lot of things seemed to have gone wrong that night at Holbeck (said the fireman) and although I had not had any real experience in firing I was sent with a spare driver to run from Leeds to Carlisle with a night sleeper from St Pancras. We had a compound, which was what was needed for the job, but I had never fired one and so I was bound to wonder how I should get on. My mate was not a top link driver but he knew the Carlisle road and had worked Leeds–London and Leeds–Carlisle for years as a fireman.

It was a very bad night with wind. We didn't need to look at the Crosby Garrett weather report to know that it was blowing. Steam and smoke from engines at Holbeck was blowing in every direction except up; it came out flat from safety valves and chimneys while the wind roared and flurried around. If there was a night to stay indoors, this was it. And it wasn't a lot better in the shed. The duck-lamps blew out more than once while we were getting the engine ready. My mate fussed a bit over that part of the job, I suppose he wasn't sure whether he should trust me to do my part right, and we didn't have a lot of time. He kept looking at the fire and telling me what to do to get the pressure up to blowing off when we were due out of Wellington but not before. He knew all about firing but I thought at the time that he wasn't too happy about the driving. Anyway that was not for me to worry about; I wasn't a bit sure how to set about firing when we got onto the Carlisle road. It was a hard road, what with the Long Drag and all that, at any time but with the wind that was blowing that night, a driver inclined to worry and a fireman who had never fired a compound before, things seemed to be all set for a bit of bother.

But my mate tried to think of all the things that could go wrong. He had a look at the lamps I'd lit, prodded the wicks a bit, and turned them up a bit higher. He had a look at the coal on the tender, and decided it could be trimmed better. So he had me go up onto the heap, to break up the bigger pieces and then move as much as I could to the front. I didn't like the look of this. Was he expecting that she was going to burn all the coal on the tender? Very likely she would. She couldn't push her way through all this wind for nothing, and it certainly wasn't going to help. To be behind us on the road, the wind would have to be from the southeast and who ever heard of a gale from that direction? No, it was pretty certain to be a west wind and probably south-west, but we should have to get out of the shed and on the road to find out all about it. What with all the buildings in a town you can't tell the true direction of a wind. But don't worry!—we were not going to spend much time in towns on this trip. A lot of the time we should be in the wide-open spaces on the hills with nothing to keep the wind off us. My mate found some string to tie his cap to his coat and had some to spare for me. 'It'll be rough on top tonight', he told me, and I didn't doubt him. It was rough enough down below.

We got off the shed right time, and as we went past it in backing down to Wellington in the dark and the wind I wondered whether I should ever see it again. When we got to the station they put us onto a platform road and my mate stopped us just inside the starter, to wait for our train from London. I must say I felt a bit nervous about being put on one of the best trains on the Midland in the middle of a windy night and I felt that I ought to be doing something about it. So I looked at the fire and started to put a bit on, but my mate said, 'Not too much just now. Wait till our train comes in and then you can put some on. You don't know how late it may be.' He took a look at the fire himself and said, 'When you see our train come in, put your blower on and then put eight down each side and eight at the back, and by then it'll be time to couple up. Till then you can be breaking some of the lumps. It's not bad stuff. I don't think you'll have any trouble with it. Keep your fire well up to the door at the back and you'll not have to throw much to the front, but if she gets much below the red mark on the gauge, have a look at what's going on down there. If it's burned a bit thin, send half a dozen down. But she'll go all right with three down each side and three at the back about every three minutes.'

He tried the two injectors and they worked without any bother. He said, 'The left one will keep her going for most of the time. Try to keep your water at half glass and if you have any bother give me a shout. If you can keep her pressure up as far as Settle Junction you'll be all right, because I can give you a hand on the Long Drag if you're getting a bit knackered by then. It's not far really as she'll run herself down from Aisgill.' This was encouraging, and I needed all the encouragement I could get. My mate made it sound easy and that gave me a bit of confidence even though he didn't seem very happy himself.

When our train ran past us alongside the next platform I knocked the blower on and put coal on as he'd told me, without wasting any time and, as he'd said, by the time I'd finished he was just backing her up to the train. I got down to hook on—the first time I'd done it, because I'd never worked on a passenger train before—and I found it was not so easy as I thought. In fact in the darkness I got into a bit of a mess, and was quite glad when my mate came and lifted the lamp from the bracket to try and see was I was doing. Between us we got tied on to the train with coupling and pipes and my mate hurried back to blow up a vacuum. By the time he was satisfied about it and I'd got the headlights set, we got the guard's green light and we were off.

Now for it! She was blowing off a bit, the boiler water was three-quarters up the glass and I'd just put a good round on the fire, so for a minute or two I had nothing to do but look ahead for signals. I couldn't say that I knew the road in darkness, and if we'd passed a red light I wouldn't have known whether it was for us or not, but a fireman is supposed to look ahead when he has nothing else to do.

The water came down to halfway pretty soon, so I started the injector and then had a look at the fire. There was still a bit of black showing among the white, and so I waited a minute before starting to fire as my mate had told me. I guessed how long to wait after each round and if there was much black showing when I looked I took the next round not so fast. With looking at steam and water gauges and breaking coal, there was not much time for looking out and anyway I couldn't help much when I did. I recognised Thackley tunnel because I'd been through before, but soon after my mate shut off for Shipley and after that I didn't know where I was. It didn't matter because it's nearly all uphill to Hellifield, the first stop.

I was interested in the firing and it meant pretty hard work all the time but I couldn't help noticing the wind in the cab and especially between the cab and the tender, roaring through from left to right and keeping your ankles nice and cool. In some places it wasn't so bad, I suppose where we were in cuttings, but most of the time it was strong. But the fire and the exercise kept you from feeling cold.

My mate eased her a bit at one place, which I suppose must have been Keighley, and after that we picked up quite a bit of extra speed and later on the side wind got worse than it had been.

My mate hadn't said a word or made a move towards my side
and I guessed that this meant that I was doing all he wanted.
I expect he was keeping his eye on steam and water and so long
as they are all right there's not much wrong with what the fireman's doing. I must have been lucky with the injector, as the
water level kept about right without any alteration of the adjustment or any shutting off.

Judging from the big-end thumps I thought that the engine
had been working pretty hard all the time, but after we'd got
through Skipton, which I noticed because my mate braked fairly
hard there, he started to pound her a bit. Even so, she was not
going as fast as she had been; we were starting on the hills and
some very windy patches. It seemed to steepen as we went on
and the steam was dropping away from the red mark. Just as I
was wondering what to do about it we must have come over the
top of a hill as all of a sudden she started picking up speed. Then
my mate shut off, braked fairly hard, and we stopped at Hellifield.
He had a look at the fire and said, 'It's hardly thick enough.' He
knocked the blower further on and said, 'Get plenty on now
while we're standing. Half a dozen at the front, ten down each
side and ten at the back. Then wait till we've done about half a
mile and start again.'

We were off again before I'd finished and as we got away pretty
fast I was soon down to it again. After two or three miles we were
going faster than we'd run anywhere so far and the wind through
the gangway was fierce; it was blowing coal off the shovel and
over the side. Then all of a sudden she started to slow down,
although my mate had wound her well forward, and after a few
minutes she was really slogging and the water was dropping
although my injector was full on. My mate started the one on his
side and left it on till the water came up to the top nut. While
this was happening he took a look at the fire and put a quick
round of coal on it. He said, 'I'm having to thrash her a bit, this
wind's holding her pretty bad. You're doing all right, but she
needs a thick fire up here. Keep it up for about twenty minutes,

and then you've finished.' So I kept at it in a hurricane of wind. I was sorry about the coal that got blown off the shovel, but there was nothing I could do about it. I wondered how much was being blown off the tender. Between rounds of firing I kept up in the front of my side of the cab, but there was plenty of back-draught even there. It must have been pretty bad on the other side. Whenever I got down to shovelling, I had a job to keep on my feet; it was not because of bad riding—she was not going fast enough for that—but the weight of the cross-wind was enough to blow you over.

In between spells of firing you could feel big-end thumps even though you couldn't hear anything above the noise of the wind and you could tell there was something unusual about the engine. On an ordinary one you get four even thumps in each revolution; on a compound you get two sets of three in a revolution. It goes 123–567–123–567—as if No 4 and No 8 were missing from an even set of eight in a revolution. You can't hear it at full speed, but when she's pulling hard and slow, you can't miss it. Of course it doesn't take anything like that to tell a fireman that he's on a compound; the length of the firebox is all he needs.

After one round of firing my mate came across and shouted in my ear and said, 'It's going to get very windy further up, so watch out that you don't lose your shovel. Push it well back under the coal when you put it down. Make sure we don't lose the bucket. Listen! Fill it with coal and then with water and put it up by the boiler.' I thought that this was a funny sort of instruction to give but of course if it really was going to get any windier than it had been up to then, it was going to be something quite special. But the old girl was plugging on and on and I had to keep slinging into her what coal wasn't blown off the shovel. I was getting a bit tired by then but even so I was surprised when my mate got down and put a quick heavy round on and then pushed the shovel well under the coal. Then he put his top-coat on. 'That's all she needs now to get to the top,' he said. 'You keep in your corner and hang on. I'm going to leave you for a bit. You'll be all right and you don't have to bother. The blower's on and so if she slips, all you have to do is to shut off and then open up again. But she'll not slip because the sanders are working.'

With that he went through the gangway on his side, swung round the stanchion, reached forward for the handrail and away on the running board towards the front of the engine. I'd heard that some of the old hands used to go forward on the slow climbs on this line to put some oil on something (nobody seemed to know what) and they even did it in the dark when nobody could have seen anything. So I was not so surprised as I might have been to see a driver leave the cab of an engine plodding along in darkness, but when a minute or two had passed and he hadn't come back I began to get a bit scared. There I was by myself on an engine pulling a sleeping-car train in the middle of the night, not knowing where we were and now with an absolute tornado screaming across the footplate. He needn't have told me to hold on. If I'd moved out of my corner I'd have been blown off.

So there I stuck, watching the steam and water and thinking that there couldn't be a better engine in the world. Nobody was doing anything about her, but she kept pounding on, not fast but not faltering, up the top end of the Long Drag while the father and mother of all gales tore at her and her train. But of course she couldn't go on forever without more coal on the fire, and as my mate had told me not to leave my corner, it meant that we couldn't be more than a mile or two from the top. Anyhow I could see the boiler water-level and so I could still do the fireman's main job. It was holding all right, nicely above half height. So long as it stopped there and so long as the engine didn't start running away, there was nothing really desperate to worry about. Perhaps I ought to look where we're going. So I did and saw nothing but blackness, but kept on looking in case we should come to a red light. So long as the water kept up and no red light showed up we were all right. But were we? Wouldn't this wind blow any light out? This made me think a bit and as I looked ahead I got worried until suddenly I made

213

out a green light. I supposed it must be a distant signal and if so that put us right for a mile or two. After a time another green light came up, then a signal cabin and a bit further another green light, which must have been the starter.

Soon after that the wind eased off. Instead of being a hurricane it was just a gale, and in another minute or two my mate came back into the cab and stopped the sanders. All of a sudden the wind died away, the fire-light shone on steam and I knew we were in a tunnel. 'Well,' he said, 'I don't know who first thought of Blea Moor Tunnel, but it was a damn good idea.'

Nobody likes tunnels as a rule, but this was the first bit of peace since we left Hellifield. We were soon going downhill and my mate notched her up and said, 'Now get plenty more on while you have a chance, we're on top now but we haven't finished with wind.' So while we picked up speed all the way down the tunnel, I threw the black on the white, and it *was* white I can tell you. But before I'd got the sides and back covered, the gale came on again and I knew we were out in the open. It was not as bad as the worst we'd had, but all the same a lot of coal was getting blown off the shovel and my mate, seeing how it was, had a look at the fire when I'd finished the round and said, 'Leave it for now, but do a quick round in the next tunnel and that'll take her to Carlisle.'

We'd got a lot of speed up by the time we went into the tunnel and she was riding a bit rough, but I did my best to put a quick round on the fire. It wasn't very quick because I'd had about as much as I wanted of shovelling for one trip and I hoped my mate was right in saying that she'd need no more coal as I was pretty sure we had still a long way to go. Before I'd had time to think much about this, my mate said, 'We've got to get some water in a minute, but I'd better do it. Watch what I do and it'll give you an idea of how to go on when you have to do it yourself.' Then he went back to his place and looked hard ahead for a minute or two. All of a sudden he opened the fire-door a bit, dropped the tender scoop and looked at the tender water-gauge in the firelight.

Then he wound the scoop up again and that was all there was to it. At the time it hardly seemed worth watching, but later on I found that picking up water without flooding the train was not as easy as it looked.

We were going well by then, but soon after I could tell we'd not got right to the top as she slowed down without any change in regulator or cut-off. In another mile or two we passed a signal-box and then she started to pick up speed like anything. My mate eased her back on the regulator and reverser but that didn't stop her. After a mile or so he shut off altogether, but she kept on going at a rare old rate and so the wind was coming more head-on than across. She rode a bit rough, and so there was more chance of being thrown off than blown off. My mate called me across and said, 'She'll go about ten miles like this, but with this wind she'll need steam again after Appleby. You can leave your fire till I open up again. Till then you've nothing to do. You've done very well. How do you feel about this job?'

I told him that it was no harder than I'd expected, but I was glad it was only fifty miles or so for the fireman. I said I was surprised that he had gone round the engine on the Long Drag. I thought that no up-to-date engine needed extra oiling on the way. He laughed at that. 'Oh,' he said, 'I didn't go out to oil anything. I just wanted to get out of the bloody wind for a bit. In a wind like this, if it's not cold, it's far better sitting on the splasher and leaning on the cab-front than it is in the cab, and you can see where you're going just as well, or even better. Of course it's warmer up by the smokebox, but there you have to stand. If you go outside in daylight, you have to take an oil feeder with you so that you look busy when you pass each signalbox, else some bobby might send "Stop and Examine" to the next box because he saw you outside. Of course a lot o' drivers wouldn't think of going outside for anything and there's never any need to, but I don't like wind and I'm glad when I can get out of the worst of it.'

So we bounced and rattled down the hill without steam, me

215

with nothing to do, my mate looking for signal lights and they were the only things you could see outside apart from signal cabins. When he did open the regulator after a long time, he looked at the fire and put half a dozen shovelfuls on. 'That'll get us to Carlisle', he said, and it did.

CHAPTER EIGHT

Conclusion

After having spent much time and effort in chasing and checking figures to found the factual parts of a book like this, an author may well sit back and ask himself why he should think anyone might be interested in them. It is probably the result of a natural desire to know as much as possible about any object of affection, even though the numerical details are unemotional. Liking for a locomotive does not in the first instance depend on the size of its cylinders, although later on it may give rise to resentment when someone announces that some dimension is not what everybody always thought it was.

What does one really remember about Midland steam? Surely the rich red colour of the passenger train engines and of their trains. 'Midland red' it may well be called, even though to many Midlanders that is also the name of a bus company. Then the double spike of the Salter safety valve and the surly pout of the chimney rim. On the tender, the big figures commanded attention but not, in every one, admiration. On first appearance they looked garishly American; one got used to them, although occasional sight of an undecorated North Western tender was a hint of better things.

Very distinctive were the letters MR on the buffer beam and the engine's number in reasonably sized figures on the smokebox. Very elegant indeed were the small brass numbers attached to the upper cab side-sheets. In this location every passenger train engine was numbered 1, 2, 3 or 4 and (one might notice)

217

the bigger the engine the bigger the number. Eventually one learned (from the *Railway Magazine*) that these numbers referred to a classification based on haulage power. For each class, a maximum train-load was prescribed for each class of duty. For example, the table below quotes Special Limit loads for trains timed to cover the 99 miles between London and Leicester in 105 minutes.

Class	Grate Area (sq ft)	Types	Load (tons)
1	17.5	4—2—2 (except 685-694) 2—4—0 Johnson 4—4—0	165
2	19.6/21.1	Rebuilt 4—4—0 4—2—2 (685-694)	180
3	25	700 class 4—4—0 (m31)	205
4	28.4	Compound 4—4—0 (m32) 999 class 4—4—0 (m33)	230

The *Railway Magazine* was always an ever-extending mine of information about all British railways and many others. In it the Midland received its full share of attention and indeed in one respect at least it was specially distinguished, but unfortunately for an unhappy reason. Editorial policy was to print nothing, or next to nothing, about railway accidents, but an exception was made in the case of the Aisgill collision in 1913, as several pages were devoted to some of the details of it and to reflections on them.

Railway accidents attracted attention by their very rarity and railway journalism lost little copy by refraining from reporting them. The *Railway Magazine* printed many articles about the

Midland Railway, and the working of Midland steam as promised in the time-table and as actually achieved on the road. From the many photographs of Midland locomotives one could discern their high standard of cleanliness and polish. The graceful singles were very frequently depicted in action as indeed were the compounds; quite often an example of each class of engine double-headed a Midland train.

Owing to the limitations of photographic techniques in those days, few pictures of trains showed any steam-cloud against the sky, although low-down leakages of steam were reproduced plainly enough. It was something of a feat to obtain a clear picture of a moving train, but it could be done and success depicted a train apparently stationary in open country with no horizontal semaphore to suggest why it should have stopped in such a place. Because of this, I was puzzled by most of the first few pictures I saw of 'moving trains' but, having got used to the idiom, I subconsciously deduced that a depicted train must have been moving because there could have been no reason for it to stop in the position shown. Convention seems to have been for the photographer of a moving train to shoot it with a sky background so that a silhouette should be obtained, if nothing else, but steam from the chimney did not appear on the picture. If the chimney were not smoking, the train looked to be firmly at rest.

Smoke from the chimney of a moving locomotive was nothing uncommon and photographers, knowing what realism smoke added to a picture, must have made efforts to take advantage of the fact, but the *Railway Magazine* published very few illustrations of British locomotives making smoke. It is a little surprising that it ever showed any such thing at all, as smoke-emission was illegal and the editor would not wish to present evidence against any railway company.

But even if a train-photograph failed to suggest motion, it might generate some excitement by tricks of light. In March 1924 the *Railway Magazine* reproduced a three-quarter front view of Midland compound No 1036 with a St. Pancras–

219

Manchester express. It was notable because the curved junction of the rear splasher and the firebox lagging sheet appeared in the picture as if it were the front part of the edge of a third splasher closely packed between the real ones. At least one reader wrote to ask whether the engine had been rebuilt as a 4—6—0.

Railway-enthusiast photographers were far less numerous then than they subsequently became, and most published pictures of trains had foregrounds as featureless as the uniformly grey sky background. The three-quarter front view was the only one that any photographer could think of, despite the fact that every engine-watcher examined engines as much from the three-quarter rear viewpoint as from any other. I do not recollect any action picture of rear-end assistance up the Lickey; certainly none with the big Midland ten-coupled banking engine at work. It is sad that the limitations of photography in pre-grouping days made it impossible to depict Midland steam (or any other steam) in action with such vivid splendour and such picturesque surroundings as became usual in the days of British Railways. One must rely mostly on memory for visions of Midland expresses at speed in the exquisite Eden gorge or high in the sky on the tall Denthead Viaduct seen from down the dale, or pounding up past Selside towards Blea Moor or streaking steamlessly at eighty down to the Junction over the main Skipton road below Settle.

At Leeds (Wellington) the Scottish trains were handled like lightning, the relieving engine backing in quickly behind the train as it ran alongside the terminal platform, getting coupled up, 'blowing up', whistling up and starting away in less than three minutes if the circumstances justified it. The driver's name was exhibited on a strip fitted into a slot on the cab-side and this enabled the guard to get this information for his journal without wasting time or breath in talking. From any North Western train running from Leeds (New) to Manchester, one obtained a bird's eye view of the Midland engines standing outside Holbeck shed, among them a fair proportion of double frame outside fly-cranked 2—4—0s and 0—6—0s. From the same train it was just not possible to see much, if anything, of a Midland engine in the Midland's Newtown Yard at Huddersfield. North Western passenger trains did not normally use any line close enough to the northern edge of the Huddersfield viaduct to admit of a good view of what the Midland was up to down there, but when you could see an engine it was usually a nice old Kirtley 0—6—0 from Royston.

From Normanton to Trent the main Midland job was collecting coal with 0—6—0s of all sizes and ages and taking it to Toton. Passenger trains, and especially fast passenger trains, were not really welcome in this vicinity but nevertheless room was somehow made for them and they could average well over 50mph through it all. Read what Frederick S. Williams wrote as far back as 1885:

> The traveller who, on a wintry or foggy night, flashes along in an express train through the railway sidings at Toton on the Erewash Valley line may well regard the scene as one of bewildering confusion. As he sees the clouds of fire-lit steam, the glancing lights, the white, green, and red signals, the moving forms of engines, trains, and men; and as he overhears, perchance, the bumping of trucks, the shouts of men, and the squeal of whistles from locomotives and from shunters, he may well consider it a spot from which he ought to be thankful to be quickly and safely extricated. Happily, cosmos reigns amidst this seeming chaos; and the multifarious and apparently bewildering transactions are carried on with order, precision, and security.

The Toton sidings were originally laid in open country. They took their name from a hamlet and they were said to be 'near Trent', which was and always remained a single island platform station in open country, but the town of Long Eaton grew up in the gap between Toton and Trent and was given its own station. In recent years that station was abandoned and its name transferred to what was previously Sawley Junction station. Even yet, though well engulfed in houses, it remains a rural station, overshadowed by trees, and with vegetation penetrating the woodenlathed railings that line the outer edges of its platforms. When the leaves are out, its appearance is purely rural.

The complex of railway lines in this region, together with that at nearby Derby, constituted the heart and brain of the Midland Railway. A railway-enthusiast who divided a day between Trent and Derby saw Midland steam intensively at work in all its phases. He could see singles and compounds moving long-distance trains into and out of Trent station in routes of surprising convolution, and he could see coal trundled from Toton at aloofly high level by the full Derby range of six-coupled engines. He might note some of the incredible Kirtley veterans from Peterborough. He could certainly see more of them at Peterborough itself, for the Midland shed there was home for several of them for over fifty years. This tended to monotony for Midland enthusiasts down there but, with Great Northern, Great Eastern, North Western and Midland & GN engines regularly serving the city, it was as gay as York in multi-coloured motive power.

Midland engines were made in only two colours, and not many classes, but there were a lot of them doing a lot of work and the organisation of their movements at Toton and Trent was an object lesson for a serious student of railway operation. When he tired of this, he might move west and see how they did things at Derby. To the Midland, Derby was very much the same as Crewe was to the North Western. Two main lines ran in from the south and three main routes started from the north end. The locomotive works of each company adjoined the main junction and traffic centre of the system. At each station many trains changed engines and many were pieced together from components that originated in widely separated places. Derby was not so big as Crewe, and neither its trains nor its engines were so big as the biggest on the North Western, but there was enough going on at Derby to keep the railway enthusiast interested for long periods. There the Midland could be seen on its toes and at its best in handling passenger trains from London, Scotland,

Newcastle, Liverpool, Bristol and Bournemouth by means of neatly dignified, dark red engines conceived and brought forth in the works just over the way.

At Derby one soon became convinced that Midland organisation and equipment were well able to keep it in its position as one of the Big Three railways of Britain. Differences in detail might be discerned from what went on at Crewe or Paddington but the overall operating results were of an excellence not surpassed elsewhere. Absorption of the Midland into the LMS made but small and slow departures from Midland steam as seen at Derby, but LMS locomotives had become common enough there before World War II began to give British railways more and slower traffic to handle. Derby was very much in the thick of this and war-time train services flooded the station platforms more heavily with train-changing passengers than had formerly been the case. I shall always remember an incident that I witnessed during that period.

Having alighted from an up train with the need to wait for some time for another, I walked forward along the platform to see the engine, although that was quite impossible because of a Mark I blackout. That's what it really was. The night itself was truly dark and out on the exposed part of the platform nothing could be seen but a few faint signal-lights; one hardly dared to move a foot. The only visible part of the engine was the underside of its black-out sheet, illuminated by the fire. Against this, the outline of the cab showed it to belong to a Midland engine, but beyond that, nothing. As I looked, a vague shape merged from alongside the tender into reflected fire-light and vanished after adding obscurity to the darkness by the audible observation, 'One out o' four'. There was a war on, strange things happened at night, civilians, let alone troops, were exhorted not to tell anybody anything and perhaps only those in a very secret 'know' were intended to be able to interpret that cryptic utterance from the gloom. It added verbal emphasis to the dark mystery of night. Only fog might have surpassed it.

223

Conclusion

Derby station was damaged, despite its complete blackout, by the operations of World War II and so was ex-Midland property at St Pancras and elsewhere, but a good deal of what was originally Midland steam survived for a long time on British rails after 1948. There was plenty of railway work for which Midland steam was as effective as anything else, but not even Midland 4—4—0s nor 0—6—0s could last indefinitely when steam itself was being abandoned. So Midland steam went with all other railway steam gradually out of use and out of existence, but not out of memory or out of record. Better still is the fact that among preserved locomotives a Midland single and a Midland compound solidly commemorate Midland steam at the crest of its wave. Long may they continue to do so!

Footnote: A great many of the knowledgeable railway enthusiasts to whom I have mentioned the Derby black-out incident (p223) confessed themselves baffled by the remark, 'One out o' four'. It was simply an intimation to the enginemen that the engine was to pick up one vehicle from No 4 Platform line.

Appendix: Steam in Midland Locomotives

COMPOUNDING

Locomotive engineers in the nineteenth century may well have been sorely tempted to try the compounding principle in locomotives. There was nothing new in it as applied to stationary engines or marine engines. In the former field, compounding had been tried even before Stephenson's *Rocket* had been built but it did win early acceptance. It was, as they say, 'before its time'. There was at the time enough for engineers to do in building single-expansion steam engines to work reasonably well, and in keeping them in good going order, without adopting any unnecessary complication. As knowledge and techniques developed, compounding crept back into steam engine practice and became accepted as necessary for the most economical operation of condensing engines. Where an engine was accompanied by a necessarily bulky condenser, space was evidently not particularly restricted and some could be found to accommodate the extra cylinder or cylinders required in a compound engine as distinct from a single-expansion engine.

The steam locomotive, however, was not (normally) a condensing engine. As it had to run through tunnels and past station platforms and round sharpish curves, its designer could find little space for extra cylinders and so it was not at all certain that the success of compounding in stationary engines and on ships could be achieved on a locomotive. Nevertheless, every now and then someone would try it and by the end of the nineteenth century

225

P

quite a number of engineers in various parts of the world were persisting with it and continuing to build compound locomotives.

The superficial advantage of compounding was obvious; a child could discern it. You watched the continuous stream of steam from the chimney of an ordinary working locomotive and after a time the thought would occur that if you could make that steam work in an extra cylinder or cylinders before letting it go you would get more pull out of it. This is the basic attraction of compounding. Use that steam in the ordinary way in a cylinder or cylinders where it helps the engine along by pushing another piston or pistons. That way you are bound to get more work out of the steam; you can't lose.

The ingenious sceptic, however, may ask, 'Why not admit steam from the boiler directly to the low pressure cylinders, and cut it off early in each stroke so that, as the pistons move, it expands down to the same pressure as it would in the compound engine you are suggesting?' In other words, 'Why not let the steam do its work by expansion in one long step instead of complicating matters by using two sets of cylinders in order to expand in two steps?'

This is a sensible question and in fact the vast majority of all the steam locomotives ever built were designed in accordance with its suggestion, but there is a technical objection to it. This is that during expansion, steam becomes much less hot than it was at first, and so on its way out of the cylinder it cools the metal it touches and this consequently cools the next incoming charge of steam. The metal picks up heat from the hot steam and lets it go into the exhaust steam. The greater the amount of work obtained from the steam by allowing it plenty of expansion, the cooler it gets, and the greater the heat loss in the exhaust. Because of this, nothing is gained by allowing steam to expand in a single stage beyond some ratio of expansion associated with the particular engine and its working conditions.

In the high-pressure cylinder of a compound engine this heat loss to the outgoing steam is unimportant because the steam itself

226

is used again. The corresponding heat lost in the exhaust from a low-pressure cylinder *is* important, because the exhaust steam takes it away from the engine altogether. So a high overall expansion ratio can be used advantageously in a compound engine, provided that the expansion ratio in the low pressure cylinders is not so high as to cause excessive heat-loss in the exhaust.

The advantage of compounding in steam locomotives was not that of using steam twice over, but that of limiting the cylinder-wall heat loss to what occurred in the low-pressure cylinders which might work at a low expansion-ratio even though the overall expansion-ratio was high. The magnitude of the possible advantage depends on the overall expansion and this is limited by consideration of the power required from the engine, the working pressure of steam produced by the boiler, and the space available for cylinders. In the conditions of the nineteenth century, the advantage derivable from compounding in a steam locomotive was never more than trivial. Later on, by use of higher boiler pressures, it could become perceptible but not every comparison was made with a single-expansion engine of the highest efficiency attainable in that form of engine. So in some comparisons, compounding might show a worthwhile advantage; in others, not. Moreover, a four-cylinder compound engine (for example) was more expensive in construction and in maintenance than was a two-cylinder simple engine. A small saving in coal could be offset by the extra cost in maintenance.

The advantage in total running cost of the best practicable compound locomotive over the best practicable corresponding simple locomotive was never great and could easily be negative. General nineteenth-century experience was in accordance with this in that there were many trials of compounding in locomotives, but few persistences. The reason why the compounding principle did not, and could not, lead to any worthwhile economy of fuel in a conventional steam locomotive is simply that in order to do so it would need to use an overall expansion ratio so high as to require boiler-steam at a pressure of about 1000psi. This is

227

Q

far above the practical limit of the Stephenson type of locomotive boiler, and no other type ever had any real success in railway service.

Non-professional students of the steam locomotive were apt to be impressed by the widespread use of compounding in France, and to imagine general British rejection of it to be evidence of perversity in British locomotive engineers. But not even French locomotive engineers were exclusively in favour of compounding and when, in 1945, the French National Railways placed orders for 700 locomotives, they were for two-cylinder simples, class 141R of the 2—8—2 type. In finally rejecting compounding, the French were some forty years behind general British practice.

In Britain, compounding was tried in a bad way by Webb on the North Western and there were those who thought that it might still be worth more rational trial in British locomotives. Among these was W. M. Smith, high in the design staff of the North Eastern Railway, and he managed to persuade his chief, Wilson Worsdell, to try a three-cylinder compound engine, fed-up though he was with two-cylinder compounds bequeathed by his brother.

A three-cylinder compound may have one high pressure cylinder and two low-pressure cylinders and may therefore be symmetrical. If the cylinders are all equal, the volume ratio between low pressure and high pressure is 2 and this is as good as anything ever used in compound locomotives, but there is nothing at all critical in this matter. If there were two high-pressure cylinders and one low-pressure cylinder, the latter had to be very considerably larger than the others. In the Webb three-cylinder compounds the low–pressure cylinder was about 30in in diameter and the other about 15in. Among the numerous disadvantages of the Webb three-cylinder compounds was the normally unremarked one that it was impracticable to provide the 30in cylinder with a flat valve of adequate size for working at an economical cut-off.

A marked disadvantage of a compound engine with only one high-pressure cylinder is that it cannot be relied upon to start from rest when the regulator is opened, because steam is admitted to only one cylinder. If the piston in that cylinder happens to be near either end of the stroke, steam pressure on it produces very little tractive effort because of the unfavourable crank-angle. So a locomotive of this type needed some special provision for starting, and different engineers produced different solutions to the problem which was simply that of feeding steam directly to the low-pressure cylinders for as long as was found necessary to get the train going. It was common to use a reducing valve that limited the pressure of steam applied to the low-pressure cylinders to about 80 per cent of the boiler pressure. Such a reducing valve could be seen attached to the smokebox on the early Johnson compounds built by the Midland.

A number of British railways tried a few compound engines in the period 1900 to 1910, but only the Midland developed anything like enthusiasm for the compound principle. Even so, it built only 45 compound 4—4—0 engines and these formed only a small fraction of its total stock of about 3,000 locomotives or indeed even of its total of roughly 400 locomotives of the 4—4—0 wheel arrangement.

SUPERHEATING

By superheating is meant the process of passing steam from the boiler through heated tubes before admitting it to the cylinders. That this might improve the efficiency of a steam engine had been recognised well back in its history, and it was tried by various people at various times in various places. Technical difficulties were encountered and it was not until the beginning of the twentieth century that sufficient success had been achieved to convince locomotive engineers that it might be worth trying out again. By about 1914 most British railways had a number of superheater-fitted locomotives and the Midland was among them.

The fall of temperature that accompanies expansion of steam in a cylinder causes some of the steam to condense unless it starts from a superheated condition. By sufficiently superheating the steam on its way to the cylinders, condensation in the cylinders can be prohibited and this saves heat. According to conventional text-book teaching, superheating beyond this point effects a further small additional economy, but this has never been convincingly demonstrated in British locomotive practice. It is traditional (and perhaps natural) to imagine that the higher the better, and that there were big advantages to be gained from high pressure and high superheat in steam locomotives. No support for this supposition is to be found either in the basic principles of physics or in the published results of testing locomotives.

One may search through text-books very industriously without finding any convincing explanation as to why avoidance of condensation of steam in the cylinder should be markedly advantageous, but the evidence from locomotives in service is that it could reduce coal consumption for any particular job by some 20 per cent. It has been suggested that wet steam, ie steam containing water as a uniform cloud of fine drops, can pick up heat more readily from a cast iron cylinder wall than can steam that is entirely free from suspended water. This is consistent with the evidence that superheating high enough to eliminate condensation in the cylinder certainly saves coal but that superheat beyond this gives no perceptibly greater advantage in practice.

A disadvantage of superheating is that the high temperature of the steam makes lubrication less reliable, and this alone could deter engineers from aiming at very high superheat with the object of effecting a dubious small gain in efficiency. (The fact that high superheat is advantageously used in steam turbines exhausting into condensers has no bearing on the question as to whether it could be useful in locomotives that do not work on the uniflow principle and that have neither turbines nor condensers.)

The contents of a paper presented by George Hughes of the Lancashire & Yorkshire Railway to the Institution of Mechanical

Engineers in 1910 on the subject of 'compounding and super-heating in Horwich locomotives' could be expected to arouse less enthusiasm about the former than the latter. The first Midland application of a superheater was to a simple (single-expansion) locomotive. There was a tendency in those times to regard super-heating as a possible alternative to compounding, but it soon became clear that the former was much more valuable and could be applied to a compound locomotive just as advantageously as to a simple.

Derby was so thoroughly convinced by 1906 of the superiority of the Deeley compound over non-compound engines that it was a little late (1910) in making its first trial of superheating. This was on one of the 999 class 4—4—0s which, when superheated, could work on some 15 per cent less coal than a standard Deeley compound required. Superheaters were fitted to the rest of the 999s but it was not until 1913 that a Deeley compound (No 1040) was so treated. This burned some 25 per cent less coal than a standard compound but only twenty-three other compounds were given superheaters in the succeeding ten years. At the end of that period the North Western Railway had over 500 loco-motives with superheaters.

The only Midland engines to be built with superheaters were the Class 4F 0—6—0s (m52) of which about 190 were produced between 1917 and 1923. From 1910 onwards, how-ever, quite a number of 4—4—0s of Classes 2, 3 and 4 (m22 to m33) were rebuilt with superheaters. It was British practice in general to use superheaters only on engines with piston valves because of difficulty in lubricating flat valves handling super-heated steam. The Midland, however, learned how to cope with this and rebuilt some engines with superheaters while retaining flat valves. The Class 3 4—4—0s (m31) were interesting in this respect as some were superheated with flat valves, some with piston valves and some were never superheated. All forty Deeley 'Flat-irons' (m56) were re-boilered with superheaters by the LMS, but retained their original flat valves.

231

LOSSES IN LOCOMOTIVE STEAM

When steam left a locomotive cylinder on its way to the blast pipe, it still had one useful purpose to serve and that was to draw smoke-box gases up the chimney. After that it was lost so far as the locomotive and the railway company were concerned. Its heat energy at the blast nozzle represented a dead loss. The only other heat loss in the engine (as distinct from the boiler and smokebox) was that from the cylinder-casting by conduction and convection to the atmosphere and by radiation to the universe in general. Consequently the word 'loss' should be used only with great caution in connection with anything that happened to the steam on its way from the boiler to the blast-pipe.

For example, it was not unusual to have steam in the boiler at a pressure of 200psi while at the outgoing side of a partly-opened regulator the pressure might be only 150psi. This kind of circumstance has sometimes been interpreted as implying a loss that might have been avoided by opening the regulator wide and thereby raising the downstream pressure to something very close to 200psi. This idea is, however, quite mistaken in that the steam loses no energy in being throttled from 200 to 150psi; there is no way for the energy to escape, apart of course from radiation from the regulator valve box, and this loss, depending only on temperature, is the same whether the steam be throttled or not.

The drop in pressure would be a loss only if the steam at 150psi could not be used so efficiently in the locomotive as it could have been at some higher pressure. If the locomotive had been the ideal heat engine that is commonly imagined as an example by which to describe basic laws of thermodynamics, the higher pressure would have enabled the engine to be designed so as to extract more energy from the steam than it could get at the lower pressure. But the steam locomotive was far from the ideal heat engine, and over the normal range of operating conditions could get as much (and it was *not* much) energy from the steam at the lower pressure as it could from the higher pressure.

So throttling of steam on its way to the cylinders of a conventional steam locomotive did not necessarily imply any loss at all.

At the blast-pipe the steam needed to have a pressure of about 5psi to produce the necessary draught on the fire. At low running speeds the back-pressure on the pistons did not need to be much higher than that because there was plenty of time for the pressure in the cylinder to drop to that level between the opening of the exhaust port and the end of the working stroke. At high speed, however, time was so restricted that cylinder pressure got down to blast-pipe pressure only after a fair proportion of the exhaust stroke had been completed and steam in the cylinder was opposing the motion of the piston over that distance.

To minimise this loss (associated with throttling at the exhaust port) the ideal would have been a valve that opened instantaneously and widely just before the end of the working stroke so that cylinder pressure was down to blast-pipe pressure by the time the piston started back. The ideal was unattainable. In practice, the best result was achieved by the use of a piston valve that began to open to exhaust before the end of the stroke and was large enough to suit the highest useful service speed. These remarks on losses are specially relevant in a book on Midland steam, because in it reference must be made to a paper presented to the Institution of Mechanical Engineers by E. L. Diamond in 1926 on 'Cylinder losses in a compound locomotive'. This paper gave figures derived from tests on Midland compounds, and listed

- (a) Loss due to pressure drop between boiler and steam chest.
- (b) Loss due to throttling at admission.
- (c) Loss due to clearance volume (between valve and the piston at the end of its stroke).
- (d) Loss due to heat exchange between steam and cylinder walls and leakage.
- (e) Loss in the intermediate receiver between high-pressure and low-pressure cylinders.
- (f) Loss due to incomplete expansion.
- (g) Loss due to throttling and back pressure.

Of these, (a), (b), (c) and (e) mean no loss of energy at all, while (d) does not apply to the high-pressure cylinder. In connection with (f) it may be remarked that in the conventional steam locomotive it was not practicable to expand the steam in a volume-ratio higher than about 5, whereas in a large steam power station 500 is possible. By its very nature the steam locomotive was unable to expand steam sufficiently to get from a given quantity of coal much more than about one-fifth of the energy that a power station could extract from it.

The throttling mentioned in (g) is that applied to the steam as it leaves the cylinder; it makes the back pressure higher than it would be with the ideal exhaust valve. The 'leakage' mentioned in (d) is something quite different from anything in the rest of the list and should preferably have been recorded as a separate item. Leakage of steam from glands to atmosphere is dead loss and leakage past valves and pistons to the blast pipe very nearly so.

By far the most valuable conclusion reached by Diamond from the material in his paper did not refer particularly to compound engines. It was that many existing locomotives were losing appreciable power in pushing steam through restricted port openings to exhaust. Sir Henry Fowler reacted quickly to this suggestion (which Great Western practice had been demonstrating for twenty years and more), and the next new design of locomotive to be built at Derby (the LMS 2—6—4T) was one of the liveliest locomotives that the LMS ever had. It was greatly to Fowler's credit that he immediately applied in a new design a recommendation made in a paper by a young man who had only recently resigned from a junior position on Fowler's technical staff. But of course Fowler and his staff ought to have seen what was needed without dependence on a junior interpreter.

The Midland compounds, with short-lap flat valves for the low-pressure cylinders, suffered severe exhaust-throttling loss unless the low-pressure valves were given long travel by setting them to work at late cut-off. This could be done on the first two engines, without using a late cut-off in the high-pressure cylinder; perhaps this has a bearing on the fact that no other Midland compound is known to have matched them in exceeding 90mph.

TABLE 1

1844   **Kirtley took charge**

1859   Brick arch and deflector (Kirtley and Markham)

1871   First single-frame Midland 2—4—0

1873   **Johnson took charge.** Dark green paint

1874   First Johnson 0—6—0T (m54). Blue-green paint

1875   First Johnson 0—4—4T (m39) and 0—6—0 (m49)

1876   First Midland 4—4—0. Lighter green paint

1880   Red paint for locomotives

1883   'Midland red' paint

1884   Joy valve-gear on ten 4—4—0s (m23)

1886   Air-sanding. Steam-sanding

1887   First Johnson single

1899   American 2—6—0s imported (m59, m60)

1900   Last Johnson single built

1901   First Johnson compound built

1903   **Deeley took charge.** Water troughs laid, Oakley, Lough-borough, Melton Mowbray

1905   First Deeley compound. Engine numbers in big figures on tenders

1907   Engines all re-numbered. Water troughs laid near Hawes Junction. First m33 (No 999). First Flat-iron, m56 (No 2000). First black paint

1908   Paget 8-cylinder 2—6—2 (No 2299)

1909   Last Deeley compound built. Paget traffic-control started. **Fowler took charge**

1910   First superheater on Midland engine (No 998) (m33)

1911   First superheated Midland 0—6—0, No 3835, Class 4F (m52)

1912   Take-over of Tilbury line

1913   First superheater on Midland compound (No 1040) (m32)
First Class 2 4—4—0 superheated, No 483 (m34)
First Class 3 4—4—0 superheated, No 700 (m31)

1919   4/0—10—0 No 2290 (m58). Retirement of Paget

1922   24 compounds had been fitted with superheaters before 1923

1923   Absorption of Midland into LMS

TABLE 2

SOME STATISTICS FOR THE YEAR 1921

Railway*	MR	GWR	LNWR	NER	GNR	GER	GCR	LSWR
Route miles	1800	3005	2067	1758	1050	1190	852	1020
Track miles	3640	6780	5830	5000	3123	2634	2690	2383
Tender engines	2275	1405	2242	1314	858	781	909	540
Tank engines	744	1743	1094	699	501	560	452	391
Coaches	6100	8680	9550	4116	3700	5650	2724	4061
Wagons Open	73300	57000	44100	39300	32160	18700	19700	9840
Covered	12600	14000	14800	9700	4012	5370	3184	3700
Mineral	24000	770	8700	59000	–	175	8106	–
Engines per track-mile	0.83	0.46	0.57	0.40	0.43	0.51	0.51	0.39
Loaded train-miles per engine per day	28	36	29	26	28	36	26	48
Percentage dividend on ordinary stock	7.25	7.25	7.50	7.50	4.50	0.38	0.00	6.0

*GCR Great Central Railway
GER Great Eastern Railway
GNR Great Northern Railway
GWR Great Western Railway
LNWR London & North Western Railway
LSWR London & South Western Railway
MR Midland Railway
NER North Eastern Railway

TABLE 3

SOME DIMENSIONS OF MIDLAND LOCOMOTIVES

Reference / Engineer	m1 K	m2 K	m3 K	m4 K	m5 J	m6 J	m7 J	m8 J
1 Wheel arrangement	222D	222D	222D	222D	422D	422D	422D	422D
2 Class	152	120	136	30	25	179	115	2601
Power class	-	-	-	-	1	1	1	2
3 Number built	2	16	14	20	60	10	15	10
4 Date of first	1845	1852	1856	1863	1887	1893	1896	1900
5 Date of last	1845	1854	1858	1866	1893	1896	1899	1900
6 Grate area (sq ft)	?	14	?	?	19.6	19.6	21	24
7 Barrel dia (in)	?	47	?	?	50	50	48	48
8 Barrel length (in)	?	132	?	?	124	124	126	128
9 Heat surf (sq ft)								
10 Firebox	75	?	?	?	117	117	128	147
11 Tubes	800	?	?	?	1120	1105	1105	1070
12 Superheater	-	-	-	-	-	-	-	-
13 NTE (1000 lb)	?	?	?	9	14	15	16	17
14 Adhesion wt (ton)	10	12	12½	?	17½	18	18½	18½
15 Engine wt (ton)	24	28	28½	?	44	45	48	51
16 Tender wt (ton)	?	?	?	?	37	37	39	52e
17 Boiler press.(psi)	?	?	?	140	160		170	180
18 Cylinder dia (in)	15	16	15	16½	18½	19	19½	19½
19 Piston stroke (in)	22	22	22	22	26	26	26	26
20 Dr.wheel dia (in)	66	80½	80	80	88/90	90	93	93½
21 Valve type & pos.	F2	F2	F2	F2	F2	8P3	8P3	8P3
22 Valve gear	S	S	S	S	S	S	S	S
23 Main mention p	63	63	-	65	68	69	70	73
24 Illustration p	-	-	-	17	17	-	-	17
25 Running numbers	*152& 153*	*120- 135*	*136- 149*	*25x 100*	600- 659	660- 669	670- 684	685- 694

Engineers   J - Johnson S W   K - Kirtley M

In Line 1 D   - double frame or outside frame
In Line 16 e - 8-wheel tender
In Line 21 F2 - flat valves between cylinders
          8P3 - 8-inch dia piston valves below the cylinders
In Line 22 S - conventional link-motion
In Line 25 *25 x 100* means 25, 100 and eighteen intermediate numbers

*Kirtley numbers

238

Table 3 continued

Reference Engineer	m8A K	m9 K	m10 K	m11 K	m12 K	m13 K	m14 K	m15 K
1 Wheel arrangement	2/240	240D	240D	240D	240D	240D	240D	240
2 Class	137	50	70	80	156	170	800	890
Power class	–	–	–	–	1	–	1	1
3 Number built	4	10	14	6	29	30	48	62
4 Date of first	1846	1862	1862	1862	1866	1867	1870	1871
5 Date of last	1846	1864	1863	1863	1874	1867	1871	1875
6 Grate area (sq ft)	12	?	?	15	14.8	14.8	16	16
7 Barrel dia (in)	?	?	?	?	47	49	49	49
8 Barrel length (in)	?	?	?	?	132	135	135	135
9 Heat surf (sq ft)								
10 Firebox	74	?	?	88	92	90	103	94
11 Tubes	773	?	?	1025	980	980	990	1028
12 Superheater	–	–	–	–	–	–	–	–
13 NTE (1000 lb)	?	9	10	11	10	10	11	12
14 Adhesion wt (ton)	?	?	?	22	22	24	24	26
15 Engine wt (ton)	?	?	?	34	35	36	36	37
16 Tender wt (ton)	?	?	?	?	?	?	26	30
17 Boiler press.(psi)	?	140	140	140	140.	140	140	140
18 Cylinder dia (in)	15	15	16	16½	16½	16½	17	18
19 Piston stroke (in)	22	22	24	24	22	22	24	24
20 Dr.wheel dia (in)	72	68	74	74	74	74½	78	80½
21 Valve type & pos	F2	F2	F2	F2	F2	F2	F2	F2
22 Valve gear	S	S	S	S	S	S	S	S
23 Main mention p	76	78	78	78	78	78	79	80
24 Illustration p	–	–	–	–	18	–	18	–
25 Running numbers	?	?	?	?	1–22	*170– 199*	23– 67	68– 126

Engineer K – Kirtley M

In Line 1   D – Double frame
In Line 21 F2 – Flat valves between cylinders
In Line 22 S – Conventional link motion
In Line 25 * – Kirtley numbers (Not all Kirtley engines survived to
                        receive Deeley numbers)

Table 3 continued

Reference Engineer	m16 K	m17 J	m18 J	m19 J	m20 J	m21 J	m22 J	m23 J
1 Wheel arrangement	240	240	240	240	440	440	440	440
2 Class	1070	1282	101	1400	1312	1327	1562	1667*
Power class	1	1	1	1	1	1	2	2
3 Number built	30	45	20	60	10	18	30	10
4 Date of first	1874	1876	1877	1879	1876	1877	1882	1884
5 Date of last	1876	1881	1881	1881	1877	1879	1883	1884
6 Grate area (sq ft)	16	17.5	17.5	17.5	17.5	17.5	17.5	17.5
7 Barrel dia (in)	49	50	50	50	50	50	50	50
8 Barrel length (in)	135	130	130	130	130	130	130	130
9 Heat surf (sq ft)								
10 Firebox	94	110	110	110	110	110	110	110
11 Tubes	1028	1096	1096	1096	1113	1200	1200	1150
12 Superheater	–	–	–	–	–	–	–	–
13 NTE (1000 lb)	13	13	12	13	13	12	13	16
14 Adhesion wt (ton)	26	30	30	30	27	28	28	28
15 Engine wt (ton)	37	41	41	41	41	43	43	43
16 Tender wt (ton)	34	37	37	37	34	34	34	34
17 Boiler press.(psi)	140	140	140	140	140	140	140	160
18 Cylinder dia (in)	18	18	18	18	18	18	18	19
19 Piston stroke (in)	24	26	26	26	26	26	26	26
20 Dr.wheel dia (in)	$74\frac{1}{2}$	78	84	81	78	84	81	84
21 Valve type & pos.	F2	F2	F2	F2	F2	F2	F2	F1
22 Valve gear	S	S	S	S	S	S	S	Joy
23 Main mention p	–	81	81	81	83	83	83	84
24 Illustration p	18	35	35	35	36	36	36	–
25 Running numbers	127– 156	157– 196	197– 206	207– 216	300– 309	310– 327	328– 357	483– 492
		217– 221	272– 281	222– 271				

Engineers   J – Johnson S W   K – Kirtley M

In Line 2   * – rebuilt to m24 class
In Line 21   F1 – Flat valves above cylinders
           F2 – Flat valves between cylinders
In Line 22   S – Conventional link motion

SOME DIMENSIONS OF MIDLAND LOCOMOTIVES

Table 3 continued

Reference Engineer		m24 J	m25 J	m26 J	m27 J	m28 J	m29 J	m30 J	m31 J
1	Wheel arrangement	440	440	440	440	440	440	440	440
2	Class	1740	1808	2183	2203	150	60	2591	2606
	Power class	2	2	2	2	2	2	2	3
3	Number built	20	35	25	45	30	30	10	80
4	Date of first	1885	1888	1892	1893	1897	1898	1901	1900
5	Date of last	1887	1895	1900	1894	1900	1901	1901	1905
6	Grate area (sq ft)	17.5	17.5	17.5	19.6	19.6	19.6	21.1	25
7	Barrel dia (in)	50	50	50	50	50	50	54	56
8	Barrel length (in)	130	130	124	124	124	124	131	132
9	Heat surf (sq ft)								
10	Firebox	110	110	117	117	117	128	128	145
11	Tubes	1200	1318	1106	1106	1106	1105	1102	1380
12	Superheater	–	–	–	–	–	–	–	–
13	NTE (1000 lb)	14	15	15	16	15	17	17	19
14	Adhesion wt (ton)	28	32	32	32	35	35	35	36
15	Engine wt (ton)	43	48	48	48	51	52	52	53
16	Tender wt (ton)	38	38	38	38	38	42	42	53e
17	Boiler press.(psi)	160	160	160	160	160	170	175	180
18	Cylinder dia (in)	18	18	$18\frac{1}{2}$	$18\frac{1}{2}$	$18\frac{1}{2}$	$19\frac{1}{2}$	19	$19\frac{1}{2}$
19	Piston stroke (in)	26	26	26	26	26	26	26	26
20	Dr.wheel dia (in)	84	78	84	78	84	84	84	81
21	Valve type & pos.	F2	F2	F2	8P3	8P3	8P3	8P3	8P3
22	Valve gear	S	S	S	S	S	S	S	S
23	Main mention p	84	84	84	84	84	84	84	85
24	Illustration p	53	53	–	–	–	–	–	54
25	Running numbers	358– 377	378– 402 473– 482	403– 427	428– 472	493– 522	523– 552	553– 562	700– 779

Engineer   J – Johnson S W

In Line 16   e – 8-wheel tender
In Line 21   F2 – Flat valves between cylinders
              8P3 – 8-inch piston-valves below the cylinders
In Line 22   S – Conventional link motion

241

SOME DIMENSIONS OF MIDLAND LOCOMOTIVES

Table 3 continued

Reference Engineer		m32 J/D	m33 D	m34 F	m35 J	m36 D	m37 K	m38 K	m39 J
1	Wheel arrangement	C440	440	440	040T	2/040T	240DTX	044DTX	044T
2	Class	1000	999	483+	1500	1528	230	690	6
	Power class	4	4	2	OF	OF	1P	1P	1P
3	Number built	45	10	10	28	10	10	26	10
4	Date of first	1901	1907	1913	1883	1907	1868	1869	1875
5	Date of last	1909	1909	1914	1903	1922	1868	1870	1875
6	Grate area (sq ft)	28.4	28.4	21.1	8.0	10.5	14.8	15.5	14.6
7	Barrel dia (in)	57	57	54	42	44	49	50	49
8	Barrel length (in)	150	150	126	96	124	135	135	126
9	Heat surf (sq ft)								
10	Firebox	153	153	127	44	64	90	107	97
11	Tubes	1405	1405	1045	490	697	980	1000	989
12	Superheater	–	–	313	–	–	–	–	–
13	NTE (1000 lb)	23	23	18	9	16	12	14	14
14	Adhesion wt (ton)	39	40	37	24	33	30	30	31
15	Engine wt (ton)	59	59	54	24	33	43	50	52
16	Tender wt (ton)	46	46	41	–	–	–	–	–
17	Boiler press.(psi)	195	220	160	140	175	140	140	140
18	Cylinder dia (in)	19/21	19	20½	13	15	16½	17	17
19	Piston stroke (in)	26	26	26	20	22	22	24	24
20	Dr.wheel dia (in)	84	78	84½	46	46	62	62½	63
21	Valve type & pos.	10P3/F2	10P1	8P3	F2	F1	F2	F2	F2
22	Valve gear	S	S'v't	S	S	W	S	S	S
23	Main mention p	93–9	101–3	86	105	105	105	106	109
24	Illustration p	71	54	54	–	72	72	72/89	–
25	Running numbers	1000–	990–	483–	1500–	1528–	*230–	1200–	1226–
		1044	999	492	1527	1537	239*	1225	1235

Engineers   D – Deeley R M   F – Fowler H   J – Johnson S W   K – Kirtley M

In Line 1   C – 3-cylinder compound   D – Double frame
             T – Tank engine   X – fitted with condenser

In Line 2   + – Nominally superheated rebuilds of m24 class engines
             but included very few parts of them

In Line 21   F – flat valve   P – piston valve
             1 – above cylinders   2 – between cylinders   3 – below cylinders
             8 or 10 – Valve diameter (in)

In Line 22   S – Conventional link motion   S'v't – Stévart
             W – Walschaerts

In Line 25   * – Kirtley numbers

242

SOME DIMENSIONS OF MIDLAND LOCOMOTIVES

Table 3 continued

Reference Engineer		m40 J	m41 J	m42 K	m43 W	m44 W	m45 K	m46 K	m47 K	m48 K
1	Wheel arrangement	044T	044T	Met	2/442T	2/442T	060	060D	060D	060D
2	Class	1252	1832	204	LTS1	A	179	232	280	480
	Power class	1P	1P	–	2P	2/3P	–	–	1F	1/2F
3	Number built	30	165	6	36	34	11	50	94	315
4	Date of first	1875	1881	1868	1880	1897	1845	1851	1852	1863
5	Date of last	1876	1898	1868	1892	1909	1845	1852	1857	1874
6	Grate area (sq ft)	16.1	16.1	19	17.2	19.8	14	15	16	15.5
7	Barrel dia (in)	49	50	48	49	56	42	50	50	50
8	Barrel length (in)	126	126	123	126	126	150	138	138	135
9	Heat surf (sq ft)									
10	Firebox	110	110	101	105	119	75	89	112	107
11	Tubes	1100	1140	913	915	1003	800	950	1067	1000
12	Superheater	–	–	–	–	–	–	–	–	–
13	NTE (1000 lb)	13	16	11	15	18	?	?	?	14
14	Adhesion wt (ton)	31	32	31	32	38	?	?	?	36
15	Engine wt (ton)	52	53	42	56	71	?	?	?	36
16	Tender wt (ton)	–	–	–	–	–	?	?	?	26
17	Boiler press.(psi)	140	150	120	160	170	?	?	?	140
18	Cylinder dia (in)	17	18	17	17	19	15	16	17	17
19	Piston stroke (in)	24	24	24	26	26	24	24	24	24
20	Dr.wheel dia (in)	66	63	69	72	78	57	60	60	62½
21	Valve type & pos.	F2	F2	F2	F2	F2	F2	F2	F2	F2
22	Valve gear	S	S	S	S	S	S	S	S	S
23	Main mention p	109	109	128	131	131	–	110–1	110–1	110–1
24	Illustration p	89	89	90/106	–	90	–	–	90	107/8
25	Running numbers	1236– 1265	1266– 1430	*204– 209*	+2110– 2145+	+2158– 2175 2146– 2157 2176– 2179+	*179– 189*	*232– 279* 290* and 291*	*280– 289* *340– 423*	*480– 499* & Misc

Engineers J – Johnson S W K – Kirtley M W – Whitelegg T (London, Tilbury & Southend Ry)

In Line 1 D – Double frame T – Tank engine Met – 2/440T with condenser

In Line 2 A – Three LT & S classes 51, 37, 79 power classes 2P, 3P, 3P

In Line 21 F2 – Flat valves between cylinders

In Line 22 S – Conventional link motion

In Line 25 * – Kirtley numbers + – Midland numbers of ex L T & S engines.
Most numbers were changed by the LMS

SOME DIMENSIONS OF MIDLAND LOCOMOTIVES

Table 3 continued

Reference Engineer		m49 J	m50 J	m51 D	m52 F	m53 K	m54 J	m55 J	m56 D
1	Wheel arrangement	060	060	060	060	060T	060T	060T	064T
2	Class	1142	3460	3765	3835	880	1620	1900	2000
	Power class	2F	2F	3F	4F	1F	1F	3F	2P
3	Number built	560	305	70	192	10	280	60	40
4	Date of first	1875	1894	1903	1911	1871	1874	1899	1907
5	Date of last	1892	1903	1908	1922	1871	1899	1902	1908
6	Grate area (sq ft)	17.5	19.6	21.1	21.1	15.2	14.8	16	21.1
7	Barrel dia (in)	50	50	54	54	49	49	49	57
8	Barrel length (in)	135	135	131	126	124	124	126	131
9	Heat surf (sq ft)								
10	Firebox	110	117	125	125	94	91	97	125
11	Tubes	1110	1200	1303	1045	935	1024	968	1200
12	Superheater	–	–	–	313	–	–	–	–
13	NTE (1000 lb)	17	20	21	25	15	16	21	20
14	Adhesion wt (ton)	40	45	44	49	37	43	49	54
15	Engine wt (ton)	40	45	44	49	37	43	49	75
16	Tender wt (ton)	26	38	38	39	–	–	–	–
17	Boiler press.(psi)	150	175	175	160/175	140	140	160	175
18	Cylinder dia (in)	$17\frac{1}{2}$	18	18	20	16	17	18	$18\frac{1}{2}$
19	Piston stroke (in)	26	26	26	26	24	24	26	26
20	Dr.wheel dia (in)	58–63	63	63	63	50	55	55	67
21	Valve type & pos.	F2	F2	F2	8P1	F2	F2	F2	F2
22	Valve gear	S	S	S	SR	S	S	S	S
23	Main mention p	110–1	110–1	110–1	111	114	115	114	121
24	Illustration p	108	–	125	125	–	126	126	143
25	Running numbers	2900– 3459	3460– 3764	3765– 3834	3835– 4026	1610– 1619	1620– 1899	1900– 1959	2000– 2039

Engineers   D – Deeley R M   F – Fowler H   J – Johnson S W   K – Kirtley M

In Line 21 F – Flat valves between cylinders
         8P1 – 8-inch piston valves above cylinders

In Line 22 S – Conventional link motion, R – with rocking shafts.

244

Table 3 continued

Reference Engineer		m57 R	m58 F	m59 b	m60 s
1	Wheel arrangement	2/464T	L	2/260	2/260
2	Class	2100	2290	2501	2511
	Power class	–	–	2F	2F
3	Number built	8	1	30	10
4	Date of first	1912	1919	1899	1899
5	Date of last	1912	1919	1899	1899
6	Grate area (sq ft)	25	28.4	16.6	15.9
7	Barrel dia (in)	60	63	56	54
8	Barrel length (in)	174	160	126	126
9	Heat surf (sq ft)				
10	Firebox	141	158	125	127
11	Tubes	1305	1560	1247	1129
12	Superheater	?	445	–	–
13	NTE (1000 lb)	19	44	20	18
14	Adhesion wt (ton)	54	74	37	40
15	Engine wt (ton)	96	74	45	48
16	Tender wt (ton)	–	32	–	–
17	Boiler press.(psi)	160	180	180	160
18	Cylinder dia (in)	20	16.8	18	18
19	Piston stroke (in)	26	28	24	24
20	Dr.wheel dia (in)	75	55½	60	60
21	Valve type & pos.	P2	10P1	F1	F1
22	Valve gear	S	W	SR	SR
23	Main mention p	134	135	116	116
24	Illustration p	143	–	–	143
25	Running numbers	+2100–2107+	2290	2501–2510 2521–2539	2511–2520

Engineers F – Fowler H   R – Whitelegg R H (London, Tilbury & Southend Ry)

b – built by Baldwin   s – built by Schenectady

In Line 1 L – 4-cylinder 0-10-0 Lickey banker

In Line 21 F – Flat valve   P – Piston valve
1 – Above cylinders   2 – Between cylinders   10 – 10 in diameter

In Line 22 S – Conventional link motion, R – with rocking shafts
W – Walschaerts

In Line 25 + – Midland numbers of ex-London, Tilbury & Southend Railway engines

245

R

TABLE 4

SOME MIDLAND RUNNING

Run No.	1	2	3	4	5	6	7
Date in Railway Mag.	1905	1904	1904	1912	1912	1904	1904
Engine No.	125	?	2788*	1032	1036	2635*	2634*
Type	422	422	440	C440	C440	C440	C440
Class	m7	m7	m31	m32	m32	m32	m32
Gross load (ton)	180	180	170	210	235	280	350

Miles	Place	Times (minutes and seconds)						
0.0	St Pancras	0 0	0 0	0 0	0 0	0 0	0 0	0 0
6.9	Hendon	10 02		8 55	10 30	11 55		11 14
12.4	Elstree		16 52	14 28	16 10	18 35		
15.2	Radlett				18 40			
19.9	St Albans	22 52	24 33	21 00	23 10	26 10	23 23	25 21
30.2	Luton	32 24	35 24	30 00	35 05	36 50	34 30	36 28
32.8	Leagrave				4 40			
41.8	Ampthill				12 35			
49.8	Bedford Nor.J	48 36	52 13	45 20	19 15	52 45	52 00	53 36
59.8	Mile Post 59¾		64 14	56 30	29 40	62 55		
65.0	Wellingboro' +				34 20	67 50		
72.0	Kettering	73 37	76 51	66 20	41 00	74 30		
78.0	Desborough				47 45	82 25		
82.8	Market Harb. +				52 15	87 25		
88.8	Kibworth				59 05	93 25		
95.3	Wigston Nor.J +				65 25	99 35		
99.0	Leicester		107 08	95 40	70 20	104 20		

C — 3-cylinder compound
* — before Deeley renumbering
+ — speed restriction

246

Table 4 continued

Run No.		8	9	10	11
Date in Railway Mag.		1915	1912	1912	1914
Engine No.		642	?	?	1041
Type		422	440	C440	C440
Class		m5	m31	m32	m32
Gross load (ton)		100	215	240	325
Miles	Place	Times	(minutes	and	seconds)
0.0	Leicester		0 0	0 0*	0 0
3.7	Wigston Nor.J		6 30	5 0	6 10
10.2	Kibworth		13 50	12 0	13 25
16.2	Market Harb.+		19 20	17 15	18 35
21.0	Desborough		25 20	23 00	24 35
27.0	Kettering		30 40	28 15	30 10
34.0	Wellingboro'+		36 15	34 00	
39.2	Mile-post 59¾		42 15		
49.2	Bedford Nor.J	0 0s	50 40	49 00	50 15
57.2	Ampthill		59 15	57 30	58 35
66.2	Leagrave		70 05	67 30	
68.8	Luton	22 25	72 45	71 30	73 12
79.1	St Albans	12 15	83 20	81 45	83 25
83.8	Radlett	15 50	87 20		
86.6	Elstree	18 20	90 05	88 00	
92.1	Hendon	22 55	95 00	93 00	94 25
99.0	St Pancras	30 35	103 35	102 00	102 40

C – 3-cylinder compound
s – start near Bedford South Junction
+ – speed restriction
* – ran through Leicester at about 30 mph non-stop
     from Leeds

247

Table 4 continued

Run No.		12	13	
Date in Railway Mag.		1912	1912	
Engine No.		1032	?	
Type		C440	C440	
Class		m32	m32	
Gross load (ton)		210	240	
Miles	Place	Time(min.sec.)		Miles
0.0	Leicester	0 0	107 00*	97.0
12.6	Loughborough	13 10	92 45	84.4
20.8	Trent +	21 00	83 00	76.2
34.3	Pye Bridge	36 20	70 30	62.7
39.6	Doe Hill	43 15	65 30	57.4
43.0	Clay Cross +	47 55	–	54.0
47.3	Chesterfield	52 25	56 30	49.7
55.3	Killamarsh	61 20	47 00	41.7
63.0	Rotherham +	68 35	38 15	34.0
68.1	Swinton	73 25	31 30	30.9
76.1	Cudworth	81 25	24 30	22.9
86.1	Normanton +	91 20	12 45	10.9
97.0	Leeds (Well.)	106 00	0 0	0.0

C – 3–cylinder compound
+ – speed restriction
* – passed Leicester at about 30 mph and
      continued non–stop to London

Table 4 continued

Run No.	14	15	16	17	18	19	20	
Date in Railway Mag.	1913	1924	1924	1903	1909	1924	1924	
Engine No.	995	998	1008	2632*	800*	998	1008	
Type	440	440S	C440S	C440	440	440S	C440S	
Class	m33	m33S	m32S	m32	m31	m33S	m32S	
Gross load (ton)	255	310	305	240	255	320	370	
Miles	Place	Time (minutes and seconds)							Miles
0.0	Leeds (Well.)		0 0	0 0			134 45	135 50	113.0
10.9	Shipley Nor.J +		16 28	16 08			121 15	122 30	102.1
17.0	Keighley		24 33	24 05			114 22	115 43	96.0
26.2	Skipton +		34 11	33 41	93 18		103 14	105 48	86.8
32.8	Bell Busk		43 19	42 45					80.2
36.2	Hellifield	0 0	47 38	47 11	83 12	94 39	92 27	92 21	76.8
39.5	Settle Junct.	4 25	50 38	50 28			88 53	89 14	73.5
41.4	Settle	6 20	52 33	52 25		88 57			71.6
47.5	Horton	14 25	61 41	61 17		83 51			65.5
52.2	Ribblehead		70 15	69 00					60.8
54.5	Blea Moor	23 30	74 31	72 59		78 28	76 29	76 58	58.5
64.7	Aisgill	36 20	85 48	84 18	57 38	66 00	64 27	64 35	48.3
82.2	Appleby	53 00	102 40	99 56	34 33	39 10	38 29	37 51	30.8
97.6	Lazonby	65 55	116 08	115 00		22 22	23 05	22 51	15.4
103.0	Armathwaite	70 45				16 27			10.0
110.3	Scotby	76 50	127 24	128 00					
113.0	Carlisle	81 25	132 27	132 11	0 0	0 0	0 0	0 0	0.0

C - 3-cylinder compound
+ - speed restriction
* - before Deeley re-numbering
S - with superheater

Table 4 continued

Run No.	21	22	23	24	
Date in Railway Mag.	1917	—	1917	1927	
Engine No.	1012	1014	1013	1049	
Type	C440	C440	C440	C440S	
Class	m32	m32	m32	m32S	
Gross load (ton)	215	215	215	260	
Miles	Place	Time(minutes and seconds)				Miles
0.0	Leicester	0 0	0 0	99 00		90.4
12.6	Loughborough	13 20	13 30	86 00		77.8
20.8	Sheet Stores J.	21 50	22 05	77 10		69.6
27.3	Spondon Junct.	28 30	28 55	70 20		63.1
29.4	Derby North J. +	32 40	33 00	67 10	67 30	61.0
34.0	Duffield	38 40		62 30	62 50	56.4
39.1	Ambergate +	44 55	45 30	56 40	57 15	51.3
45.9	Matlock	51 45		49 25	49 40	44.5
50.4	Rowsley +	58 40	60 00	44 55	45 05	40.0
53.7	Bakewell	61 30	63 00		42 05	36.7
56.1	Longstone	65 25	67 05		39 25	34.3
60.2	Millers Dale	72 25	74 30	35 10	36 30	30.2
64.8	Peak Forest	80 05	83 00	30 30	32 00	25.6
68.5	Chapel-en-le-Frith	84 45	88 05	23 25	23 55	21.9
70.4	Chinley	87 00	89 50	20 20	20 25	20.0
73.1	New Mills S.J.	90 00	92 15			17.3
78.2	Hazel Grove	94 45	96 35	8 00	8 40	12.2
82.2	Cheadle Heath	98 15	100 05	0 0	0 0	8.2
85.2	Withington		103 10			5.2
88.9	Throstle Nest J. +	107 00	108 55			1.5
90.4	Manchester (Cent.)	110 35	112 35			0.0

C — 3-cylinder compound
+ — speed restriction
S — with superheater

250

Table 4 continued

Run No.	25	26	27			28
Date in Railway Mag.	1925	1925	1925			1919
Engine No.	1057	773	520			1295*
Type	C440S	440S	440S			240
Class	m32S	m31S	m34			m17
Gross load (ton)	200	275	185			115

Miles	Place	Time (min.sec)			Miles	Miles	m s
0.0	Derby	0 0	0 0	44 00	41.2	55.5	63 20
1.4	Pear Tree	3 30	3 30	41 50	39.8		
6.3	Repton	9 40	9 40	36 35	34.9	49.2	
11.0	Burton +	14 25	14 25	31 05	30.2	44.5	51 12
12.6	Branston	16 25	16 45	29 35	28.6		
16.5	Wichnor Junct.	20 05	21 15	26 00	24.7		
19.6	Elford	23 20	24 35	23 15	21.6		
23.9	Tamworth	27 30	29 05	19 10	17.3	31.6	38 22
29.4	Kingsbury	33 10	34 50	13 45	11.8	26.1	32 50
33.5	Water Orton	37 15	38 55	9 50	7.7		w
35.9	Castle Bromwich	39 45	42 45	7 30	5.3		
39.1	Saltley	43 25	46 25	4 00	2.1	15.2	20 43
41.2	Birmingham	47 10	50 10	0 0	0.0		w
	King's Norton					8.7	13 37
	Blackwell					2.2	6 19
	Bromsgrove					31.3	38 31
	Abbot's Wood					18.0	21 05
	Ashchurch J.					7.3	8 10
	Cheltenham					0.0	0 0

+ - speed restriction
* - Kirtley number
S - with superheater
w - via Camp Hill and Whitacre Junction

251

Table 4 continued

Run No.		29	30	31	
Date in Railway Mag.		1925	1925	1925	
Engine No.		522	773	521	
Type		440S	440S	440S	
Class		m34	m31S	m34	
Gross load (ton)		230	275	245	
Miles	Place	Time (min.sec.)			Miles
0.0	Birmingham	0 0	0 0	23 50	14.2
0.9	Five Ways	3 50	4 05		13.3
3.3	Selly Oak	8 25	8 15	18 40	10.9
5.5	King's Norton	11 15	10 50	15 55	8.7
10.5	Barnt Green	17 55	16 30	10 00	3.5
12.0	Blackwell +	19 40	18 15	7 20	2.2
14.2	Bromsgrove *	23 25	21 55	34 25	31.3
20.9	Dunhampstead	30 10	28 20	26 40	24.6
25.0	Spetchley	33 50	32 00	22 30	20.5
27.5	Abbott's Wood J.	36 05	34 20	19 40	18.0
32.3	Defford	40 05	38 20	14 40	13.2
36.1	Bredon	43 20	41 40	11 05	9.4
38.2	Ashchurch J.	45 15	43 40	9 00	7.3
41.7	Cleeve	48 30	47 00	5 45	3.8
45.5	Cheltenham	52 45	51 40	0 0	0.0
52.0	Gloucester	60 40			

+ — momentary stop in down direction
* — stop to take banking assistance up
              to Blackwell
S — with superheater

Bibliography

1 Barnes, E. G. *The Midland Main Line 1875-1922*. Allen &
   Unwin
2 Hamilton Ellis, C. *The Midland Railway*. Ian Allan
3 Nock, O. S. *The Midland Compounds*. Ian Allan
4 Radford, J. B. *Derby Works and Midland Locomotives*.
   Ian Allan
5 Williams, F. S. *Our Iron Roads*. Bemrose

Acknowledgements

The writer is indebted for information and inspiration not only
to the books enumerated above but also to innumerable articles in
    The Engineer
    Engineering
    The Locomotive
    The Railway Magazine
    The Journal of the Stephenson Locomotive Society
    Trains Illustrated
    The Railway World
In using the vast volume of available material to produce a
book of this size, one difficulty is in deciding what to omit and
another is in resisting the temptation to suppress original thought
on the ground that there is no room for it.

Acknowledgements

Photographs of its locomotives during the period of the Midland Railway proper are far less numerous than those of the same locomotives in much later years, and it is hard to find reproducible ones that have not already been reproduced.

Mr J. Edgington of British Rail has been most helpful in this connection and so also were Mr W. A. Camwell, Mr R. F. Roberts, Mr W. O. Skeat and other members of the Stephenson Locomotive Society.

Many Midland locomotives survived with little visible modification right through the life of the LMS group and even after nationalisation in 1948. Pictures of such locomotives are reproduced by courtesy of Mr T. G. Hepburn of Nottingham.

Sources of illustrations :
T. G. Hepburn 17 (centre), 35 (centre), 35 (below), 36 (above), 36 (centre), 53 (centre), 54 (above), 72 (above), 89 (above), 89 (centre), 90 (centre), 90 (below), 108 (above), 108 (below), 125 (centre), 126 (centre), 126 (below), 143 (above), 144 (above), and 144 (below)
LMS official photograph 125 (below)
Midland Railway official photographs 17 (below), 35 (above), 53 (below), 54 (centre), 54 (below), 71 (above), 71 (centre), 71 (below), 89 (below), 125 (above), 126 (above), 143 (centre), 143 (below)
Photomatic Ltd 35 (above), 18 (above), 18 (centre), 18 (below), 36 (below), 108 (centre)
Railway Magazine 53 (above), 144 (centre)
Stephenson Locomotive Society 72 (centre), 72 (below), 90 (above), 107

General Index

255

Index

Index

Place Index

(Each number in brackets represents the mileage by Midland from St Pancras)

Index

Name Index